Michael Brosnan

Against the Current

**How One
School
Struggled and
Succeeded
with
At-Risk
Teens**

Heinemann

Portsmouth, NH

Heinemann
A division of Reed Elsevier Inc.
361 Hanover Street
Portsmouth, NH 03801-3912
Offices and agents throughout the world

The names of all students and other minors mentioned in this book have been changed to protect their identities.

The author wishes to acknowledge the students, faculty and staff at the Urban Collaborative; Kathy Connolly, formerly from the Rhode Island Skills Commission; Rick Richards of the Rhode Island Department of Elementary and Secondary Education; Dan Challener, head of the PROBE commission; Barbara Cervone of the Rhode Island Foundation; Jan C.G. van Hemert, general manager of Patriot Metals; Henry S. Woodbridge, Jr., president of the advisory board of the Providence Dropout Collaborative; Joe Maguire, former head of Roger Williams Middle School in Providence; Steven Raffa, attorney; Rhode Island State Senator Charles Walton; Elizabeth Brown; Irene Brosnan; and Beth, Molly, and Samuel Brosnan.

Library of Congress Cataloging-in-Publication Data

Brosnan, Michael.
    Against the current : how one school struggled and succeeded with at-risk teens / by Michael Brosnan.
      p.   cm.
    ISBN 0-435-08140-3
    1. Socially handicapped youth—Education (Secondary)—Rhode Island—Providence—Case studies. 2. Education, Urban—Rhode Island—Providence—Case studies. 3. Urban Collaborative Accelerated Program (School). I. Title.
    LC4093.P9B76   1996

    371.826′24—dc21
                                           96-47299
                                              CIP

Production: Renée Le Verrier
Copy editing: Renée Nicholls
Cover illustration: Michelle Wegler
Cover design: Barbara Werden
Manufacturing: Louise Richardson

Printed in the United States of America on acid-free paper
00 99 98 97 EB 1 2 3 4 5 6

To Robert Emmet and Irene

The very least you can do in your life is to figure out what you hope for. And the most you can do is live inside that hope. What I want is so simple I almost can't say it . . . the possibility that kids might one day grow up to be neither the destroyers nor the destroyed.

—Barbara Kingsolver, from *Animal Dreams*

If there is no struggle, there is no progress.

—Frederick Douglass

Introduction

LET'S START WITH A CONFESSION. ROB DEBLOIS, THE FOUNDER and director of the Urban Collaborative Accelerated Program—and the key figure in this book—is a friend of mine. We went to high school together, played lacrosse and hockey on the same team (he once played with a shaved head and wore underwear in place of his helmet). In college, he'd visit me in Boston, and I'd drive up to New Hampshire to check out his world. He was the best man at my wedding and I at his. So when we first talked about this book, I was reluctant to take on the project. Isn't there a rule against writing about one's friends? Isn't this something akin to—and as risky as—a husband and wife going into business together?

I don't know. But I've known for years, even before we began discussing the book, that there was a story brewing, a very good story, and that it would need to be told. My hesitation, in truth, was based more on the seriousness of the undertaking—that I would have to work hard and that I would not be able to bow out in the process.

What's the story here? It's a story of struggle and weary triumph—of a hearteningly original school that has had great success educating inner-city adolescents at risk of dropping out. It is also the story of the students who attend and the people who work there. But before I can talk about the school in detail, I need to say something more about Rob. For he is at the heart of the matter.

In high school, Rob was a whirlwind of physical energy, fueled by high-octane enthusiasm for the possibility in each day. We stayed close friends through college. Rob studied literature at the University of New Hampshire and spent much of his free time hiking in the White Mountains.

One of my fondest memories is the Thanksgiving I joined Rob and friends for a hike to Zealand Falls Hut for a backcountry feast. Tired of all the freeze-dried camping food, Rob had begun carrying "real meals" with him on his overnight hikes up the four-thousand-foot peaks. That Thanksgiving he went all out, stuffing his backpack with a few clothes and a cooked turkey ample enough for a hungry soccer team. The rest of us carried vegetables, potatoes, bread, and drinks. He was right; one of the keys to a good adventure is good food. The hike up the snow-covered trail was invigorating. But the meal was pure pleasure, heightened by the setting deep in the woods at the side of a fantastic, half-frozen waterfall.

And then, at the end of that school year, everything changed. Always one to seize the day, Rob decided to go for a swim on a warm spring afternoon. He drove out to a local river, stood on the shore just above a small cascade where the tannin-rich water is dark, and dove in. But he did not see the rock just beneath the surface. On contact, Rob's neck broke, leaving him, at age twenty-one, a quadriplegic for life.

The story really begins here—with a man whose life has been instantly and irrevocably altered by a single act. For a man who now can't even get himself out of bed in the morning without help, his achievements have been astounding. Following the accident, he struggled through rehabilitation and the hard adjustments to his new life; completed his undergraduate work at UNH; got married and settled in Massachusetts near Providence, Rhode Island; taught high school English a while; and then earned a master's degree in English from Brown University.[1]

During this time his interest in education sharpened. With the same sort of energy and optimism he once brought to his physical activities, Rob began taking a hard look at the shortcomings of our educational system, particularly at how the current system fails urban schoolchildren. Dropout rates in many cities nationwide have climbed to 35 percent or higher. In Providence, the home of the Urban Collaborative Accelerated Program, this translates into thousands of students leaving school each year, never to return. Such failure has not only taken its toll on the lives of these teenagers but, more important, it has also thrown into question the whole American notion of egalitarianism and social mobility.

To Rob, these weren't abstract failures; they were a personal affront to his sense of justice. So he set out to help rectify the problem at the local level, first with a summer school program he started for urban children,[2]

---

[1] Rob later went on to earn a master's degree in education from Rhode Island College.

[2] The program, called SPIRIT, is another success story—and is still in operation today.

and then, beginning in 1989, with the creation of an independent public school for inner-city youth at risk of dropping out, the Urban Collaborative Accelerated Program.

I have to admit I didn't think much of the name when I first heard it. And its nickname—UCAP—doesn't help much. But you can't argue with the results. The school itself has been winning praise from just about everyone who visits, works, and learns there.

Why is this school important enough to be the subject of a book? Because the Urban Collaborative has much to teach us about the problems in public education today. Because the school has turned much of the current educational philosophy on end with impressive results. Because it has succeeded with the most difficult population of students: disenfranchised, inner-city youth. Because it adds a great deal to the dialogue about nationwide school reform at a time when such reform is vital. And, finally, because the people who run the program have struggled immensely—at times against frightening odds—to achieve all this.

The Urban Collaborative's one-hundred-plus students come from some of the poorest and most violent neighborhoods in Rhode Island and share backgrounds of family chaos and instability. Many have had poor attendance at previous schools and all are academically at least one year behind their peers. Nearly all arrive with poor reading and math skills, low self-esteem, and a tendency toward either hostility or apathy. Many of them resent and distrust authority and have histories of multiple suspensions from school. Some have used drugs and alcohol to debilitating excess. A number have hooked up with street gangs, engaged in prostitution, or taken to crime. In short, these young teenagers lead tough, disheartening lives. Without intervention, the majority would have little chance of making it through high school. Without intervention, they would eventually find themselves on the welfare roll, perpetuating the cycle of poverty and despair.

Of course, the Urban Collaborative Accelerated Program is not the only alternative[3] urban school. Far from it. We are in the midst of an educational reform movement in this country, and one could list many noteworthy programs, including the great work of Ted Sizer and the Coalition of Essential Schools (another Providence-based program). There are impressive, young magnet programs in New York City. Certain California public schools, under the direction of Henry Levin, are proving the value

---

[3] Rob DeBlois dislikes the label *alternative* because it conjures up images of schools with low standards. For my purposes, however, it is the simplest identifier—one most readers will readily accept. As you will learn, the academic standards at the Urban Collaborative are far from low.

of accelerated learning. Meanwhile, numerous states are experimenting with variations on the theme, especially the idea of charter schools, whether run by nonprofit groups or for-profit businesses. It's heartening to know that Walter Annenberg is also putting some of his immense wealth to work improving urban schools.

But even amid these worthy, better-known efforts, the Urban Collaborative stands out. The school is distinctive, unique, and one of the most successful. It also comes from far more humble beginnings than the others. It was not the brainchild of a university's education department. It did not start with much foundation support. Rather, it began with the determination of a man in a wheelchair.

At the heart of this book is a snapshot of the Urban Collaborative in its fourth year of operation. For the most part, I try to tell the story of the Urban Collaborative through the eyes of those involved with the school. In order to do this, however, I need to explain up front the school's basic framework—the five distinguishing components that make the school educationally significant. The first is the school's radical structure. Although a public school, the Urban Collaborative is an independent legal entity with total control over all aspects of its operation—including budget, curriculum, and personnel—a forerunner, really, to the way most state charter schools operate. The school's board is comprised of school superintendents from the three participating cities: Providence, East Providence, and Pawtucket. They, in turn, have given Rob, as director, a great deal of freedom to establish the program as he and the teachers see fit. The value of this kind of independence, virtually unheard of in public education, cannot be overemphasized. The fact that policy at the Urban Collaborative is not directly controlled by any single school committee means the director and teachers have the flexibility to create a program that best serves their students. All other features of the school exist, in essence, because of this.

The second distinguishing characteristic is the school's emphasis on individualized instruction. While this may seem like an obvious and logical directive for any school, it is, in fact, highly unusual. In the vast majority of schools nationwide, instruction is group centered, and advancement in grade is based on the time one spends "in seat," almost regardless of competency. This is why some can graduate from high school without learning how to read at the twelfth-grade level, or how to read at all. At the Urban Collaborative, students advance academically only after they individually complete established criteria for each grade. This system comes with its own set of problems, but it helps motivate and engage students who would otherwise disappear into the urban woodwork.

The third noteworthy characteristic is the required involvement of teachers in virtually all aspects of the school. This notion of "school-based management," as it is called, has received a lot of attention lately because it places critical decisions about a school in the hands of those closest to the students. At the Urban Collaborative, the teachers and the director work together to establish, among other things, curriculum, methods of instruction, school policy, and scheduling. The greatest benefit of this collaboration is that the teachers, by helping to design the program, feel a sense of ownership; as a result, they work harder to make the school succeed. At a recent parents' meeting, a number of parents commented on the energy and dedication of the teaching staff. One mother said they were "blessed" to have such teachers for their children. While this may be true, it is also true that the Urban Collaborative teachers generally perform better, or at least more eagerly, than their counterparts in most other public schools precisely because the school is a direct reflection of each of them. There is no administrative "system" to blame; they are, in effect, the system.

The fourth distinctive element of the school is the degree of responsibility given to all students. In the area of discipline, for example, students take part in developing school rules, then oversee adherence to these rules through a student-run committee. Thus, students also feel a certain sense of ownership and belonging. By being able to speak their minds on a variety of issues, students learn that their individual lives matter, that they are as much a part of this community (and society at large) as the teachers. It also helps narrow the traditional divide between students and teachers.

Less obvious, though equally important, is the role each student plays in deciding his or her own pace of work. Instruction is set up so students can see a causal relationship between academic effort and rate of promotion. While students are urged to work hard and are given numerous incentives to do so, the final decision is theirs. The point is to help them find motivation and take responsibility for their education. This is intended not only to help build self-esteem and character but also to give them the best chance of succeeding when they progress to larger, less personalized high schools.

The final component is the Urban Collaborative's relationship with the private sector. The financial reasons for a strong relationship are obvious. Money raised from private sources is used to enhance the educational experience by allowing for a variety of programs, by funding needed equipment, and by giving the staff the freedom to initiate new projects and offer learning incentives (anything from free lunches to a science-class trip to Love Canal). But the relationship with the private sector has other mutual benefits. Community business people and other volunteers often work in classes and serve on committees that help shape the school's future. In turn, such involvement helps the private sector realize the challenges facing public schools today and how it might help meet those challenges. At a time when American corporations are spending an estimated $25 billion a year teaching employees skills they should have learned in school, such a collaboration is clearly necessary.

My intent in writing about the Urban Collaborative is twofold. First, because Rob DeBlois' story is worth telling. His tenacity, his endurance, his vision, his skill, and his love for his profession are remarkable and inspirational—not even counting the physical limitations he must overcome daily.

The second reason is a bit more complex. As we know, the public educational system is awash in problems—inequality between urban and suburban systems, high dropout rates, low SAT scores, increased violence, teacher dissatisfaction, administrative frustration, lack of parental involvement, moral confusion, community indifference, and so on. At the same time, there are perhaps more theories and programs designed to address these concerns and improve American education today than there have been at any point in history. The question arises: Why is the system still foundering? Why aren't we able to affect real and lasting change? Why can't we solve this serious problem—for the sake of the children and the future of our nation? This is where the story of the Urban Collaborative becomes vital. On one hand, we can point to the school's innovation and achievements and say, Yes, reform is clearly possible. On the other hand, we can look at the enormous difficulty of establishing and running such a school and realize the magnitude of the task. Yes, educational reform *is* possible. But, as you will see, it takes tremendous effort and will, and more energy than most of us have.

In short, this is a tale of one determined school and what it can teach us about educational reform. This is also a tale of human suffering, confusion, desire, dedication, and perseverance—all in the effort to make a real and lasting difference.

1

AROUND 7:40 EACH MORNING ROB DEBLOIS AND HIS PERSONAL
assistant, Catalina (Cati) Martinez, cross the I-195 bridge over the Seekonk
River into Providence, Rhode Island. Just upriver to the north is the site
of the first Rhode Island colony, established in 1636 by Roger Williams,
who came here from England, via Boston, to found a settlement based in
part on religious freedom. Williams, by all accounts, was a rare man,
respectful of individual rights and the sovereignty of Native Americans.
His colony earned a reputation as one of the more admirable colonies in
the New World—until the 1700s, when the port of Providence became a
major player in the African slave trade.

In a Ford van modified to accommodate Rob's wheelchair, Rob and
Cati escape the highway, skirting College Hill and the city's financial district.
They cross the forlorn Providence River just north of the Fox Point Hur-
ricane Barrier, which was erected in the 1960s to protect the city from
hurricane-driven high tides. From the river it's a short ride uphill past the
aging Narragansett Electric plant, Planned Parenthood of Rhode Island,
and some renovated factories and warehouses, to the south end of the
city. Here, at the corner of Somerset and Prairie, is the home of the Urban
Collaborative Accelerated Program, an alternative middle school that Rob
started in 1989.

Although only a mile or so from three of the nation's top colleges
and the state's marbled capitol district, the South Providence neighborhood
enjoys few of the opportunities such institutions offer. One wonders what
Roger Williams would think of this region today. There is, for those who
care to take advantage of it, the religious freedom for which he advocated

so tirelessly. But there is little sense that this is, as its founder had hoped, the land of providence. In the past two decades, much of the white middle class has moved out of the city to the suburbs. At the same time, an influx of poor immigrants, many who don't speak English, have moved in. Today the city's population is mostly African American, Hispanic, Portuguese, and Southeast Asian—many of whom live within an arm's length of the poverty line.

In the early 1980s, Providence experienced an economic boom that made it one of America's hottest cities.[1] Construction went hog-wild. An office/residential complex shot up in the heart of downtown; the city refurbished its waterfront and its renowned jewelry district; new industrial parks were erected on the city's outskirts; new train and bus stations were built; 148 parks and recreation areas received substantial face-lifts; and smack in the center of town construction began on an expansive convention center with retail stores and a glitzy hotel. The general impression in Providence (as in other American cities) was that things were going just fine. But even before the economic tailspin began in the late 1980s, the quality of life in South Providence was already on the decline.

During the decade of supposed economic prosperity, poverty increased in the city. In the 1990 census, 50 percent of the households were in the "low" or "very low" income brackets, the latter being below the poverty line. Sixteen percent of the city's residents were on public assistance. What was good news for property owners—skyrocketing real estate prices—was horrendous news for those renting their homes. Income did jump 120 percent between 1979 and 1989, but the average rent price jumped 224 percent during the same period. In the city's poorest neighborhood, the percentage of income spent on rent rose from 25 percent to 42 percent.

When the nation finally slipped into a recession, it hit particularly hard in Providence. Like the rest of New England, Rhode Island had prospered in part because of lucrative defense contracts. Once these contracts dried up, so did the economy. At the same time, corruption in management led to the failure of a number of the state's credit unions—a scandal so serious it led protesters to block off Interstate 95 for a time and cost taxpayers millions to repair. As a result, 24,000 jobs were lost, jobs that had brought in $300 million to the state's economy. Unemployment statewide climbed to nearly 10 percent. And nowhere in the state did the recession sting more severely than in South Providence. Housing became less affordable, jobs less available. This was compounded by the general

---

[1] Some of the statistical information about Providence was provided by Patrick J. McQuillan, from his research as a doctoral candidate at Brown University's Department of Anthropology. In his thesis, after analyzing urban schools, McQuillan challenges the oft-stated notion that educational opportunity is equal for all Americans.

reduction in the federal government's support for low-income housing, human services, and job training. The City of Providence, with a sudden reduction in its tax base, also found itself hard-pressed to meet the needs and demands of its residents. In particular, the city's support for public education decreased—at a time when the needs were greatest.

By 1990 the makeup of the city's schools had changed. Not only did many white families migrate to the suburbs, most of those who stayed behind began to send their children to private and parochial schools. The Hispanic and Southeast Asian portion of the student population grew from less than 10 percent in 1978 to 34 percent in 1990. At the same time, 22 percent of the students came from families in which English was not the primary language at home. And most of those families were headed by a single parent.

All this would suggest the need for more money in the schools, for English-as-a-Second-Language programs and bilingual instruction, and for more social workers, health specialists, and counselors. At the very least, these stresses on the school system suggest the need for smaller class sizes. But these things have been slow in coming, if they've come at all. The schools are crowded. Kids are discouraged. As a result, in 1989, the city's cumulative high school dropout rate climbed to an intolerable 47 percent— sadly, a rate not uncommon in many large cities.

As Rob often points out, South Providence is not without hope—and certainly not without a sense of concern and compassion for its residents. A short distance from the Urban Collaborative is a homeless shelter; in another direction is a house for the poor afflicted with AIDS. Brown University has helped establish community gardens in a number of empty lots. In the spring these gardens are patterned with neat rows of seedlings; by the start of school in fall, they are full of well-tended vegetables. The Urban League of Rhode Island, a tireless advocate for the poor, is adjacent to the school. Beyond the Urban League is the newest branch of the Community College of Rhode Island. Directly across the street from the school is a modern community center complete with an outdoor swimming pool and a lined basketball court, one hoop with its net still intact. And just down Somerset Street is prospering Rhode Island Hospital, the largest employer in the neighborhood, with its original stately manse dwarfed by modern wings. A new women and infants building faces the Urban Collaborative. And under construction is a state-of-the-art children's hospital bankrolled in part by Hasbro, a Rhode Island company and one of the nation's leading toy manufacturers.

But these signs of hope are more than matched by signs of despair. Driving through South Providence, one can't help but notice the number of down-at-the-heels housing projects. A small billboard on Point Street advertises "single-family homes starting at only $79,900." The sign is worn, as are a growing number of empty, burned-out, boarded-up, or simply dilapidated houses in the neighborhood. Most are typical three-story tenements lined up tightly along the littered streets. There are, to be sure, some well-kept homes with neatly trimmed yards, but these are the exception.

One also can't help but notice that not many white people live in the area. Racial polarization is so sharp that seventeen of the city's thirty-four schools are out of compliance with federal desegregation laws. And there is little to indicate that this will change in the near future. In a 1991 *Atlantic Monthly* article, Thomas and Mary Edsall point out that the contact between whites and minorities, particularly blacks, "has routinely violated every standard necessary for the breakdown of racial stereotypes. Most white contact with the underclass is through personal experience of crime and urban squalor, through such experience related by friends and family, or through the daily reports about crime, drugs, and violence which appear on television and in newspapers. The news includes, as well, periodic reports on out-of-wedlock births, welfare fraud, drug-related AIDS, crack babies, and inner city joblessness." What is true for the nation at large is true for Providence. The underclass of minorities has become increasingly alienated from the middle and upper classes. As Patrick McQuillan concludes in his recent study of Providence and its school system, the needs of the schools that service these poor minorities are great, greater now than in years past. The schools need to play a larger role in the lives of their students. But, McQuillan notes, "politically, it [has] become increasingly difficult to secure the funds to address these needs since urban concerns may appear insignificant and inconsequential to suburban voters," who now hold most of the clout.

It was in this atmosphere that Rob decided he wanted to start a school for kids at risk of dropping out, not only for children from Providence, but from East Providence and Pawtucket, two neighboring cities with similar struggles and dropout rates.

Rob and Cati ease left onto Prairie, certainly an ironic name for an inner-city street, though an apt location for the pioneering notions of the Urban Collaborative. After a quick right onto Somerset, they turn into the school's parking lot. The entire property is surrounded by a tall chain-link fence and a gate that is locked each night. The building is a former Catholic school, built in 1959. It has that clean, no-nonsense look of most parochial schools: three stories, flat roof, pale bricks, and classroom-length metal-framed windows. A sign directing people to the fallout shelter in the basement—a relic of the Cuban missile crisis and the following cold war—is fading on the wall. The building is owned by a private school, Community Prep, which occupies the second floor. The Urban Collaborative is housed on the first floor.

Cati parks the van in the handicapped space and wheels Rob out with the help of a hydraulic lift. Life as a quadriplegic, Rob points out, is twice as difficult as life as a paraplegic, perhaps more so. Rob has some control of the muscles in his head, neck, and shoulders, but that's all. So he must depend upon many people every day for every need and bodily function. Still, he tries to lead a life as normal as possible. Although school doesn't start until 9:00 A.M., he makes a point to arrive early. It's a good time for some banter with students before schoolwork starts. Today a number of students are already here. Some sit on the red park benches anchored to the parking lot. Miguel, a sturdy, slow-moving boy of Mexican descent, is shooting baskets across the street as usual. It's what he does. Easy jump shots from the perimeter, followed by easy lay-ups in which he gives the ball a casual, practiced spin off the backboard.

Rob calls out, "Good morning, Miguel." It's one of those spring mornings that promises afternoon warmth.

Miguel looks over, smiles faintly.

"OK, Miguel," Rob says with a hint of mischief. He waits for the boy to station himself a fair distance from the basket. "One shot from there."

Miguel dribbles the ball. He doesn't look at Rob, but clearly he has heard the challenge. He draws a deep breath, bends his knees, then lets go a jump shot with near perfect form, the arm held high and the hand limp in the follow-through. But the ball overshoots the basket and bounds off the juncture of backboard and rim. When Miguel makes "the morning shot," as he occasionally does, Rob gives him a dollar, or, more accurately, asks Cati to give him a dollar from the wallet Rob keeps in a pouch on the back of his wheelchair. If another student shows up, Rob may offer him the same challenge. Either way, he pays up quickly for baskets. Missed shots usually provoke a groan of mock disappointment. Miguel and the other early arrivals would like to take the shot again, but they know there are no second chances here. It's just one shot for one dollar.

Rob looks to Cati and shrugs. "Incentives," he says. "It's all a question of incentives." He's not talking about basketball, of course. Most of these kids need no incentive to play basketball. He's talking about school, about making kids feel at home here, making them want to come, making them want to work. So much in life is driving them the other way. All the kids in the Urban Collaborative have stayed behind at least one year in school and will in all likelihood drop out by their sixteenth birthdays if someone doesn't give them reason to stay. Rob's whole passion is giving them that reason.

As Rob talks, he gestures with thin arms that barely work. Both hands, permanently bent at the mid-finger knuckles, are wrapped in braces used for holding either an eating utensil or a stick needed for turning pages or dialing phones. With strength from his shoulders, he throws back his arms over his head to stretch—an oft-repeated motion—and calls out, "Next time, Miguel." If Rob were healthy, he'd punctuate every conversation with animated hand gestures. As it is, his flailing arms occasionally catch a passerby in the hip, especially in the crowded hallway of the school.

When he last stood, seventeen years ago, Rob was six feet tall, skinny yet taut and muscular from many weekend hiking expeditions. (The leather boots he wore hiking, as well as his old hockey skates, still hang from a nail in his basement.) Now he sits slightly hunched with the paunch all quadriplegics eventually develop, though his upper body and face are still thin. Much of his appearance speaks of practicality. His brown hair is straight, cut short, and requires no fussing. He'll muss it up often in a day, pondering thoughts, and pay no attention to the results. He has also let his beard grow, even though it's a bit scraggly, so as not to be forced to depend on someone shaving him each morning. He wears a tie and jacket only when he has to, and sometimes not even then. Instead, he prefers loose layers of clothing that can be put on or taken off to adjust to the day's temperature. He looks his age, thirty-eight. The only sign that his condition is taking its toll is in his eyes. Above his hawkish nose, they show the strain of sleepless nights, the effects of periodic bouts with infections and antibiotics, and the general weariness of having no real privacy.

Still, Rob is a happy man—by nature and circumstance. He is not the type to dwell on his injury or slump into self-pity. After a year of recovery and therapy, he returned to the University of New Hampshire to finish his undergraduate work in English and education. Later he completed his master's degree in English at Brown University and has taken a number of courses toward a master's in school administration. A native of Pawtucket, he married his college girlfriend, Bonnie Hunt, a school librarian, and settled in neighboring Massachusetts. With the help of medical science, his wife, Bonnie gave birth to their son, Justin, who is now six years old.[2] Rob

---

[2] Rob and Bonnie have since adopted a Vietnamese boy, Eric, and are now in the process of adopting a girl from Guatemala.

may not be able to take care of himself physically, but he takes solace in what he has—security, the love of his family, the support of friends—as well as in what he has accomplished. More than anything, perhaps, he loves a challenge. One can't help but notice how happy he is to greet each morning with a sense of purpose, his thoughts running full tilt from the moment Cati wheels him out the door of his house.

If the weather is nice, Rob will remain in the parking lot momentarily, enjoying the morning sun and some bantering with the kids or with faculty members. While Rob waits, Cati, a trim, twenty-six-year-old, often scurries across the street to shoot a few baskets with Miguel. Although she is employed by Rob and not the school, Cati is both a fan and a friend of the kids at the Urban Collaborative. She misses most of her shots, shoving the ball two-handedly at the rim on an unfavorably low trajectory, kicking one heel up behind her as no real ball player would. But the point is not to make baskets. The point, as she will quickly tell you, is to share one's time and one's self with one child. To smile at Miguel, join his activity. Most of the time, adults only give these kids directions, bark out orders, and command them to be still. That Miguel is here almost every morning, when he could be hanging out anywhere else in the neighborhood, is a clear indication that he enjoys these encounters. Even if he won't say so.

Cati knows firsthand the troubles these kids face. She grew up near Smith Hill, a poor area of Providence not far from the state house, and dropped out of school in the eleventh grade. Later, unlike most, she returned to school and got an associate's degree as a medical assistant. That's how she hooked up with Rob the summer before the Urban Collaborative opened. Attendants generally come and go with the seasons, but Cati has stayed with him all this time, in part, she says, because of the school. And in her own right, she has become a vital member of the Urban Collaborative staff.

"Good morning, Rob," says a heavy-set girl in a flower-print dress, her black hair pulled tight in a bun.

"Good morning, Maria," Rob says in return.

All the students call the adults here by their first names. Some educators don't like the idea; by their old-fashioned code of ethics, it is a sign of disrespect. But clearly the kids are happy with the arrangement.

"Want me to close your van?" Maria asks.

"Maria," Rob says, "that would be wonderful." And then, because he knows it will draw a response, he adds, "You're so sweet, Maria."

"Oh, shut up, Rob," she says.

But she likes the compliment nevertheless, and, with the help of a friend, carefully folds away the hydraulic lift and shuts the van's doors.

"I mean it," Rob says to her when she is out again. "You're a good kid, Maria."

She feigns a punch.

"Do you have your speech ready for graduation?" he asks her.

"Not yet," she says. "I'm working on it."

"I need it by tomorrow," he says.

"It'll be there."

Maria is heading back to the local high school after two successful years at the Urban Collaborative, and she is not shy about extolling the school's virtues. Because of this Rob has asked her, and a few others, to write a short statement to deliver at the graduation ceremony—or "closing" ceremony, as they prefer to call it, since technically the students aren't graduating. It's also a good way to help Maria clarify what she has done at the school and what she needs to remember for the future. While she is happy about her success, she is also a little nervous about leaving.

Maria and her family—her parents and three younger brothers—came to Providence seven years ago, new arrivals from the Azores, a group of islands some seven hundred miles west of mainland Portugal, where Maria hated school. The teachers were allowed to hit students, she will tell you. What she means is that they hit her, for reasons she will not say. The Azores were beautiful and clean, she says. She misses it. But she wouldn't go back there for anything now. She wants to be a teacher and work with inner-city kids. There is no reason to doubt that she will make it through high school with decent grades. Although just an average student in terms of ability, she has determination. A few years back she hated school, missed most of the year, didn't like the way the teachers or other kids treated her. In two years at the Urban Collaborative, however, she has completed three years of work—missing only two days the past year—and is ready to tackle the regular school system again. She knows now that she can do it. She knows she *has* to do it.

Although she never complains, Maria leads a difficult life. Her father left the family shortly after arriving in America. Without him, they have survived on welfare. Maria's mother, fearful for her daughter's well-being in their Providence neighborhood, has Maria on a tight rein, rarely letting her out of the house, even for school functions. Maria doesn't complain. And when she can get out, she usually takes on projects to help other poor families. One day, Chris Cuthbertson, one of the school's two social studies teachers, spied Maria lumbering down the sidewalk under the weight of two huge bags of day-old bread. She had collected the bread free from a bakery and planned to distribute it to her neighbors. As Rob says, "The world needs people like her."

A half hour later, after Rob has gone inside to start planning the day, a crowd of boys has gathered on the basketball court. Some days they play a full-court game. Other days they just shoot and contend with each other for rebounds. This day, they are trying to "school" one another, as they call it, by driving toward the hoop and attempting to lay a shot in the basket over the outstretched arms of a single defender. This is the sort of scene from professional basketball that these kids admire most: a direct challenge of another player, sometimes won, sometimes lost—much like life on the street. Other kids, girls mostly, and those boys who don't find solace in sports, gather around the set of benches and hang out. Those who have permission from their parents to smoke, smoke. Some who don't have permission smoke too. One boy who has brought his trumpet to school shyly plays a few unadorned bars from a popular song.

From a visitor's perspective, all seems rather calm and orderly at 8:30 in the morning, a few weeks from the end of the school year. And, in part, it is. But this only masks the challenges to come, for both students and staff. The day will be crazy. Kids will act up. Crises will arise. This is a small school, with 105 students. But these are tough kids, poor kids, unpredictable, and mostly troubled. That the Urban Collaborative has gotten most of them to care about their education—or, more precisely, to care about themselves—has helped. But life here is never easy, never calm, never settled.

Jack's father was recently convicted of murder in a Mafia-related shooting and locked up for life; his mother wants nothing to do with Jack. Joe's father died earlier this year from an overdose. Randy's mother committed suicide last year, after her husband, Randy's father, announced that he was gay and left her. Mela, a fourteen-year-old Vietnamese girl, had been coerced into prostitution by her live-in "boyfriend" because he knows there is good money for young prostitutes free of HIV infection; a few days earlier she was found wandering a back road in a rural town far from Providence, dumped there by three "customers" who apparently were angry at her bold refusal to fulfill their wishes. Jan, at fifteen, gave birth to a daughter in September. Roberto, also fifteen, fathered a child the previous year. Kane's father died a few years back; shortly after, his mother abandoned him; then his grandfather died and his brother was arrested for possession of heroin. Malinka missed most of school last year because she was testifying in a court case against her sister, who had given birth to a child and then tossed it out the window to its death. Don, too, has spent time in court, in connection with the death of two friends in a botched arson case.

Each student in his or her own way has struggled with pressures that most middle- and upper-class Americans never have to face. Broken families, alcoholism, drug addiction, teenage pregnancy—those things often born of the weight of poverty. In light of their troubles, it is difficult to get them to care about their education, to learn binomial equations, to name the major mountain ranges of the world, to read and debate *Romeo and Juliet*, or to understand the relationship between water pollution and macro-invertebrates. But here, somehow, they do it. At the Urban Collaborative, about 90 percent of those who come here make it through the program, many having completed three years of work in two, or two years in one. Most important, more than 80 percent of those who make it go on to finish high school.

2

ANOTHER DAY. SHORTLY BEFORE 9:00 A.M., ALBERTO LEMOS, THE school's full-time counselor, strides purposefully over to the fence, cups his hands over his mouth, and calls out to a group of kids playing basketball across the street. "Let's go, gang. Let's go." The boys keep racing from one end of the court to the other like excited, involuntary cells of some microorganisms in a petri dish. Al claps his hands, repeats his message. By the third request, the players start to give up the game, gather their belongings, and filter across Somerset Street into the school parking lot to join their more sedentary schoolmates.

Peter Case, a math teacher, herds the dawdlers, who take this chance to let fly one last three-point bomb, a buzzer-beater to start the day. Within a few minutes, they are all of the same mind and begin to head indoors. There are no bells here, though it is understood that no one should push too hard on the good will of the faculty. The faculty, for its part, would like the students to learn to come of their own accord, to take enough responsibility to be at the right place at the right time—though it is also aware that this is more than many of these kids can realistically give at this juncture in life. It's also true that many of the teachers arrive a minute or two late for meetings and classes on occasion. Military precision is not the goal here.

Al and Peter continue to urge the students toward the door, calling out to the sluggish and reluctant. Eventually all file inside, down the stairs, and into the basement community room—the boys hot and sweaty, wearing baseball caps, untucked shirts; the girls dressed mostly in sweatshirts, stretch pants, myriad earrings, and hair fixed in one of a dozen complicated

11

patterns. Many pose desperately as adults. They gather in small boisterous groups around the lunch tables, somewhat divided by race, but not strictly so. The student population is well mixed here with an equal number of white and African-American students; the remaining portion contains Hispanics and Southeast Asians. Some kids strut to the sound of their own private music. Some scuff their heels, their minds elsewhere. Some head directly for the soda machine to buy their first dose of sugar and caffeine for the day. Mark, a short, round-faced boy wearing a Chicago Bulls hat and jacket, arrives with a tray full of donuts, which he is hoping to sell to raise money for the school's explorer's club. He finds a few buyers, turns away two boys looking for handouts. "Come on, Mark ol' buddy," they plead. He scowls at them, says nothing. The donuts he doesn't sell here, he will sell in the faculty room on the honor system. Most of the teachers, as everywhere, are hopelessly addicted to donuts and coffee.

The first fifteen minutes of each day at the Urban Collaborative are dedicated to community meetings. It is the one time when students and faculty gather together, when the faculty members can make announcements, check attendance, offer bits of public praise or criticism, and generally reinforce the notion that the Urban Collaborative is above all a community.

Some days, like this one, the kids arrive full of vigor and are unwilling to settle down. It is springtime after all. Sunny and warm. And the city sounds invite their minds away through the open windows. The teachers work their way into the room. Peter Case immediately begins circulating among the students, shaking hands, offering easy good-mornings, congratulating individuals personally for their achievements, small or large. Sometimes John Howard, a senior-banking-V.P. turned social-studies teacher, joins him. There is something about John's style that makes him look more like a campaigning politician—sincere, yet a bit stiff—but the kids he greets seem to appreciate the effort nevertheless. Cati Martinez, too, makes the rounds. After she wheels Rob in, she locks the brakes to his chair and heads out to say good morning to some of her favorite students, greeting them with exuberance. Younger than the staff, Cati is the most at ease among the students, a quality that makes her seem like an older sister to them. She does not teach and is not responsible for discipline. She is free to play the role of confidante, friend, and occasional critic. Having once dropped out of school herself, Cati clearly understands their hardships and is inclined to help them make their experience better than her own. To this end, she likes to share in their excitement and offer encouragement to keep them on track.

The other teachers ease themselves in among the students or lean up against a free wall. They wait like nervous athletes before a big game.

Then it starts. Jim Snead, a science teacher, begins. "All right. Quiet down, ladies and gentlemen. Quiet down, please," he says. His voice rises above the din, yet remains utterly respectful of the crowd he addresses. The decibels drop by half. "Quiet, please," Jim repeats. He stands by the unadorned stage, shifts his considerable weight, looks around patiently. The other faculty members help out in their quadrants of the room by asking individuals to give their vocal chords a rest. The room never reaches pre-symphony silence. But it gets close enough. Someone always has his or her back to the proceedings and chatters away as if they all were still out in the parking lot.

"Corina. Jane. Shh," Jim says.

A quality to good parenting, experts will tell you, is the ability to tolerate noise. If this is true, the Urban Collaborative teachers earn high marks as parents. The general feeling is that any attempt to demand complete silence of the kids will be the beginning of the end of the school. These kids are antsy. They don't mean to be disruptive. But they truly can't sit still. For the staff, this is all right. The kids are here. They are at ease. And, generally, they pay attention. As Rob likes to say, "Just getting them to come to school is half the battle." Still, there have been days when the noise is simply too much. In a meeting the first year, for example, Rob grew angry at the group and told the students they would stay right through lunch period if necessary until they quieted down. Forty-five minutes later, they were still waiting. He hasn't used that threat since.

As the leader of the school, Rob would like to be able to command the instant attention of the group, but he needs Jim's voice; in his condition, Rob is unable to do much with his own voice amid such background noise. No diaphragm muscles to speak of, or with.

"Any announcements?" Jim asks.

Cati raises her hand. "Yeah. I just want to remind all those who took part in the walkathon . . . ."

"Shh. Quiet, please," Jim implores.

"I just want to remind all those who were in the walkathon to get your money to me as soon as possible. So far I've received very little money. So come on, folks. The walkathon does no good if you aren't going to get money from those who pledged and bring it in. I need it by Friday."

There is some giggling. The noise level rises again as a flurry of private conversations start up.

"Quiet, please," Jim says. "Tonya. Brandon. Liz. Quiet. Please. Any more announcements?"

Al holds up his hand and reminds those in the probation group that he will be meeting them in the community room later in the morning. "Remember to bring work," he says emphatically.

Connie Zeeland, the librarian, reminds those with library books to return them by the end of the week.

Peter urges kids to sign up for Aim High summer basketball camp, adding, "Especially if you are a girl." Then he says, "I'd also like to announce that Harold Greene has accelerated in math."

Everyone cheers for Harold, a small, thin boy who sits staring at the floor with a half smile.

Lynne Abbott, the school's full-time English teacher, announces that James Williams, Carrie Hart, and Ray Edwards have accelerated in English. Ray stands up and takes a bow. The others receive the applause with more humility.

After announcing the English accelerations, Lynne says, "I think Martin has something to say to the group." She raises her chin and fixes Martin with a stare.

Martin stands and glances at Lynne, then at Cal. "I just wanted to apologize for hitting Cal yesterday," he says quickly and sits down.

Another student apologizes for cheating in English. Lynne walks over and hands him a visor with a small sign across the front that reads, "I will not cheat." He puts it on to the sound of jeers and catcalls.

A boy named Phillipé apologizes for lying to the discipline committee and apologizes to Connie for being disrespectful.

Every few days there is an apology or two. Even if they are spoken half-heartedly, they are solid reminders that each student is responsible for his or her actions and that those actions affect the whole community. The staff believes this one lesson can mean the difference between success and failure.

Jim announces that the science class will be making a trip to the river this afternoon. "Last trip of the year," he says.

Gloria Merchant, the art teacher, holds up her hand. Teachers of electives are not required to attend these meetings and most don't; their elective classes are late in the morning and many of them have other jobs. But Gloria came this morning just to make a special announcement.

"Gloria," Jim says, giving her the floor.

"I just wanted to let everyone know," she says, smiling, "that Emmett has won a scholarship to Rhode Island School of Design for this summer."

The room erupts in cheers.

"I should also say," she adds above the tumult, "that Emmett had to compete against dozens of artists from all the middle schools in the area for this. It's a great achievement."

Again, the students cheer and pound their fists on the table, chanting "Emmett, Emmett, Emmett." Gloria pumps her fist in the air.

A shy, lanky boy whose clothes have little to hang on to, Emmett ducks his chin into his chest and sits still as friends tousle his hair. He had never done much with art until this year, when he discovered he had a real talent. He won the scholarship with a series of stylish sketches of African-American men, a few comic clay sculptures, and some delicate pastel landscapes. These days he can be seen walking proudly with his portfolio tucked under his arm.

Amid all the noise for Emmett, a girl sitting by the stage says to another girl, "You're real funny looking."

"Shut up."

"No. You are. You don't have no lips hardly at all."

"Shut up."

"No, you shut up."

"Girls, quiet please," Jim says. "Melanie. Tina. Shh."

Jim quiets the room again. "Rob has an announcement," he says. "Quiet, please."

"First of all, I want to apologize to Andrew for accusing him of lying," Rob says. "Sorry, Andrew." He nods to the boy. (The apology was the result of a decision by the discipline committee. Although Rob disagreed with the decision, he felt he had to honor it.) "Second, I want to remind you all that the drawing for the lottery will be on Friday, so keep working hard. The prizes," he says, "include backpacks, cosmetic kits, movie tickets, a calculator, pizzas, baskets of food, and a turtleneck of your choice from my closet." The latter is meant as a joke, since Rob seems to have an endless supply of turtlenecks.

"And remember, tomorrow is school colors day," he adds. "Anyone who wears the school colors gets a free donut." The lottery and the donuts are part of an effort to keep the kids engaged late in the year. Wearing the school colors—black and red, chosen in honor of the Chicago Bulls—is simply a way to make the day different. The lottery, which was Connie Zeeland's idea, is designed to keep them working, to give them a short-term goal. And so far it has worked well.

The kids start chattering again and begin to get out of their seats, thinking the meeting is over.

"One more thing. One more thing," Rob says. He needs Jim to get their attention.

"Quiet, please," Jim booms. "Rob has another announcement. Quiet."

"I want all the kids who take the Providence bus by the hospital to stay here briefly after the meeting," Rob says. "Everyone else can go to class."

The kids filter out. Some try to buy another snack at the vending machine, but Rob tells them forcefully to do that later. As they leave, Rob calls a few out of the crowd and tells them to stay.

"Howard," he says. "Stay."

"What for?"

"You take the Providence bus?"

"Yeah, but I didn't do nothing."

"I asked you to stay. Take a seat, please."

Most mornings, Rob approaches these meetings cheerfully. But this day he seems perturbed. A few other Providence bus riders try to sneak out the door, but he calls them back curtly. And when he has them all assembled, he asks Cati to close the door.

"I've been told there was an incident at the bus stop yesterday afternoon," he says. "Anyone want to tell me about it?"

"Nothing happened," one boy says, sounding a bit peeved that they are being accused.

"That's not what I've been told," Rob says. He throws his arms back to stretch, then rubs one hand beneath his left eye. "I heard that some of you were getting out of hand and that when a security guard at the hospital asked you to move, one of you threatened him."

"No. We didn't do anything. The guy was just being a jerk," Howard says.

"Look," Rob says, hitting his hand against the padded arm of his wheelchair, "I'm going to have to take the hospital's word on this. They called me. And this is not the first time there has been an incident at the bus stop. The guard wouldn't have asked you to move if you hadn't done something."

Howard starts to protest, but Rob won't let him. "When an adult in authority asks you to do something, the last thing you should do is threaten him. As I hear it, one of you was stupid enough to threaten the guard with a gun."

"It's not true."

"I don't know whether or not anyone actually threatened this person. But he certainly feels that he was threatened. I also hope to God that those of you who might have been involved didn't mean this and don't have any intentions of carrying this further."

"There was no gun," one student says.

"I just wanted to let you know what has happened because of your actions," Rob continues, ignoring their protests. "There happened to be a woman at the bus stop who is the mother of the girl from Pawtucket who was shot in the head over the weekend. The girl is in critical condition and may not make it. The mother had been sitting by her daughter's side at the hospital all day. When one of you mentioned that you had a gun, the woman broke down. Whoever said that, you should know you put this woman through hell—and for what? Because you didn't want to move?"

Rob scans the group. Generally speaking, the kids don't take well to such direct criticism. Their gut reaction is to defend themselves, guilty or innocent. But now they all sit still, apparently unaware until this moment that their actions had had such an effect.

"I don't want any of you using that bus stop for the rest of the year. You understand? You can all walk down to catch the bus at the next stop. I want you to stay away from the hospital and hospital grounds. Now, go on to class and think about this. OK? This is serious stuff."

Duly humbled, they leave.

Cati releases the brakes to Rob's wheelchair and wheels him out of the room without a word. As is her habit, she stops to check the girl's bathroom to make sure no Urban Collaborative students are hiding out. Earlier in the year girls dallying in the bathroom was a problem. But not this day. She then hefts Rob into the small, dark elevator and takes him upstairs.

Out in the hall again, he asks Cati to leave him by the office door so he is facing down the hallway. Classes are about to start, and Rob likes to be part of the hubbub.

A boy tries to squeeze by him into the office. Rob says to him, "Martin, where are you supposed to be?"

"In English. But I just want to tell Aisha something."

"Later," Rob says.

"Come on, Rob. I just want to get a donut."

"You had your chance earlier. Go."

When need be, Rob doesn't mind the role of bad cop. Someone has to do it. The student-run discipline committee can handle certain infractions. Teachers generally rule their classrooms. But there are numerous small things (like getting Martin to class on time) and large events (like kids pulling knives on other kids) that Rob handles, always with the advice of Al and other teachers. If the school had more money, he acknowledges, he would love to hire an assistant principal to deal with the daily discipline problems. An independent evaluation of the school suggests that this would be a valuable addition. But for now, Rob is comfortable putting on this hat. Confrontation has rarely bothered him.

Al comes out of his office to tell Rob that he just got a call from Jasmine's mother, who said that Jasmine, who days earlier collapsed from the effects of anorexia, will be voluntarily spending time in the hospital.

"That's great news," Rob says. "How's her father doing with all this?"

"Apparently, he's OK about it."

"That's wonderful." After Jasmine's initial collapse, her father has come to school at Al's request to discuss the girl's health. Instead of being sympathetic, he threatened to slap her.

"Yeah, and her mother says Jasmine asked if we could get together some work for her while she's there."

Rob turns his head slightly and gives Al one of his patented expressions of disbelief, as if to say, "What? An Urban Collaborative student *asking* for work?" Instead, he says, adding a hand gesture, "Fine. I'll gladly get some for her. This is not the sort of thing we should question."

This bit of good news seems to lift Rob's spirits. He turns to Cati and asks her to write down a note to remind him to get work for Jasmine.

"Better yet," Rob says. "Why don't you go now and get some assignments for her. We can run them over at lunchtime."

While Cati starts down the hall, Rob asks a visitor—one of many in the course of the year who have come to see how well the school functions—to wheel him over to a group of girls. "Watch this," Rob says. "I won't even have to say anything. My presence will scatter them."

The visitor laughs.

"No, watch."

They approach the group. And, as Rob guessed, when he gets within two feet of the girls, they disperse without a word.

Everyone who knows Rob knows he is a gamesman. He likes the thrill of competition—once physical, now mental. He likes the joy of surprise. He likes challenge. He likes engaging his mind in everything from liar's poker to presidential politics. In high school, he was as full of mischief as he was of energy. A good student, Rob played football, hockey, and lacrosse—in love with the intensity and the immediacy of competition. He also studied Greek, shaved his head, experimented with drugs, created comical Super-Eight films, and joined in food fights. Anything that shook up the day.

In college he studied literature and gave up varsity sports for the thrill of the outdoors. For him, there was nothing quite like reaching a mountain summit, setting up camp, and engaging the mind in the wonder of the wide-open night sky. Spontaneity and creativity were at the heart of his existence then. The days were to behold. After he and a friend were picked up by the state police for hitchhiking on the Maine Turnpike *twice* on the same spring day, they were brought to the York County jail, where inmates shaved Rob's head. Asked to respond on the evening news to this breach of his civil rights, Rob rubbed his head and told the grimacing reporter that he thought the inmates did a passable job. Sitting in a bar one Friday night, he convinced a group of friends to go skydiving because it was something new and thrilling and because they might never get the opportunity again. Such was the way he moved from week to week, one eye on literature, the other on the potential in each day. This is also the sort of impulse that led him to dive into an unfamiliar section of river and break his neck—and to start an alternative school for kids at risk.

Rob has Al station him in the hallway beside a handmade poster of a black bull on a red background, the school mascot, with the title phrase from M. C. Hammer's hit song "Too Legit To Quit." It has become the school's unofficial motto. Across from the poster in the entranceway is a Michael Jordan "Wings" poster, and below it is a bulletin board announcing the ongoing race among the randomly assigned student groups to see which group will get the most accelerations in the final month of school. The winning team earns a day at the beach. Rob's group is dead last. Over the doorway is the Urban Collaborative "Wall of Fame," a John Howard creation in which students' photos are posted with a notation of their achievements. At the moment, there are two students on the wall, Kara Connell and Mark Korda; Kara for helping out with the walkathon, Mark for his work tutoring young math students.

Things have quieted down in the hall, and Rob and Al talk about two girls who are on in-house suspension—a new idea being tried for a few repeat offenders of minor infractions. In-house suspension requires them to wear a tag around their necks, like security clearance IDs, and between every period of the day they must check in at the office. This makes life rather annoying, and perhaps slightly humiliating, for the two girls. But it also allows the school to keep a very close watch on them for an entire day or two. The hope is that after going through this for a day, the girls will think twice about skipping out of class or sneaking a cigarette in the bathroom. Maybe. Maybe not.

"I'm surprised they are doing it so willingly," Al says.

Rob agrees. He tells Al that for last Saturday's detention, in which students came in for a few hours with parents (another of the school's ways of dealing with end-of-the-year trouble), all but one of fifteen kids showed up. "That's amazing," Rob says.

"That's another thing we probably shouldn't question," Al says as he heads back to his office.

Rob asks Aisha, the school's secretary, to wheel him into his office while Cati is out. Aisha readily agrees. In addition to her secretarial work and the occasional push for Rob, she has proven indispensable to the school—at times playing the role of traffic cop, mother, friend, and nurse.

Rob's office is a simple, utilitarian space. The only hint of luxury is an aging air-conditioner stuck into a sheet of plywood in one of the window casements. There are three folding tables: one for Cati, one for Rob, and one to catch all the miscellaneous stuff. Along the windowsill are samples of clay sculptures from art class and one besieged spider plant. There are two paper-recycling bins that collect paper only after it has been used on both sides—an office rule. The walls are a distant cousin to off-white, fairly scuffed from chairs, tables, and shoes. Off in the corner is a private bathroom, which holds a standing coatrack, a school boom box, and an assortment of items needed for Rob's personal care.

The days, Rob will tell you, seem terribly short, and he hates to waste time. First, he calls a state legislator on his speaker phone to discuss the school's funding for the following year. Pawtucket and East Providence have committed resources for another year, but the Providence School Committee, in an effort to cut $3 million from its budget, decided not to fund the Urban Collaborative. The same thing happened in each of the past two years, but Rob is more worried this time. The mayor, the governor, and nearly everyone else in a position of authority support the school. The parents support the school. The students support the school. The other public schools support the school. The *Providence Journal* supports the school and recently named Rob as one of ten people in the state who will likely make a difference in the 1990s. But these are desperate times in Providence. A month back, Rob had been forced to give his teachers layoff notices. They are free to look for other jobs, but for the moment they have all decided to hang in there, hoping that Rob will be able to work something out with the city, as he has in the past, and that this foolish funding method will end soon so they can concentrate on teaching. Rob is publicly hopeful but privately worried that this time there might be no rabbit to pull out of the hat.

A student named Jack walks into Rob's office. Jack had been suspended for a week for a number of small infractions—from smoking cigarettes between classes to skipping out on detention to harassing another student on the bus.

"What are you doing back?" Rob asks. "You're supposed to be out until tomorrow."

Jack, tall and imposing, sits down at the chair by Rob's desk. "I thought I was supposed to be back today."

"Tomorrow," Rob says.

"Oh," Jack says. He takes off his baseball hat and twirls it. "You want me to leave?"

Rob thinks about it. He's pretty sure Jack knows he is back a day early. But the fact that he is may be a good sign. He decides to let him stay. "Since you're here you might as well stay. But I should warn you, Jack, that you are very close to getting thrown out of here. Do you understand that? You mess up again and you may be gone, even if it is the last day of school."

"You keep blaming me for everything . . . ," Jack starts.

"I don't blame you for everything," Rob cuts in, taken back by the suggestion that he, or the school, has been unfair with Jack. The truth is to the contrary. They've given him more chances than they give most students. "If occasionally you are accused of doing something that you didn't do, you've got to realize it's only because you have done so many things wrong this year. You've got to understand that nobody is willing to give you the benefit of the doubt anymore."

Jack—six foot three, sixteen years old—is finishing his second year at the Urban Collaborative. He entered at the seventh-grade level, and in the first year here he managed to complete two years of work. During the second year, Rob hoped he would complete two more years of work, but Jack opted to do only one. As Rob says about him later, "Jack is very smart and basically flew through the criteria the first year. Our plan was to push him to complete two more years of work. He is easily capable of this. But Jack had other ideas, and, as usual, he prevailed."

"Get yourself to class," Rob tells him. "And keep out of trouble."

"Hey, Rob," Jack says, flashing a wry smile. "Do I look like someone who would cause trouble?"

"Yes. Now go." As Jack stands up, Rob adds, "Hey, Jack. I'm serious."

"I know, Rob. I know." Jack ambles out of the office, self-consciously cocky.

Rob worries about Jack. He is capable of college. But he is also capable of finding himself in jail someday. His father is serving a life sentence for killing a man at the behest of a Mafia leader, and sometimes

Rob suspects that Jack is unconsciously steering a course in that direction—
not murder, but lawlessness. When Jack first came to the Urban Collaborative, he was living with his grandmother and an aunt who has Down's
Syndrome. His grandmother says that Jack would often be very helpful
around the house, cutting the lawn, washing her car, or helping to care
for his aunt. But he kept late hours and bad company, and he often skipped
school. His grandmother disapproved and asked him to come home earlier
and to attend school regularly. Jack would not listen. After a while his
grandmother decided he had to move out. At this point, his twenty-three-
year-old stepmother, who is also caring for Jack's younger sister, reluctantly
took him in. His older sister dropped out of school at sixteen and has her
own apartment in Central Falls. But he is not welcome there. His mother,
also living a short distance away in Central Falls, made it clear two years
ago that she did not want him living at her home. She's a registered
nurse, working on her master's degree, and wanted only to start a new
life. Once or twice a month, he visits his mother. And every week, he
makes a trip to the maximum security prison to visit his father.'

During his first year at the Urban Collaborative, Jack stole his grandmother's car and ran away with another boy, who had been sentenced to
the state training school in Massachusetts. Jack apparently decided he
wanted to help this other boy avoid doing time. No one knew how to get
in touch with them, but Jack managed to stay in contact with Jim Snead
through the help of another Urban Collaborative student. One night around
midnight, Jim Snead got a call from Jack, who had just slammed his
grandmother's car into the back of another car near a shopping mall. He
was scared and wanted to end this episode and come back to school. "In
many ways, he's a little kid in a man's body," Rob says, "and this is the
source of much of his trouble. The funny thing is, I think he is really
afraid of many things—especially, for some reason, blacks. He won't even
travel on the city bus because he's afraid he'll end up in a fight."

Jack broke nearly every rule that could be broken at the Urban
Collaborative. But he never got into a fight or brought in a weapon.
Instinctually, he knows where the lines are. He also knows how to beat
the system, how to complain loudly of injustice, how to argue for leniency—a
trait, perhaps, that he picked up from his father, who tried to beat the
system one too many times.

"It's hard to say what is going to happen to Jack," Rob says privately.
"I do know, however, that he is a master at manipulation. His father cares
greatly about him and has high hopes, which is right. But he doesn't have
much control over Jack. Jack's father dropped out of East Providence High

School. And now he hopes Jack will go there, get involved in sports, and get his diploma. Jack's a great wrestler. But I doubt he will put up with a regimented sports program. His life is one of constant frustration and futility, and, as much as I would hate to see it, I'm afraid there is a fair likelihood he'll end up behind bars one day." He pauses. "It's so damn complicated. The lives of these kids. The bizarre and painful ways in which they grow up. You look at a kid like Jack and you see great potential, and you see all the social ills working against him. But who knows? Maybe not. That's the thing. We never know what will turn a kid around. So we just keep trying."

Between classes, Chris Cuthbertson, a social studies teacher, tells Rob she overheard someone saying that Randy Boyer boasted that he had a weapon in his pocket earlier this morning.

"Shit," Rob winces. "Any idea what it might be?"

"I don't really know," Chris says. "But I don't think it's a gun."

"It better not be."

"I just thought you ought to know about this before anything happens."

Rob nods his head and thanks Chris as she leaves.

Cati enters with a donut, and work assignments for the girl in the hospital.

"Cati, could you straighten me out?" Rob asks.

"Sure." She puts her donut on her desk, which is covered with school financial records and letters. She stands behind Rob, slips her arms under his, and locks her fingers together in front of his chest. In the quick motion of a weightlifter, she pulls Rob up, then lets him down gently into a better, more erect sitting position. Next, she comes around front and adjusts his pants.

"A little more on the left," Rob says.

She gives another quick yank.

"That's good." Then she leans him forward, straightens out the back of his shirt and sweater, and leans him back again.

"Thanks," Rob says. "Could you get Randy for me?"

"Uh-oh. What's Randy done now?"

"He may have some sort of weapon."

"You're kidding."

"I don't really know. But I'd better make sure."

"This should be interesting," Cati says. And she leaves to find Randy.

Rob, meanwhile, looks at his notes, then buzzes Aisha on the intercom and tells her that a woman from the Rhode Island Foundation should be arriving at any moment. Would she ask the woman to wait five minutes? He has to talk to a student first. Then he calls Al and asks him to come in and help him with Randy.

Al arrives and Rob fills him in, then Cati returns with Randy. She sits at her desk and busies herself with a stack of bills. Randy is wearing a leather coat. He is a tall, slim boy with raw skin and short, spiked hair. His life, Rob and Al know, has been difficult and confusing. His father left his mother and announced he was gay. His mother later committed suicide. Randy seems confused by his own sexual identity. What frustrates Rob is that Randy is constantly taunting other students and then becoming upset when they fight back. Earlier in the week, he walked away from the outdoor physical education class, ignoring the teacher's requests that he stay. He said afterward that a former student had come by and thrown him to the ground. If it happened, Rob would like to offer Randy some help, press charges even. But no one else saw the other boy, and, more to the point, Randy broke school rules himself by ignoring the teacher and leaving class. It's always like this with Randy. He may have legitimate complaints about abuse from other students, but he won't trust the school and won't work with the system. He blames everyone, including Rob, for making his life miserable. Meanwhile, he takes direction from no one.

"What do you want?" he asks Rob, his tone defiant.

"I want you to empty your pockets."

"What for?"

"Because I heard you might have a weapon."

He gives Rob a look of exasperation. "I don't have a weapon."

"Then you won't mind emptying your pockets."

"This is ridiculous."

"I don't think so."

Randy takes a few items out of his pockets. A pen. A pack of gum. His wallet. "There. That's all. Satisfied?"

"Take off your jacket and give it to Al."

"You're always accusing me of something," Randy says, sounding hurt.

"We are not always accusing you of something," Rob says, raising his eyebrows because he had just heard the same line from Jack Longo. "We've heard you may have a weapon, and we need to find out. Please take off your jacket."

Randy does with a huff and hands it to Al. "You won't find anything."

Al pats it down, finds something in the inside pocket, takes it out, and shows it to Rob. It's a jagged top to a small tin can. Glued to it are a dozen short copper nails. On the back is a piece of string that apparently allows this homemade device to slip over Randy's fingers and rest in the palm of his hand.

"What's this, Randy?"

Randy turns red. No explanation comes immediately to mind, so he explodes with anger. "You won't protect me, so I have to protect myself. All right," he screams. "I've got a right to protect myself."

"You've got a right to get an education here without fearing for your safety. But you don't have a right to bring in a weapon."

"I hate this place," he says.

"Look. We'd like to help you as best we can, Randy. And we will. But whatever else might be going on, you can't bring weapons into school. I want you to call your father. You're going to be suspended for the rest of the week."

Randy protests. But Rob effectively cuts him off and asks him to wait in the hall while he talks to Al. Al agrees with Rob. They could, in fact, expel him from school. But this isn't the most dangerous of weapons. Still, the idea of it is disturbing. That Randy feels threatened is probably true. But he has to learn to get along better with both students and faculty.

"I just wish we could get him to stop thinking the world is out to get him," Rob says.

Al and Rob briefly talk over their strategy, then Al departs. Rob asks Cati to make a note for him to call Randy's father that night. Randy is sent back to class. Then Rob checks with Aisha to see if the woman from the Rhode Island Foundation is waiting. She hasn't arrived. So he stays at his desk and once more rifles through his battered blue folder for notes of things to do. Rob doesn't trust his memory. Every day, from the moment he wakes up until the moment he goes to bed, and sometimes later, he is instructing people to jot down thoughts, names, phone numbers, comments, things to remember to do, letters to write, errands to run. By the end of each day there is a fistful of notes in varying handwriting crammed in his folder. To a stranger, it might seem chaotic. But Rob has his own system and knows what to reach for with his rubber stick—a short, pencil-like device tipped in rubber that allows him to painstakingly turn pages or, in this case, pull out a piece of paper from his folder. He ponders each note. Some he puts aside with a soft curse—Rob's way of dealing with the never-ending stream of work. Other sheets go directly into the recycling bin.

On the wall to his right is a photo of a casual, windblown John F. Kennedy with his arm around his daughter, Caroline, at the beach. The caption reads, "It's okay to dream." Below this are a number of snapshots of happy Urban Collaborative students: on a whale-watching trip, in acting class, at a Halloween party. On the opposite wall is a photograph of the staff and students in the 1988 SPIRIT program, a summer program for at-risk students.

Over Rob's desk is another board filled with lists and notes and letters and announcements: a flyer for Frank "Happy" Dobbs Basketball Camp at Brown University, applications to the Urban Collaborative, a fire-drill schedule, a conference announcement for the National Association of Independent Schools, an invitation to Community Prep's graduation. There are also some family photographs. One of Rob's six-year-old son, Justin, with their golden retriever and a soccer ball. Another of Rob, his wife, Bonnie, and Justin smiling in the White Mountains. Even now, the mountains remain an elixir in Rob's life. Each summer, he finds at least a few days when the family can escape from Rhode Island to Franconia Notch in the White Mountains, the one place he is drawn to again and again, to sit on the porch of a chalet, breathe the mountain air, and stare down on the Littleton valley and the hills rolling away toward Canada; or to sit by the shores of Echo Lake, a deep, cool, glacier lake puddled between the towering peaks of Cannon and Lafayette Mountains, where he can watch his family swim as afternoon clouds spill over the peaks.

Before Rob finishes checking his notes, Karen Voci, the woman from the Rhode Island Foundation, arrives. She has come to talk with Rob about the school's five-year plan. Although funding for the following year is in doubt, Rob is going ahead with a plan that will help make the Urban Collaborative a more financially sound institution in five years. "It's best," he says, "to keep looking ahead."

Optimism is one of Rob's greatest strengths. Another is his ability to raise money and rally support for the school. In the past year, he was able to raise $112,000 from private sources. The Rhode Island Foundation has been particularly generous, giving the school a total of $44,000 during the past three years. One of Rob's hopes is that the foundation will contribute again for next year, this time with a $10,000 challenge grant that will help in raising contributions from individuals. Rob could go after bigger dollars, but he says he does not want to raise money on the scale of most private schools. He doesn't feel it's right. "It's important to me that the public sector supports us," he says. "I have been adamant about this from the start, and I will continue to be adamant about this." In Rob's struggles to get funding from the City of Providence, it has been suggested to him more than once that he raise operating money privately. There are not many comments that make him more angry. "I think this betrays ignorance and a total lack of understanding of what this school is about," Rob says later. "First of all, it is a public school. It is the public's responsibility. These students are still the obligation of the public school system. Simply because we've raised money from private sources, about 10 percent of our budget, some people think we could raise all of it privately. But money we receive from private sources is given on the very clear understanding that we'll use it not for basic operating expenses but for additional things in the school, to extend our influence beyond the school day, the school year, the school building, to build in those components of the school that make it special, that make a kid feel as if there is a real reason for being here." He also points out that the private sector wouldn't be able to support the school completely if asked. A community like Providence is too small to afford that kind of money year in and year out. "But the biggest reason I'm opposed to asking the private sector to fund even a portion of the operating expenses," Rob adds, "is that the minute the private sector does this, the public sector will never pick up on that again. It will be gone forever. And part of my hope with this school is that it offers ways to improve public education."

Another of Rob's goals is to build an endowment so the Urban Collaborative can eventually have a home of its own, at the very least, and a steady flow of discretionary money that will allow the school to continue to be flexible. At the moment, Rob and members of a volunteer building committee are eyeing a former factory closer to downtown Providence than the current building. It is a large brick and timber structure, a former commercial cleaners, adjacent to Classical and Central High Schools and their athletic fields. Nearby is a community center with two gyms. The current building is adequate for now. But space is tight, and, more important, it could all be taken away from them in a moment's notice. What Rob wants is a secure home.

Karen Voci asks Rob about the public funding situation for next year. Rob explains that nothing is clear but that just about everyone wants the school to remain in existence. "I understand even the mayor has told the school committee to find a way to fund us for next year," Rob says. "So I feel pretty confident that we're going to be here. On the other hand, we keep hearing the same refrain: 'You have a worthy program, but we just don't have the money this year.' So we'll just have to wait and see and not panic."

Karen shakes her head at the thought of the school committee cutting off funding for the Urban Collaborative. She, like so many others, is a firm supporter of the school. "It's crazy for the school committee to say that what they have is the best they can expect when there is a program like this as living proof that there is a better way," she says.

Rob shakes his head in agreement. Then he talks bluntly about the school's needs. And when he asks Karen for $10,000 that he hopes to match with other sources, she doesn't blink. In fact, it seems like a rather small amount to her, given the program's success. Karen agrees to come to a meeting of the building committee to figure out how the foundation could get involved in the school's long-range planning.

She leaves, and Rob calls a student's mom on the speaker phone. He dials the number, then forgets who he is calling. A woman answers and Rob asks, "Who is this?"

The woman responds, rather perturbed, "Who is *this?*"

"This is Rob DeBlois at the Urban Collaborative."

"Oh, hi, Rob. This is Gloria," her tone changing.

"Gloria. Yes. Forgive me. I actually forgot who I was calling."

"It's OK."

"I'm calling because of Denny. He seems to be heading the wrong way. I think he needs a lot of attention here and at home or we might lose him."

"I know. I know, Rob. He stays out real late. He won't listen to me no more. I can't do anything with him. That's the problem. He comes home whenever he wants. Does what he pleases. He ignores punishment. Sometimes he don't get home 'til eleven o'clock at night, or midnight. I call his father, but his father don't want to be bothered."

"Well, we are losing him here, too. He isn't doing any work, and he seems to be getting into trouble at least once a week. If he won't listen to you, maybe you'll have to file wayward charges."

"You think so?"

"Something has to happen. I think he's a bright kid, Gloria. And I think he's a good kid. But he's getting himself mixed up with the wrong crowd, and pretty soon he'll be in bigger trouble than he can handle."

"What should we do?"

"I guess I'd suggest you keep trying to talk to him this week. He's coming back to school tomorrow. Tell him it is absolutely essential that he comes and does his best for the next few weeks. If that doesn't work, maybe you'll have to file wayward charges. He started off real well, and I'd hate to lose him. He's too good a kid to lose."

"I'll try, Rob."

"Thanks, Gloria."

"Thanks for calling. And please give me a call any time."

"Don't worry, I will."

The day goes on like this. Rob heads downstairs during lunch to talk with kids and members of the faculty. He usually doesn't eat anything—no breakfast, no lunch—until he gets home for dinner. There is no time. After lunch, he takes his turn running a class that the school has labeled "criteria," an hour each day when kids can work on whatever subject they like. It's his way of keeping in touch with the academics of the school, to get away from his role of director and do one of his favorite things: work with students, mostly one-on-one.

Later, he has to deal with three girls who got caught using a stolen telephone credit card. They made more than six hundred dollars' worth of calls, many to a boy in New York City. Rob questions them individually to make sure their stories are the same. One girl stole the number from her mother and, not understanding how the billing system worked, passed the number along to her friends, figuring they'd be able to call anywhere for free. Once he is satisfied they are telling the truth, Rob tells them that they'll have to pay for the calls. The girls seem humbled and scared by the experience.

The school day is drawing to a close, and Rob shifts into high gear. A boy named Kane knocks on his door. Apparently he had pulled down another boy's pants before English class. Few other students were in the room and because he was wearing a long shirt, the boy suffered little embarrassment. But Rob wants to make sure this isn't the beginning of a feud. In Rob's youth, he might have done something like this. But he also knows the circumstances are different with these kids. Such an act can be the beginning of war, and he wants to defuse it before it can start. Rob decides to give Kane detention after school and warns him not to let this get out of hand. Kane smiles and assures him it won't. "I've paid him back. We're even."

Ray and Calvin enter the office and tell Rob they have been sent for wrestling in math class. Rob lights into both of them, particularly Ray. It is his third offense in as many days. Apparently, on a science trip to the river, Ray picked up a sizable rock and threw it at science teacher Jim Snead as Jim was standing midstream collecting samples. The rock, Ray contends, was supposed to hit nearby and splash Jim. But instead it caught Jim in the leg. Another girl threw a rock and hit Jim in the head. She was expelled. "You know doing work here is not the only thing that matters. It's also how you play the game," Rob says. "You understand, Ray?"

Ray is wearing a Bart Simpson shirt and a Syracuse University hat. He looks down at his feet and doesn't answer.

"You know what you are doing, Ray? You are telling me you don't want to stay in this school," Rob says.

Because he is tired of Ray's antics, or simply tired, he does not offer to let them tell their version of the story. Instead, he tells them to call their mothers. They do, and as is typical, neither one is home. Rob suspends them for a day and sends them to the time-out room for the rest of the day, or until he can reach their parents.

They leave and Maria arrives with her graduation speech. Rob thanks her. Steven West, a part-time counselor, comes in to ask if he should cover science class tomorrow while Jim is working with the singing group. Al pops his head in the door to say he needs to talk about a student. Another girl, Leanne, waits outside Rob's door until Rob calls her in. She is concerned that her absenteeism will affect her chances of getting into high school. Rob sends her back to class with a promise to check into it. After she leaves, he looks at his notes and says, "Ah, shit." He calls in Muriel, the school's teaching assistant, and asks her to get a few buckets and hoses out of his van and drive them to a woman who has planned a car wash fund-raiser for Saturday. He calls a state representative about the funding for the school next year, asks him to see what he can do to put some pressure on the Providence School Committee. He hangs up, dials another number. A man, half-asleep, picks up the phone and says hello. Rob says, "Who is this?"

The guy says, "Who is this?"

Rob tells him, then remembers that he was calling a girl's mother, but evidently he has gotten her boyfriend instead. On a whim, he asks the man if he is interested in helping out at the car wash. The boyfriend laughs and says no way.

Rob hangs up and dials a woman who has allowed science students to use her land to study the Moshassuck River. They are planning an end-of-the-year picnic in her yard for students with good attendance, and he wants to talk over the food—pizza, burgers, and whatever else she wants to include.

He looks at the clock, turns to Cati, and asks her to straighten him up again and check his leg bag. She does, and empties the bag into a soda can.

That evening, Rob sits in his living room, exhausted. He isn't feeling well, again. The catheter is causing trouble and he may have another infection, one of many he gets each year. For the first time, he is starting to show his worry about the possibility of the school closing because of lack of funds. He shakes his head. The Urban Collaborative is an easy target, despite all it has done for the kids and despite the fact that the program can save the city and state money in the long run. For a half hour, at any rate, he doesn't want to think about it. His habit before dinner is to watch the national news on both the Boston and Providence stations, flicking back and forth between them at commercial breaks, while Bonnie prepares their food. This night, by chance, he catches a segment on alternative schools. According to the report, all such programs will take a beating this year because of budget cutbacks. Most of them are successful, the reporter notes, but they generally cause headaches for mainstream schools and teacher unions and don't garner enough support from the public sector.

"It's crazy," Rob says, "cutting programs that work and continuing to fund a system that has proven year after year that it does not work. It's so fucking crazy."

This is the first night Rob dares to utter the possibility that his school might close. He has held on to the belief that the forces of reason and common sense would prevail and the city would come up with a way to keep the Urban Collaborative going. Seeing this news report, he can't help but wonder.

Justin, who is recovering from chicken pox, runs into the room to tell his dad that dinner is ready. Rob throws his right arm out to encircle Justin but only manages to catch him on the head and muss his hair.

"Sorry, Justin."

Justin laughs and runs back into the kitchen.

Bonnie serves up a spaghetti dinner with a loaf of crusty Portuguese bread and a salad. She, too, is tired from the challenges of her day.

Justin says grace. They eat. It's a warm spring evening outside. A mockingbird is singing. After dinner, Rob will once again make numerous phone calls—to parents, to teachers, to those who may help keep the Urban Collaborative going yet another year. But there is no sense in thinking about that now.

"So," Rob says to Justin, "how did you get all those mosquito bites?" With a mouth full of bread, Justin laughs.

3

CONFUSION. YOU CANNOT START A SCHOOL WITHOUT IT. PLAN all you want. Hammer out the details. Arrange the hours into neat units. Line up your lesson plans. Assure that everyone is in sync, the buses on time. Still, confusion will stand firmly by your side like a nagging younger cousin. When the Urban Collaborative opened in the fall of 1989, confusion strolled through the front door with the wide-eyed teenagers. And it resisted leaving for the entire year.

At the start, even simple things didn't work out. Take the first lunch, for instance. Lunch? In all the planning, Rob DeBlois admits, neither he nor the rest of the staff thought much about feeding the kids the first day. They assumed the students would pack their own. But after sending the students around to get acquainted with classes and the concept of accelerated learning, the staff discovered that many of them didn't bring a thing to eat. Quickly, a teacher ran to the local market to pick up jars of peanut butter and jelly and a couple sacks of bread. It seemed like the perfect solution: quick and somewhat nutritious. But it was the last thing the students wanted. Even the hungry refused this meal. "This was our first lesson in dealing with our student population," Rob says, laughing about it now. "I think they saw peanut butter and jelly as little kids' food. Even though they had nothing else to eat and were excruciatingly hungry, they were too embarrassed to eat what we offered." It was a sharp reminder that for teenagers image *is* a staple of life.

The drama of lunchtime aside, to watch the unfolding of the Urban Collaborative is to understand why it is so difficult to offer alternatives in

32

education. Traditional public schools may not work well, but at least they are familiar. Turn on the machine in the morning and it runs fairly orderly and efficiently. It has been doing so for most of this century. That it now cranks out defective products and discards those who don't mold to the system is easy to overlook when all seems to be running smoothly.

In the beginning, the Urban Collaborative jolted and jumped, shuddered and stalled. Of the 102 students accepted, 95 showed up the first day—a good number by any school's standards—but this was due in part to Al Lemos and some Brown University students who drove all over Providence, East Providence, and Pawtucket rounding up stragglers. Of those who didn't show, some had moved away without telling anyone. Some silently decided not to come because the school didn't have organized sports at the time and didn't offer driver's education. One girl called to tell Rob she wanted to come but was stuck at her aunt's house in Pennsylvania without enough money to return to Providence. (Rob wired her money for the bus fare, figuring if she didn't show up it wasn't the worst way to gamble $60.) A few students gave it a try for a day but, not at all comfortable with the new system, decided to head back to their familiar old schools.

Another student, a fourteen-year-old Hispanic girl named Martita, called on the second day of school to tell Rob that her four-month-old baby was sick and she couldn't come. Martita had missed much of the previous year of school because of her pregnancy and decided to enroll in the Urban Collaborative because she felt she needed to make a better life for herself and her child. She and the father of the child also decided to get married. But at the start of school Martita was having trouble with her husband, who apparently had little interest in helping care for the child.

As Rob puts it, he was prepared to hear from mothers of students calling to say their children were sick, but not at all prepared to respond to a girl struggling through the eighth grade calling to say *her* daughter needed her at home.

"The first couple of days we spent mostly in crisis control," Rob recalls, "much of it on the phone trying to reach people or returning calls, tracking down student records, arranging transportation, locating absent kids, talking with parents, figuring out the payroll, ordering needed resources for the school—desks, tables, substitute teachers, you name it. I had the feeling that we were always two steps behind where we should have been—and that we might never catch up."

On his first weekend, Rob spent nearly all his waking hours creating a student roster, setting up an accounting system, writing a report for the board of directors, and getting a mailing out to parents describing the program in more detail and offering advice on how they could get involved. By the next Monday he was exhausted. And by then, the students of the first week were getting to know each other better and were starting to stir things up.

During the second week, the school had its first fight. A boy named Tom had boasted that he "was going to kick the shit out of Hugo," another student, after school. Hugo didn't hear the boast directly, but someone else kindly told him about it. Hugo confronted Tom. Tom tried to back away sheepishly, but Hugo punched him in the face anyway. When Tom didn't respond, Hugo taunted him, then kicked him in the stomach before someone stepped in.

The first real crisis: The school's position on fighting was clear from the start—it would not be tolerated. When the teachers interviewed students the previous summer, again and again the students said they did not like their schools because they were always forced into fights. Even the supposedly tough kids said this. The promise then, to students and parents, was that the Urban Collaborative would be a safe place. In the first week the staff had the students sit down and work out a basic set of rules they all agreed they could live with. Near the top of the list was "no fighting." After Hugo hit Tom, the staff discussed the fight. Some wanted to keep Hugo in school and give him another chance. Others thought he should be expelled because his actions were vicious and he showed little remorse. Rob ultimately decided to expel him to make "a clear and unequivocal statement" that the Urban Collaborative was going to be that safe place he promised it would be. Keep Hugo, he felt, and they risked further chaos.

Crisis: Melanie, the girl from Pennsylvania, showed up smiling and anxious to work, only to grow distant, quiet, and unwilling to participate in classes. Not long after she arrived, she announced that she wanted to leave.

Rob and Al Lemos learned from a counselor in her previous school and from her school records that she had received counseling for depression and attempted suicide. Apparently she came to the Urban Collaborative looking for a place where she could feel good about herself. When the school tried to accommodate her, ironically, she pulled back. Part of her problem, Al speculated, was that she was more or less on her own. Although she said she lived with her mother, Al was never able to contact the mother by phone, mail, or personal visit. Rob and Al tried to help Melanie, but in the end she opted to return to Pennsylvania, where she claimed she had a more supportive living arrangement with her aunt.

Crisis: A shouting match broke out one morning between two girls and a boy, apparently over a love triangle that had begun to disintegrate. The boy was African American and one of the girls was white. The two had been going out, but evidently the boy had dropped her for the other girl, who was African American. The word among the students was that the boy had been threatening the white girl and telling her that his new girlfriend was going to beat her up.

It was not the worst incident, since it never got beyond accusations and shoving. Rob met with the students and extracted from them a promise to work out their differences with civility. The worst of it came later when the father of the white girl told Rob that he was withdrawing his daughter from school because, as he put it, he "had no use for black people" and saw them "only as trouble." The irony of the situation was that he planned to put his daughter into another public school that had at least as large a percentage of African-American students as the Urban Collaborative. The tragedy was that the Urban Collaborative would have been a more nurturing environment for this girl.

Crisis: A boy named Curtis had been acting up since day one. All the teachers complained about him. During the second week of school, Rob and Al discussed the matter with Curtis and his mother. "We drew up a list of his errant behavior," Al recalls, "little nagging things like his habit of constantly getting out of his seat and 'cracking' on other students. Nothing terribly bad, but stuff that constantly annoyed everyone. And we handed it to him, figuring this would give him something to think about and work on for the next few months." When it was his turn to talk, Curtis began speaking quietly and deliberately. But his emotions quickly escalated. He started banging his hands on the table and yelling at his mother, saying the problems began at home. "It's at home; it all starts at home!" he shouted. Then Curtis stormed out of the office and yelled some more. His mother, a large, strong woman, took off after him and tried to punch him. The hook she threw missed. But she got ahold of her son, shoved him up against the wall, and began beating him in earnest. Neither Rob nor Al had ever seen anything like this—and certainly weren't expecting to referee a fight between a mother and her son. Another woman had accompanied Curtis's mother to the meeting and had brought along her own young son. When Curtis started in, the child, as if on cue, said, "Curtis is no good"—words, no doubt, he had heard often enough to mimic.

Al broke up the fight. But the whole event had been too much for the boy, and he ran off down the hall screaming. Al ran after him and tried to calm him down. Eventually, Al says, "we asked the mother to leave because the situation clearly was not going to get any better with her there—especially if she was going to continue to brag, as she did, that she had 'whupped' her boy good."

Crisis: To solve the lunch problem, the school was able to get a federal lunch program to serve hot meals to students who wanted to participate. Shortly after the program began, however, a boy named Steve slapped the lunch aide for refusing his request. The lunch aide, young and already intimidated by the kids, decided to quit right then and there. Consequently, the school lost the lunch program for the remainder of the year. When Steve's mother came to school, Rob asked her to take Steve home and told her that the school would consider expelling him. In contrast to Curtis' mother, Steve's mother was very understanding. She told Rob not to feel sorry, that the school had done what it could for Steve. The boy was hyperactive, she said. But she had taken him off his medication a year earlier without consulting his doctor because it was making him too dopey. She said that she had a job but had been unable to work the past two weeks because she had been running back and forth between three different schools trying to keep her sons in school. The other two boys were like Steve, she said. Her eyes were bloodshot and puffy. For a while she held her head between her hands and rocked quietly. After a minute she asked Al if he could take her to the hospital. "I have a terrible headache and I don't feel well at all," she said. "I don't know what I'm going to do. I don't know what I'm going to do."

Crisis: Near the end of the same day, another fight broke out in a classroom. This one began with the passing of gas. The students decided to pin the act on a boy named Luis. One of those who singled out Luis was Lamar, who stood more than six feet tall and weighed close to two hundred pounds. When he accused Luis of the deed, Luis responded quite simply by saying the one thing he knew would get to Lamar, "Your mother farted." At that Lamar flew across the classroom, picked up Luis, slammed him against the wall, and was about to pummel him. Then the teacher stepped in and grabbed Lamar by the collar.

Two things you don't do with these kids, all the teachers will caution, is criticize their mothers or roll your eyes.

This time, Rob decided to suspend the boys rather than to expel them. Since no punches were thrown, and since both boys apologized readily, Rob wanted to let the students know that there was a way out before they went too far.

When Rob got home that night, shaken from the day's activities, he learned that a friend—who had been in a coma for a year as a result of an auto accident—had died.

"The next day, I remember that I commented to Cati that the good thing about the previous day was that things couldn't get worse," Rob recalls.

But they did.

Crisis: On arriving at school late the next morning, the teachers discovered a dead body outside the school building. Apparently a car had driven up onto the lawn. Inside the car, a man's body slouched over the steering wheel with two bullet holes in his stomach. The students also saw the dead man as they came to school. The police arrived, asked some questions, and then took the car away. "In late morning," Rob says, "I got a call from the mother of one of our students. She had told me that her daughter had called and wanted to go home. So I told the woman it was probably because of the murder outside. The mother's response was, 'Oh, my daughter is so dramatic. These kinds of things happen every day. Why doesn't she just learn to get along with it?'"

Crisis: At lunch one rainy day, a girl approached Rob and English teacher Lynne Abbott and told them that she had smelled alcohol on the bus driver's breath. Rob took note of this, and Lynne seized this opportunity to ask the girl about an incident rumored to have taken place on the bus a few days earlier. When pressed, the girl told them candidly that one of the boys had approached a girl named Tiffany on the bus, put his hand down her pants, then pulled her pants down. Or something like that.

After lunch, Lynne spoke with Tiffany in private about the incident. Tiffany was hesitant at first, then seemed relieved to finally be able to let someone know what had happened. She said she was sitting in one of the bus' back seats riding home. There were only four students remaining on the bus, including a boy named William, whom Tiffany had dated briefly at the end of the summer. William came to the back seat, she said, sat down beside her, and put his hand in her pants. Then he pulled down her pants as well as his own and proceeded to have intercourse with her. She said she told William she did not want to have sex.

When Rob confronted William, William admitted to having sex with Tiffany on the bus, as if it were no big deal. He said she had consented, not at first, maybe, but when he had asked her if she wanted him to stop, she said no. He also said that he had had sex with her because he had just smoked pot with another student on the bus—as if this were a legitimate excuse.

Rob contacted the school's lawyer. Then he and Al contacted both sets of parents and explained what happened. He told Tiffany that the school would back her if she decided to press rape charges against William. When they spoke with William's mother, she did not seem duly surprised. "Her reaction was one of sorrow for us for having to go through with this," Rob says. Apparently, life with William was no picnic. William, for his part, got angry at the school for, as he put it, dredging up the affair. As far as he was concerned, it should all be behind him. Earlier he told Al that Tiffany was "just a whore anyway," and that it didn't really matter what happened to her.

They learned later that William had a drinking problem. He had been found two weeks earlier passed out on the stairs to a building and had been taken to the hospital unconscious. There had been similar incidents of drunkenness throughout the previous year.

Tiffany's father spoke little English. And when Rob tried to explain what happened, it became apparent that he did not understand. Al then told him the story in Portuguese. "It was at that moment," Rob recalls, "that I suddenly understood just how terribly difficult life is for new immigrants, how they dream of success but are constantly beaten back by disappointment and tragedy." As Al explained things in Portuguese to the father, the man suddenly broke down and cried. Tiffany, too, was crying, pained by the hurt the incident had caused her father—even if it wasn't her fault.

Later they learned that Tiffany had tried to kill herself with an overdose of pills less than a year earlier. The staff made every effort to comfort her and offer support. Al gave her the number to a twenty-four-hour suicide prevention hotline as well as his home phone number.

Eventually Tiffany decided not to press charges. Instead, she left the Urban Collaborative and returned to her old junior high school. Rob and the staff decided to expel William.

Instead of focusing on academics at the start of the first year, the staff found itself dealing with an avalanche of outside issues, or at least with issues the teachers were not expecting right off the bat: the effects on students when they get involved with drugs and alcohol, the emotional and physical complexities of becoming sexually active, the seeming lack of respect many students have for each other, and their seeming inability to make positive decisions about their lives. Interestingly enough, the staff discovered, when one tries to make decisions for these students they tend to get angry and insist that they are old enough to make their own decisions. "Perhaps one of the greatest lessons of their age," Rob says, "is when they actually do make responsible decisions, when they see their own role in causing pain or sorrow for themselves and others. More often than not, however, they seem to make very bad decisions—react thoughtlessly, behave selfishly or destructively."

The school was faced with fundamental questions. Where do you start with these kids? Do you start with counseling on alcohol, on drugs, on sex and pregnancy? How do you persuade a fifteen-year-old that it's important to work on math when she is about to bring a baby into the world? How do you get a student to work on English when he has had a few bottles of beer before class? How do you get them to care about photosynthesis when their parents are struggling to pay the rent?

Crisis: In social studies class one cool morning in fall, Eric put his head down on his desk and began to cry. Chris Cuthbertson, the teacher, spoke to him briefly, then escorted him to Al's office, where he apologized and said he was simply tired and cold. Eric owned only a thin windbreaker and said he nearly froze every morning waiting for the bus. His mother promised she'd buy him a decent jacket, but she was still waiting for money and didn't know when it would come.

That afternoon, Al bought Eric a winter coat and gloves with his own money.

Crisis: A fifteen-year-old girl named Rhonda didn't show up for a week, and Al began to worry about her. Rhonda was a bright girl, but explosive and headstrong. And her life was extremely chaotic. She was being raised by her grandmother, her legal guardian, because her father had abandoned her long ago and her mother had a serious drug addiction. So one afternoon Al drove to Rhonda's home in a housing project to see if she was all right. As it turned out, Rhonda had stayed out of school because she had discovered she was pregnant. She had already decided she would keep the child, but she didn't know what to do about school.

Al asked her to come back to school, but she wouldn't. A week later Rob told Rhonda that if she wasn't going to return, he'd give her place to someone else. Her grandmother took Rhonda down to the school to talk things over with Rob. There, Rhonda admitted she did not like to go to school. At the same time, she said she did not want to drop out. Rob told her she could stay if her attendance improved dramatically. Rhonda agreed to try. But when Rob asked her what class she would attend that day, she said that she would come to school regularly starting on Monday. Rob, sensing that she'd be lost forever if she delayed, told her that if she walked out the door, she was walking out for good.

Her grandmother urged her to stay, then left the building. Rhonda started crying and ran after her grandmother. Four hours later, she came back into the office looking tired and sad. She said she had walked around the neighborhood trying to sort her thoughts. Out in the streets, looking around at the decay and poverty, she said, she decided that she really did want to come back to school.

She needed it.

For herself and for her child.

4

"WE BUILT OURSELVES A NICE LITTLE SCHOOL. THEN THE students came along and ruined it," says John Martin, who taught English at the Urban Collaborative during its first year. He is partly joking. But there is an element of truth to the sentiment. After a summer of planning, no one on the faculty was adequately prepared for what came that first September.

"I think we envisioned the kids coming in here, getting right to work, and accelerating quickly, in part because that was our hope," says Al Lemos. "But the truth is we really had no clue what we were in for. The type of kids who arrived took us completely by surprise. They were by and large tough and difficult to deal with—more difficult than the kids we have today. I think, to a certain extent, the other schools saw the Urban Collaborative as a way to get rid of kids who were really pains in the ass for them. And that was partly our fault. We didn't really know what we were about, so how could we expect the other schools to know? So, yes, that first year we struggled quite a bit.

"The other problem," he continues, "was that the kids who came here were not prepared for this. We tried to push them to work, but the idea was foreign to them because most of them hadn't done any work in years. There is so much going on in their lives that school has never been a priority. At the same time, the kids could sense that we were not as confident about what we were doing as we should have been. And they definitely took advantage of this. No question about it."

"The first year was totally bizarre," adds Lynne Abbott, shaking her head. She laughs a little, reruns the year in her mind, frowns, draws a deep breath. "I think part of the problem was that this was a brand new school. When we were recruited we didn't have the luxury of walking in here and seeing a school in action. We had no way of knowing ahead of time what it would be like, what we could expect. Rob gave us a general idea, but all of us, I think, arrived with different images of the school. And the truth is that none of us was right. It was bizarre. That's all I really can say. It was totally bizarre."

Pauline Hilgers, a math teacher who often opposed Lynne on many issues the first year, agrees. "I have to admit that when I took the job, what Rob described to me that first summer and what I walked into in September were like night and day," she says. "He made it sound, or at least I perceived it this way, as if the kids who were coming here had been interviewed and hand-picked because they really wanted to do the work. Yeah, they had had trouble in school and they had family problems, but there was a desire there to do . . . something. I assumed the focus of the school would be on accelerating the students as quickly as possible. And I expected at least some willingness on the part of the students to do work. And I was wrong.

"The point is, however, that none of us really knew what to expect. We spent much of the first year trying to figure out what we were doing. We had no past to fall back upon, no precedent to start with. We had to create everything. We designed our own schedule, created our own report cards, wrote our own curriculum, invented our own rules of conduct, and so forth. We did agree at the start that we would require mastery learning. But everything else was more or less up for grabs. It was intense. It was definitely intense. We had a bare bones plan that we scraped together, and we prayed that it was going to work. And parts of it did. But parts of it didn't."

Peter Case, who team teaches with Pauline, is more philosophical about the troubles that first year. "When you try to invent something new, something in education that has not been tried before, you run into problems," he says. "The creative process is not without its stumbling blocks." He smiles. "And believe me, we've stumbled. We've encountered all that we could encounter. It's as if the whole first year we were on a spaceship riding through a strange and unfamiliar landscape. The kids were older and bigger than they are now and therefore tougher to manage or motivate. Only Lynne and Al came from schools that were at all similar. The rest of us were more or less clueless. Opinionated, but clueless.

"I thought about giving up numerous times, to tell you the truth. I thought this was too much. But since I had no concept of what it could be like, I had no sense of how much punishment I should take. I kept saying at home, 'You're copping out if you quit now. This is what you've wanted to do all along. And if you don't give it at least a year you will never forgive yourself.' So I decided that I was in it for at least the year. No matter how bad it got, I was going to stay. And it got pretty bad."

Down the hall, Chris Cuthbertson looks across her momentarily empty classroom. "I had some expectations based on my experience with the SPIRIT program," she says, referring to the summer program Rob had started in 1983 and where the two had met. "But I would say on the whole that the kids here the first year were more challenging than the kids in SPIRIT. They were older and less hopeful about their futures. I think the biggest surprise, however, was trying to work with the staff. Not to criticize anyone individually, but we did not work well together as a group. I don't know if this would happen with any new school, but it was really quite painful at first. Communication was not good from the start. The staff meetings were vicious. I went home in tears almost every day until November. It was that bad."

While staff members couldn't agree on much at the start of the year, they all agree now that the process of becoming a school was one of the most painful experiences of their lives. Even Rob, who prides himself on his ability to deal with adversity, was shaken.

"Well, yes, I guess I would have to say that we were flailing at the start," Rob says. "I kept hoping everything would fall into place quickly. But it didn't. Instead, we ran up against one problem after another. And we spent hours arguing over everything, even the smallest detail. The tension was incredible in part, I think, because of everyone's feeling of ownership of the school. Everyone had a vision of the school and everyone tried to move the group in his or her direction, which in retrospect, I suppose, makes perfect sense. We were not only creating a product, but we were struggling to define the process by which we would create that product."

From the beginning, Rob wanted this to be a school run by the teachers. He had read enough to know that other schools were trying similar experiments in school-based management and were reporting good results. He also knew that teachers in traditional schools too often feel as if they have no control over anything. Bureaucracy, with the best intentions, can enervate. Here's your curriculum—your books, your schedule, your extra duties, your roster, the school policies—now go teach. Eventually, many teachers grow cynical. They lose a sense of purpose.

Rob's goal was to let the teachers have as much authority as possible. "I knew this would be best in the long run," he says. "I knew that if you give the teachers authority, not only in their own classrooms but in the entire school, they will work hard and be productive and, hopefully, successful."

As simple as the concept might be, however, the process was never easy. Right from the start, the staff members fought over ideology. Bad feelings erupted into verbal confrontation. Nerves frayed. Some of the teachers wanted stricter discipline: "No hats or gum chewing in the school." Others were more liberal: "Yes to hats and gum—and portable cassette players, for that matter—and let them call us by our first names." Some wanted to throw out the troublemakers: "They disrupt class for those who want to work and make it impossible for us to keep order." Others thought they had an obligation to work with all of the kids: "If we let the trouble-makers go so easily, they will drop out and we'll have lost sight of our mission."

At one point early in the fall semester, as a reminder that what he was witnessing was not unexpected, Rob reviewed an article he had written on alternative education just before he began the steps to create the Urban Collaborative. It ended this way: "Without a doubt, both teachers and students will have to get used to a new way of ordering their day. They will be forced to define how their day will be productive rather than let a set schedule allow them to just go through the motions of teaching and learning.

"There will be times when some administrators, teachers, and students will not know what others are doing. There will be a certain level of organizational ambiguity to which both staff and students will have to adjust.

"At times the school will appear to be chaotic. But it will not be boring. It will not be the kind of place where a student can easily pull back, turn off, and remain untouched."

Chris likes to describe the summer before school opened, when Rob invited the staff on a retreat of sorts to the rural town of Exeter, Rhode Island. Rob had hired a specialist in team building and management consulting to come help the staff learn how to work together. Chris laughs about it now. "This guy put up a big sheet of newsprint on the wall and asked us all sorts of questions. 'On a scale of quiet to talkative, where would you place yourself?' That sort of stuff. 'Who are the people who have influenced you most in your life?' It was a good idea, I suppose, but it was way too premature for us because nobody trusted anybody enough to say anything meaningful. We were all incredibly guarded. I remember we brought a lot of beer along, thinking that after our formal session we could hang out and get to know each other. But it turned out to be a horrible scene. There we were, standing on the concrete patio of this odd little raised ranch where we were staying, and we were fighting mosquitoes, drinking beer, and trying to pretend this was a jovial occasion—and I know everyone was thinking this was an incredible waste of time. No one knew what to say. We just smiled and coughed out pleasantries. And, afterward, part of the plan was that we were to make our own dinner so we could get a sense of what it means to work together, or something like that. So we made dinner." She laughs some more. "And a month later it came out that so-and-so was mad at so-and-so because she criticized the way she cut up the salad fixings. Incredible stuff like that."

This may have come as a surprise to Chris and the others, but such behavior is fairly standard for any new group. According to psychologist M. Scott Peck, the first stage of building a community is exactly this sort of false joviality, which masks doubts and concerns. "The first response of a group in seeking to form a community," Peck writes in *Different Drum*, "is most often to try to fake it. The members attempt to be an instant community by being extremely pleasant with one another and avoiding all disagreement." The problem is, it never works.

The second stage, Peck notes, is chaos, in which each member tries to "convert" the others to his or her way of thinking—and usually without success. It would be nice to think that such a stage is avoidable, but Peck argues that, human nature being what it is, the convergence of wills is inevitable.

"It was extremely frustrating at first," Pauline says. "I have to say that this is the most incredible group of professionals I have ever worked with. Fantastic people, all talented in their fields and gifted teachers. But you also have a group of incredibly strong personalities. We don't always see things eye to eye. And when we clash, boy do we clash. We ended up having huge battles among the staff. Are we an accelerated school or an alternative school? What is our focus? Truthfully, I think we spent most of the first year not really answering that question. I felt the focus of the school should have been on the accelerated program. Others really felt the focus was on the alternative elements. And no one wanted to give much ground. That was real hard for me. I'm from the Midwest, from a very conservative upbringing. It took me almost two-and-a-half years before I would admit to any of them that I voted for a Republican, for instance. It may sound silly, but I knew they'd just pounce on me. So I came at this whole project from a different angle oftentimes, and still do. The staff meetings the first year were absolute torture. I would walk out of there every week with a splitting headache. John Martin—a strong, athletic English teacher who left after the first year—once slammed his fists on the table, leaned over at Rob, bright red in the face, and screamed at him. I thought John was going to belt Rob. I really did. I don't even remember what the argument was about. There were so many of them, about every single aspect of the school. Things were so volatile I remember a couple of times I piped up with my conservative values, only to be attacked by the whole lot of them. It was horrible. At one point I didn't say a word in staff meetings for two weeks. I couldn't."

Peter Case was one of those at odds with Pauline in the meetings. "We had a staff that was essentially split between the notion of being an accelerated school, a place where we were trying to get kids to zip through the curriculum and catch up, and an alternative school, where we were going to help those who for whatever reason couldn't make it in a traditional school, those who had been labeled as problem kids," he says. "I was more interested in the latter. I just assumed that if you are in the inner city there are going to be problems. But a number of people were pushing for a school that would be more elite and take in selected kids who were less problematic and more anxious to learn. This became the heart of our struggle. All the smaller problems seemed to revolve around this central issue. The hard part was that we never were able to resolve things. We'd talk and scream and fight and go home. The next day we'd do it all over again. In the meantime, we had to teach and take care of these kids and try to live our private lives."

Adds Al Lemos, "Often the arguing reminded me of teenagers. You know, as a teenager you nag and nag your parents until they give up, say 'Fine, go ahead, do what you want,' even though they don't really think it is fine. They just get tired of it all. And that's how we often came to decisions. We'd just get so tired of fighting."

At one point early in the year, concerned about the staff, Rob called the director of another alternative school, who had been in his job for ten years. He reassured Rob that it was normal for a new program to go through these kinds of growing pains and that differences in philosophy were bound to create tension among the staff—especially in a school where the teachers are given equal voice. In the case of the Urban Collaborative, he speculated, the tension was exacerbated because there was so much about the school that was undefined.

This at least gave Rob the reassurance that they were not way off base—or that there wasn't something fundamentally wrong with his school. But as the director of the Urban Collaborative, he was still stuck with the problem of resolving the tension and differences. During the first month of school, he hired a substitute teacher to spell each teacher for a half hour so he could get their individual views on the school. What he learned, essentially, was that everyone was hanging on fiercely to his or her vision of the place.

By the end of September, things were beginning to unravel. Jan DeUbl, who taught science, talked openly about quitting if things didn't get better quickly. Jan was having the toughest time, in part because she had one of the largest classes. She and Chris, who taught social studies, had twenty-four students each, while the others taught only twelve at a time. Rob would have liked to make all the classes small, but the school financing would not accommodate this wish. Even before the end of September, Jan was extremely distraught and told Rob that she felt like a failure as a teacher. She demanded that some of the troublemakers be kicked out of school immediately. She was trying to hold on to her sanity, she said. If these kids stayed, she wouldn't make it.

Jan was twenty-eight, experienced in teaching at the college level and in alternative schools. She held a master's degree in science education from the University of Pennsylvania and had taught on a Navajo Indian reservation in New Mexico. She knew and loved science, and she knew how to teach. But nothing had prepared her for this. By October she caved in. She called Rob one night and said she simply couldn't come back to school, not even for a day. Rob didn't push the matter. "Just listening to her voice I knew there was no arguing the point," he says. "The work load, the sheer size of her classes, and the difficulty of setting the school's course had all taken their toll on her. To tell you the truth, I think it was the best thing for the school. If she hadn't called me, I was going to talk to her the next day."

Rob was perplexed by this, however. Jan was a talented teacher with a lot to give. She came with high hopes but lasted only a month. He could chalk up her quitting to her personal life, perhaps. For whatever reason, she was not well equipped at that point in her life to deal with the struggles of inner-city youths. She was too easily angered, too impatient with kids who more than anything needed patience and understanding. But he also felt Jan could have made it if things were less volatile among the staff. Ironically, Rob says, the school has now moved closer to Jan's initial vision.

With things seemingly falling apart, Rob was tempted to step in and simply set policy. He could tell the teachers how things were going to be and that they'd have to abide by his decisions—for the sake of order and sanity. And, in fact, this is what half the staff was begging him to do. "At times we'd just sit there and argue and argue and go around in circles," recalls Al. "We were beating a dead horse, but nobody knew enough to say stop. It frustrated me very very much. I think we were looking to Rob to draw the lines. I know I was. I wanted him to listen to our arguments, then make a decision on his own. But that was not his plan at all. I tell you, at times it drove me crazy."

M. Scott Peck, again, is familiar with this stage of community development. "Since chaos is unpleasant," he writes in *Different Drum*, "it is common for the members of a group in this stage to attack not only each other but also their leader. 'We wouldn't be squabbling like this if we had effective leadership,' they will say. . . . In some sense they are quite correct; their chaos could easily be circumvented by an authoritarian leader—a dictator—who assigned them specific tasks and goals. The only problem is that a group led by a dictator is not, and never can be, a community. Community and totalitarianism are incompatible."

Rob did not have the benefit of M. Scott Peck's wisdom at the time, but he knew he should refrain from laying down laws, figuring this would set a lousy precedent. If he did this, eventually he would have to mediate every battle, play judge and jury to every faculty dispute. And this would definitely move them away from his goal of having the school policy set by the faculty. It would also begin the undesirable movement toward shaping the Urban Collaborative more like a traditional school with its sharp division between the administration and teachers.

Of course, Rob was not without his opinions, and he voiced them strongly. On certain matters he would not compromise—particularly on the constituency the school would serve. But for most issues, the group had to come to a consensus. Better, he decided, to let them have this out now. Better to let them scream in his face, blame him for the problems, if they wanted. Eventually, they would find their way through this. "I knew at times that the staff wanted me to just step in and say, 'This is how things are going to be, period.' And maybe at times I should have. But I think that we still would have ended up with immense problems and that we would not have grown in the way we have. More important, I think I would have damaged the very valuable process we have established of hammering things out as a group—as painful as it might be."

5

AS ANY TEACHER AT THE URBAN COLLABORATIVE WILL TELL you, suffering, failure, fear, and tragedy are never more than an arm's length away from the students here, or from most inner-city children. It makes learning anything other than basic survival very difficult. If the educational opportunities for these children were equal to that of other children, they might be able to make it. But one of the grand American fallacies is that educational opportunity is equal for all. So much is stacked against the poor, particularly the urban poor. For one, housing is less affordable than it is for the middle or upper class. This is compounded by a host of social and health problems and by the steady reduction in federal support for low-income housing, human services, and job training. The out-migration of the middle class from the cities to the suburbs has also added to the problem by draining away the tax base, leaving cities with fewer dollars to spend on students. With most public school funding coming from local property taxes, inner-city children end up with far less than their suburban counterparts.

The Urban Collaborative teachers have discovered that this inequality has created enormous barriers. Along with all their other problems, most of the students come to school with deep-seated anger and distrust for authority. As Jonathan Kozol said, "The greatest injury being done to kids today is not financial parsimony, though that's bad enough. It's to have them grow up believing the government isn't on their side." By high school age, many poor, urban youth are firmly in the camp that believes government and society are working against them. Some of the Urban Collaborative students have crossed that border of cynicism, though most teeter on the edge. This is why the Urban Collaborative targets middle school children. It's an age that offers more hope. It's an age when school can still make a big difference in their lives. In the Urban Collaborative's first year, the average student age was slightly higher than it has been in subsequent years.[1] Couple this with the fact that the staff was struggling all year to find its direction, and it is easy to understand the staggering list of problems everyone had to endure that first year.

Perhaps the saddest commentary on student troubles is how commonplace these troubles seemed to most students. One morning in the middle of the first year, for example, a teenager not enrolled in the Urban Collaborative strolled into the building, held a knife to a boy's throat, and stole his new jacket. When the boy who lost the jacket was later asked to identify the thief, he declined, saying that he did not care about the jacket anymore, that it was probably full of lice by now anyway.

Every day someone suffered. Every week brought trouble and sometimes tragedy. During the year, the friend of one student committed suicide. The cousin of another accidentally shot and killed himself while playing with a gun. After a school basketball game, two girls got into a fight, and one slashed the other across the face with a scalpel, then cut the hand of a boy who tried to interfere. The mother of the injured girl would not bring her daughter to the hospital for fear the hospital would blame her for child abuse and take her daughter away. Another girl had trouble staying awake in school because she was prostituting herself at night. When a boy sat in the wrong seat in math class one day, a girl attacked him and bit him in the face. Trouble came in rapid-fire succession. Drug and alcohol abuse, unwanted pregnancy, family problems, fights, arguments settled with knives, you name it.

Halfway through the first year, a girl named Karla dropped out. Her story epitomized the confused thinking of many Urban Collaborative students. Karla was intelligent and doing well in the program. But earlier in the year she had accidentally broken a car's windshield. The school paid six hundred dollars to replace the windshield, but Rob had asked Karla to repay the school when she could, as a matter of principle. Friends organized a fund-raiser to help her earn money. Yet, for some reason, she declined the help and decided to leave the school to take a job. Rob received a letter from Karla's mother soon after, in which she wrote, "I have tried to convince her to finish school, but she wants to work and make money. I think her whole problem stems from the time when she broke a man's car window. The price was six hundred dollars and change. We do not

---

[1] The school now recruits mainly from sixth and seventh grades.

even have five dollars to spare. My husband is out of work and I'm working to keep us going, which isn't enough to support seven people. I told Karla don't worry, after Christmas my husband will have a job, and we'll help to pay for the window. [But] she does not want us to pay for it. Please try to understand, I've tried, but she's going to be seventeen and it's tough to convince someone at that age to go back to school." In a postscript, the mother said Karla would be sending money to the school as soon as she could. Karla became pregnant a month later and kept the child. A year later, her younger sister enrolled in the Urban Collaborative. Before the year was out, she, too, gave birth. The school never received money for the windshield.

One October weekend, the *Providence Journal* ran a story about two teenagers who died while setting a pizza parlor on fire so the owner could collect insurance money. Both were killed when the gasoline they used exploded prematurely. To illustrate the story, the newspaper ran a photograph of a tall, heavy-set Urban Collaborative student named Dexter, sitting sullenly on a car outside the school. Apparently Dexter had helped the kids fill the gas canisters and had at least some idea of their plans to set the fire. For the first month of school Dexter missed many days because he had to testify before a grand jury about the incident. The boys who died allegedly had been promised $1,000 by a man who had been contracted to torch the pizza parlor. But something went wrong and they couldn't escape the building after the fire started. The most plausible theory suggests that they were dousing the place with gasoline when a stove's pilot light ignited the gas. The attorney general was seeking to indict the man for murder. Dexter, dejected by the death of his friends, knew he had to cooperate with the grand jury. But he was also afraid, knowing there was a chance the man he was testifying against could be set free.

Another *Providence Journal* article that same weekend discussed adolescent drug dealers. These children, from eleven to seventeen years old, are employed by local adults to sell drugs. When the police catch these children, the children are usually given a slap on the wrist and sent home. At worst, they are sent to a training school. But they never get hard time, as an adult would. It's a neat trick, having the children act as a buffer between the dealers and the law. The *Providence Journal* article mentioned the man who was shot to death outside the Urban Collaborative a few weeks earlier. Apparently the man had bought some crack cocaine from an eleven-year-old. The police were unable to determine whether or not the man's purchase of cocaine was directly connected to his murder— though, as any Urban Collaborative student would tell you, the probability was high. Nor was there any indication that Urban Collaborative students were involved. Nevertheless, it was a strong reminder of the pressures on these kids. In all schools, community problems leak into the classroom. But not to the extent they do in inner-city schools. Which is why many educators argue that inner-city schools need more money and better-trained staff and better facilities than the average school—just to hold their own. The reality is that these schools get fewer resources to deal with far larger problems than the typical suburban school.

All the trouble took its toll on the staff, Rob in particular. Late in the first year, it would affect his health and actually send him to the hospital. He got out of the hospital for the school's graduation ceremony and struggled just to talk coherently. The next day he returned to the hospital. Like the rest of the staff, Rob looks back on the first year with wonder and amazement, and, sometimes, sadness.

"None of us were quite prepared for the barrage of student problems. It also took us a while to recover from Jan DeUbl's leaving in October," he says. "But in some ways I think her leaving marked a turning point for the rest of us. We all knew that we had to learn to work together better if we were going to survive. And I think we had to learn that we weren't going to perform miracles overnight with this group. We had to measure progress not in terms of our goals but in terms of the students' lives. Many of these kids would have dropped out if not for us. We had to remember this. We had to remind ourselves that we were accomplishing a lot in getting them to school and getting them to think about their studies. When students fall a year or two behind in the regular school system, the system generally doesn't know what to do with them except shuffle them about until they drop out in despair. What we were doing was letting these kids know that some people do care, that there is a way to succeed, and that we would do what we could to help them. And despite some troubles that first year, many of the kids were beginning to flourish.

"At the same time," Rob continues, "trying to solve crisis after crisis made me understand why the American system of education, as faulty as it is, developed the way it has. It would have been far easier for the faculty to set down the rules hard and fast than to weigh each incident, consider the needs of each of a hundred troubled kids."

Between the crises of the first year—any one of which might have been the crisis *of* the year in most schools—the faculty did meet with success, albeit slowly. One week late in the fall, Chris Cuthbertson walked into Rob's office smiling. She told him that she had had an excellent day, an amazing day. Three classes in a row in which the students were all happily engaged in work. Rob didn't say anything, waiting for the punch line, the bad news. In the beginning, in a class of twenty-four kids, Chris might have had four or five on task, with the rest of them bouncing off the walls. Rob had heard all this a number of times. But now she said, "I'm serious. It was a great day. No joke." And they both started laughing.

Afterward, Rob visited some other classes and found that kids, indeed, were engaged in work. "For me, having to deal with problems most every day, it was very encouraging to see things going well in the classrooms," Rob says. In the English classes, the teachers were finishing up John Steinbeck's *Of Mice and Men*. When Rob visited, he found students discussing the book intently, preparing for a mock trial in social studies class. In Steinbeck's novel, Lennie, the simple-minded protagonist, accidentally kills Clara, a lonely young woman. The students decided they wanted to put Lennie on trial, weigh the extent to which he was guilty of manslaughter and the extent to which society was guilty of neglect. Chris' social studies class was studying law and government at the time, and Chris was taking small groups of students to the Rhode Island courthouse to view trials. "It was so nice to see these kids engaged," Rob says. "And they were enjoying it, too. Which, for this group, must have felt extremely good after years of hating school."

In one math class, some students had conducted a survey by polling people in the community about popular and controversial issues. They recorded the opinions and, in class, were busy tabulating the results, figuring percentages, and preparing oral explanations to present to the class. Meanwhile, others were working on oral presentations about famous mathematicians and important concepts in mathematics. One of the girls giving a presentation was a shy girl named Portia, who earlier presided at a ceremony in which two Providence businesses formally adopted the Urban Collaborative. During the ceremony, Portia was so petrified that the paper in her hand rattled against the microphone as she spoke. But in class, she had gained a great deal of confidence and gave an excellent presentation on the life and work of Galileo. She did not refer to her cue cards, which she held in her hand. What impressed observers most, however, was how Portia concentrated her remarks on Galileo's youth. Clearly, she knew her audience.

In meetings, when not fighting over policy and ideology, members of the staff began reporting successes in their classrooms. Each of them had students who had told them directly that the school was helping them. One student matter-of-factly told a teacher that the Urban Collaborative had saved his life. Outside of school, he had been involved in a gang. He knew both of the boys who died in the botched arson incident. The Urban Collaborative, he said, had allowed him to withdraw from the gang and focus on education. Life was better, he said. He knew now what he wanted, which was an education.

One girl, unbeknownst to the staff, had gotten into an extraordinary number of fights in school the previous year. Somehow this information was withheld in the screening process. Had the school known, it probably would not have accepted her. The remarkable thing was that she had not gotten into a single fight at the Urban Collaborative. The staff was shocked when it found out about her past. She was coming to school. She was working. She had made friends among the faculty and students and was happy.

One Saturday night, another girl called Rob at home just to talk. Earlier in the year she had contemplated suicide. Al Lemos spoke with her then and had spent much of the week getting her good outside counseling and connecting her with a group of students with whom she could talk. This girl, Veronica, had been sexually abused by her father from the age of eight until fourteen. Trying to get psychologically free of it was extremely difficult for her. But Rob was very happy that she would call him. What she needed more than anything in her life were adults she could turn to with trust.

The first "acceleration" occurred in December. Myra, a girl from Pawtucket, had come to the school late in September. Myra understood from the start the value of this system and worked hard, even taking home extra assignments each night. In a community meeting, when it was announced that she had accelerated in one of her classes, a boy said, "Hey, why is she accelerating, and I'm not a quarter of the way through my work, and I've been here longer than she has?" At that, a friend whacked him over the head with a baseball cap and said, "That's because she works, dickhead."

As Rob puts it, "Our philosophy in an eloquent nutshell."

By late winter, more and more students were accelerating in grade— and some of these kids were unlikely leaders, former troublemakers who normally didn't revere school work. Each morning at the community meeting, it seemed, someone else would accelerate in a subject. This generated momentum for the day and encouraged those who previously thought they couldn't do it. After all, they were all once marked as failures.

The small things added up. The school brought in a specialist on peer mediation to help students resolve their own problems. A system was instituted to encourage work by offering points to those who did well. In turn, these points could be traded in for anything from lunch at a local restaurant to movie passes. The school also began offering a community service program in which Urban Collaborative students volunteered at food banks, nursing homes, and other agencies. One group helped remove graffiti in Providence and became the focus of a short segment on the evening television news.

Once, in midwinter, two teachers were asked to apologize to the school in a community meeting for throwing snowballs—which is against the school's rules. When the teachers did so graciously, the students were impressed. Apologizing, admitting mistakes, are among the hardest things for these kids. To see two grown-ups do so without fear of losing face made it that much easier for the kids to do so in future incidents, of which there were many.

At another point, Pauline Hilgers was in her room when she heard banging coming from an adjacent closet. Pauline tried the closet door, but it was locked. She stood quietly for a few minutes until a student stuck his head out. It turns out that several students, all but one from another program within the building, had been smoking in the closet. When Pauline instructed the kids to leave, some of the students made disparaging remarks. To Pauline's surprise and pleasure, the boy from the Urban Collaborative stood up for her, telling the other kids not to talk to *his* teacher that way.

If you ask anyone on the staff exactly how things turned around, how the school moved from its chaotic beginning to its present success, they will all give you a genuinely puzzled look. There were no major turning points, no single event that suddenly made life better at the Urban Collaborative. It was a series of steps—often slow and painful—that began the moment they walked into the school building and that continues today. By the end of the first year, ten students had quit or had been expelled. But most of those who remained, and those who came in mid-year, succeeded in varying degrees. Not all of them accelerated a whole grade, but they did come to school. They were making an effort, finding a community, developing good habits. Given their past school records, this was remarkable.

Chris Cuthbertson will tell you that simply surviving the first year gave everyone a boost. "It was that chaotic," she says. "We just weren't sure we were going to make it. For me, aside from everything else going on, I realized early on that a lot of the stuff I had planned for the social studies curriculum wasn't the best." The criteria sheets—those elements the students were supposed to master in each grade—were far too general, she says. The seventh-grade criteria sheet for social studies, for example, noted that the students would be "able to formulate questions at the knowledge and comprehension level of cognitive development," and that the students would be able "to correctly and effectively use the dictionary, the encyclopedia, and the phone book." These are fine criteria, but the difficulty came in finding ways for students to achieve such mastery—and for Chris to measure it. The second year, the criteria became more specific. For example, the new list included the following: "Student is able to list factual information or answer questions about at least five different topics by using various sources available in library," and "Student identifies an article of interest and summarizes it in a paragraph or two." This year, the list was further refined and simplified to make each item as concrete as possible. For social studies, another important change came with additional staff the second year. "The first year I had twenty-four kids in each class, and it was just too much," Chris says. "From a personal standpoint, I was the only person working to figure out how to teach social studies in the context of this criteria-reference grading. And that was hard for me. I like to work in collaboration much more than I like to work by myself. In the second year the groups got smaller, and I tried to make the curriculum more responsive to the students, to what was going on in the world—the Gulf War and all. And I tried to make sure the activities were more hands-on. In class, these kids need to be engaged in a social studies activity or they will invent their own activity to engage in."

Chris is also quick to point out the changes in staff dynamics. "It was not a warm and cozy supportive group by any means. By the second year, however, we were working together much better. We had more staff, for one thing. We also had a year's experience. We had the summer to regroup. We became smarter recruiters. We knew better what type of kid would work well here. Our systems—such as the disciplinary committee— were working better. The library was a little more functional. Our arrangement of classes was better. We used to hold staff meetings on Friday afternoons, for instance, when all any of us wanted to do was get the hell out of here. We started to develop policies on fighting that made one's reaction to a bad situation less personal. I think a lot of the conflicts we got into the first year were made worse because they ended up being personal. Everything was so intense because the stakes were high. The second year, we all felt a little more secure. We had made it through a year. The system was beginning to work. We could see this in the classroom, in which more and more kids were engaged. And we could see it outside the classroom."

Al, who is the one who dealt with most of the problems outside the classroom, agrees with Chris. "What made things better for me the second year is that there were fewer problems with the kids themselves," Al says. "I think our selection of students was far better the second and third year. That first year, we arrived, opened the doors, and discovered a group of kids with severe problems. They were just a little bit older than our students today and therefore just that much more hardened. At the same time, a lot of our problems with the kids had a lot to do with the staff and how we operated. Because this place was new, everything was an experiment. We learned through trial and error. And we made plenty of errors. If this school were a shortstop, it would not have won the rookie-of-the-year award. But we also did plenty of things right. What helps, of course, it that we have the freedom to experiment. We've gotten where we are today because everyone recognizes that we need to be flexible, to take chances."

"If I had known what was coming that year," Peter Case says, "I wouldn't have done it, and I'd never do it again. But I have to say that it is wonderful here now. I am very proud of having been here from the start and having achieved what we have with this group."

The problem in the first-year math class, Peter points out, was that he and Pauline were thinking mostly about the method of teaching and not the curriculum itself. For instance, they worked hard to get students involved in cooperative learning. "While the idea is good," Peter says, "we ended up asking them to multiply and divide and nothing else. They didn't feel as if they were getting anywhere. And this was just the sort of stuff that turned them off in years past. On top of that, we also made the curriculum too big. In order to get through the seventh grade, a student had to do more work than any other seventh grader in the city. I think this was true in other courses as well. So we learned to cut it down. We learned to make the projects more interesting. Instead of just asking the kids to add and subtract all day, for instance, we'd have them do a packet on banking, which, of course, required them to know a lot of basic skills such as balancing a checkbook, writing numbers in words, calculating interest. We also added far more art to the curriculum, using math to make interesting and complex designs. And the next year we had more kids accelerate in math. Now it has reached a stage where we feel the curriculum works well.

"We were such high-powered people," Peter continues. "We had teachers coming from Brown and Harvard, all across the country, people with years of experience and know-how. Everybody wanted to try the newest thing. But we were thinking wrong. We were thinking about new techniques such as cooperative learning. For some reason we thought if kids didn't do well in a traditional school, we would just give them more of what they got in the traditional school in some slightly altered form. What we needed to do, however, was make the curriculum, not just the teaching methods, more alternative. Hell, what works with these kids is just to focus on caring and attention and making sure the work you have appeals to an alternative way of looking at things."

Because Peter worked with Pauline, he says, he was able to learn some in-class lessons that he could apply to the group at large. "Because

Pauline and I were so different, developing some sort of model of professional integrity was the only way that we were going to be able to communicate with each other, or gain each other's trust," Peter says. "Pauline was a strict disciplinarian the first year and would go ahead and zap kids right away for any infraction. I was totally unable to be a disciplinarian. So, in order to get more consistency, we both had to make shifts." Over time, Pauline ended up being more liberal and Peter learned to enforce classroom rules more strictly. "We learned that in order to be effective team teachers, we had to be consistent and honor the other person's example, even if we didn't agree with it. It was more important to honor the other's example than it was to own it. In other words, there was room here for different ways of thinking. We didn't have to make converts of each other. We just had to make compromises. And this lesson carried over plenty of times to the broader group."

"I'm very happy that this is the system here," Peter adds. "I don't always enjoy it. It can be very difficult. In fact, that first year it was downright insane. It was also a huge transition to make, getting used to not being told what to do. Gigantic. I mean, we all just came from jobs where we were told what to do. And I remember the reason why Rob took so much shit the first year is that we were looking for him to guide us. We'd think, 'Rob, you're the boss, just tell us what to do.' And Rob would say, 'No, *you* guys are boss, *you* decide what you want to do.' And we couldn't do it. Not the first year. We couldn't look each other in the eye and say we were willing to be responsible for all these kids. It took a really long time. Now, we are doing it. We've learned. And it is so incredibly simple. I think, in a painful way, we've come to the understanding that we've all got to figure out a way to agree, because we've had to endure one too many quagmires in the group decision-making process."

Strangely enough, for Peter, after watching the process unfold over two-and-a-half years—hating it with a passion most of the time—he suddenly began to enjoy it. "It is an amazing experience to be part of a school that is just starting. And then to just watch it stay alive somehow and grow and develop. I feel lucky to be part of all this."

The others might not embrace the process as wholeheartedly as Peter, but all of them will praise school-based management, headaches and all.

"I think that we all really do feel a sense of ownership here," Al says. "Right from the start, we were all working to get this place in shape—from planning curriculum together to setting up tables in the classrooms. In the beginning, no one quite knew where the boundaries were. But, of course, we have evolved. There is a lot more confidence among the staff now, and we are much better at discussing issues. I still get impatient. But we have come a long way, and, as painful as it was, I think it has been a valuable experience—and it certainly has enabled us to create a school that helps these children."

Lynne Abbott concurs. "I think school-based management is very valuable because it makes teachers connected to and responsible for not only their own classrooms but what is going on in the school," she says. "And this is very important. Most teachers go to school and know that the only thing they are responsible for is inside their classrooms. They can close the door and forget the rest of the world exists. And a lot of them do it in order to survive. And that's tragic. Because no one ends up taking responsibility for what happens in the school, what happens to a child beyond a particular course. This way helps teachers look at the whole child, rather than just what he does, say, in ninth-grade English. I know how all my kids are doing in social studies and math and what sort of trouble they are getting themselves into. I know what their lives are like outside the school. And this is bound to make me a better teacher.

"I should also say, however, that we must never get complacent," Lynne adds. "There is a danger in saying we know what we are doing now. Because these kids challenge us constantly. And the minute you think you've got it, you haven't. Learning to adapt is important for all of us. Fortunately, I think most of the teachers here are open to change and see change as necessary. This is the secret to our success."

Pauline, who went home every night with a headache during the first two months, has also become a staunch advocate of school-based management, "I think it is fantastic," she says. "The beginning was tough, but eventually things got easier. We're a little more civilized now and give each other the chance to talk without attacking each other. I really do feel safe now saying what I believe, even if I know I'm still the odd person out most of the time. I suppose that's the process we had to grow through. A violent clash of wills followed by the recognition that we have to get along better if we want to accomplish anything. And what's impressive, I think, is how willing most of us have been to stick it out through a very painful process, and how much we have been able to accomplish with this population of kids because of that process.

"I often refer to this as my dream job, with all its frustrations and aggravations and times when I think I'm not going to get through the day. With all of that, with what I wanted out of my career, I think I've found the ideal job. I've peaked out in my first full-time teaching job. This is it. To be able to have a say not only in how my classroom is run but in how the school is run is a gift, because if you've got a say in creating a school, then you can't help but believe in it. You have a personal investment in it, and you are going to do more to protect it."

Chris defends school-based management as well. "I've never taught in a public school of a more traditional nature, and I probably shouldn't sit in judgment. But I know a lot of people who do teach in public schools. My brother does. And it took him about five years, working with the system, to get a new English textbook for his classes. *Five years.* The old book was twenty years old. That was incredibly frustrating to him, and he had to pour a lot of energy into simply getting a better textbook. I think school bureaucracies, by their very nature, are entrenched and difficult to work with. They are very resistant to change, very self-protective, as a lot of big institutions tend to be. For teachers and students, that sort of life can be debilitating.

"I think that everyone who works here has a real investment in the success of the school. And that, more than anything, is going to keep us pushing hard in the right direction—until we get it right. I particularly like how it allows us to be responsive to the kids and to be spontaneous. Education this way always seems fresh and alive."

6

BY CERTAIN MEASURES THE URBAN COLLABORATIVE LOOKS and sounds like a traditional school. There is no way around this in an aging parochial school building. The tiled floor and walls of the central hallway resonate with the exuberant voices and shuffling feet of youth. The metal doors are dented at foot level and the door windows are laced with wire to prevent the glass from spraying in the event the windows should shatter. The office is the first room at the top of the entrance staircase, and five classrooms (one converted into a small library and computer center) line up dutifully along the central corridor. One journalist profiling the school called the facilities "shabby." It might be better to say the space is serviceable. And, more to the point, affordable.

Tradition, however, stops with the look of the facilities. Walk into any classroom in the Urban Collaborative and you'll know you're not in the academic equivalent of Kansas anymore. First of all, there are no individual desks. A few of the teachers have their own desks, but these are used mostly for storing personal items, classroom supplies, and the mountain of paperwork one needs to run a class. None of the teachers sits at the desk to lecture or lead discussions. Instead, they sit with the kids at one of the large tables, as in the English and science classes, or wander from table to table assisting and coaching individual students, as in the math and social studies classes. The chalkboards are used sparingly; most of the time they serve as bulletin boards or as places to hang information or inspirational messages.

The first classroom at the right is Chris Cuthbertson's social studies class. Chris has arranged her tables in a square, open in the middle so she can move easily from student to student. At the front of the room are two maps of the world, one political and one geographical. During class periods this time of the year, these maps are the focal point. Most of the students are working on their geography unit, trying to earn points to accelerate a grade before the end of the year. Some, like a thin, quiet boy named Lester, have already completed their work in social studies and are using this period to catch up in other subjects. In typical fashion, students at the Urban Collaborative tend to tackle first the subjects they like best, then take on the other subjects only after goading and prodding from the staff. Lester is engrossed in a banking project and has the latest edition of the *Providence Journal* open to the business section—this from a student who stayed back the previous year and showed little interest, if any, in his education. Later, Lester says how glad he is to be here at the Urban Collaborative. "In my other school, they didn't care what you did," he says matter-of-factly. "Here, it's real nice. They help you realize you can do the work."

There is much fussing around at the start of class—the sharpening of pencils, the gathering of materials, the carry over of talk from the morning school meeting, the expected groans and complaints about being asked to do work. At the Urban Collaborative, kids are allowed to wear just about whatever they want. Hats are permitted in class, and stereo cassette players with headphones are tolerated. It's all part of the hope that more tolerance of individuality will make the kids more comfortable, and thus help them to learn. They also call Chris by her first name.

"Some people might frown on these practices," Chris says during a mid-morning break. "But we need to take down some of those barriers that kept them from learning in the past. When I first came here I was surprised how many spoiled brats there were. Before this I taught at a private girls school on the east side of Providence, where one would think there would be more spoiled brats per square inch than anywhere else on the planet. But the kids here are incredibly spoiled, especially the boys. As they see it, their will is law. Whatever they want to do, they feel they have a right to do. Given this, it's understandable that they had a hard time fitting into the rigid structure of most public schools. In the lunch room of one local middle school I visited, the students were required to sit quietly and get up only when permitted. After they ate, a guy blew a whistle, barked out some instructions into a bull horn. Then the teachers came down and the kids lined up and followed the teachers back to the classrooms. And every classroom I've been in has straight rows, with kids sitting quietly, teacher sitting at the desk, completely regimented. I under-stand why with eight hundred kids in a middle school they might feel compelled to do this. I'm not criticizing them. But it's hard for our more exuberant folks to fit in there, especially when they are not used to having their wills challenged and restricted.

"Part of the problem," she continues, "is that these kids don't have a lot of family support, for whatever reason. It's not a question of intelligence. Most of our kids are very bright and creative. It's a question of finding a way to reach them. So we have to work with them very carefully."

Chris, thirty-seven, has no children of her own, yet there is a certain maternal quality to her, partly because of her stocky build, but more so because of her gentle, reassuring nature, and a voice that could calm a pent-up hound dog. Her black hair is cropped short and is graying slightly. Yet what one notices more than anything is her eyes, bright blue and steady.

Chris pats a girl named Jan on the shoulder as a gentle reminder of where she is. Jan, a sixteen-year-old who has a one-year-old daughter at home and no husband in sight, slouches in her chair, more or less ignoring the class. She has "chosen" not to do any work this day. Instead, she has put on her Walkman and listens to the tough, in-your-face rhythm of rap music. Chris lets her go for now. Moves on.

Most of the kids are working on the geography unit, trying to fill out detailed information sheets that give the essential facts about a country. Their job is to pick a series of countries, preferably covering a number of continents, and learn something about each of them. In a complex point system that will earn them credit toward each grade, this exercise carries good weight. One girl is standing by the wall map looking confused. She tells Chris she is searching for a particular continent, but from her expression, Chris understands that she is lost.

"Name a continent, Liz."

Liz pauses.

"Any continent."

"United States?"

"No, that's a country."

Another girl, Maria, steps in to help Liz. "The United States in part of the continent of North America," she tells Liz. Liz writes down "North America" on her sheet, glad just to have her answer, then returns to her place at the table.

A frail Asian boy named William, who wears an overcoat and tie even though it's a warm spring day, asks Chris if he can go to the library. He has a pencil in his hand and is tapping his exercise sheet. He tells Chris he needs to find information about Peru that is not available in the class' few resource books.

She nods and he's gone.

"Chris, Chris," Calvin calls out. "Chris."

She is working with another student and asks Calvin to hold on.

"Chris," he continues, "Is Berlin in South America?"

She finishes helping the other boy, then turns to Calvin, and tells him, no, Berlin is a city in Germany. She takes him to the map on the wall, points out Berlin, and explains briefly the division of East and West Germany and the recent events that brought down the wall. It's all news to Calvin.

What one notices about this method of teaching is that it allows Chris to teach one-on-one. Calvin, who might otherwise disappear in the back of a classroom, is now, momentarily, the center of attention. Shortly, questions from other students fly: Is Cairo in China? Is Caracas in Mexico? Is "be able" one word? What is a monetary unit? Where is Providence *at* on this map, anyway?

She takes each question in stride. One of the questions is fielded by a female student. "It's in Egypt, stupid." Chris turns to her, and without acknowledging that she is right, says, "Can't you say that nicer?"

"Well, he called me stupid," the girl replies.

"Try it," Chris says. "Just try saying it nicer and see how it feels."

"Cairo is in Egypt, Phil. On the continent of Africa," she says with schoolmarm sweetness.

Chris smiles.

When Chris looks away, the girl leans over to Phil and whispers, "Stupid."

Some of these questions might surprise a visitor. But what is important here is not what the students don't know but that they are not afraid to ask questions, that they are curious enough to ask. In past years, the majority of these kids—if they had come to school at all—would open their mouths only to disrupt class. Otherwise, they'd just frown at the teacher lecturing the class, or stare at the clock and numbly watch the seconds tick by.

Later, Chris smiles again, thinking about how little they know. "I'm still shocked sometimes by how many students will come up to the map and not be able to find the United States," she says. "There is so much they don't know. They don't know how to read maps. They don't know how to use a ruler. You ask them to figure out scale and they can't do it. Unless the measurement falls exactly on the inch, they are in big, big trouble. So I try to keep it simple. On one hand, all I want to do in social studies is increase their awareness of the world. On the other, I want to teach them how to communicate effectively. We do a lot of reading and writing in here to improve their comprehension and their ability to communicate. We don't do a lot of specifics of history. To ask them to know the policies of the Eisenhower Presidency, for instance, is absurd. Eisenhower means nothing to them." The unit that focused on American history started with the 1940s and ended with the 1960s. To make that sort of learning fun, while studying the 1950s, her class listened to fifties music, whirled hula-hoops, and ate Twinkies. "They'll remember that, and maybe later can build upon it."

This doesn't mean the work is any less demanding here than elsewhere. To accelerate in social studies—which means to complete a year's worth of work in social studies in whatever amount of time it takes—a student needs to complete the geography section, pass twelve vocabulary tests, complete projects on the use of graphs and charts, clip three news articles of interest and summarize, complete twelve reading comprehension assignments, conduct outside reading, take part in debates, and complete three special projects. There are, however, very few set lesson plans. Each student works more or less at his or her own pace, choosing from any number of worksheets in any order. Chris is there mostly to coach and cajole, keep them focused, and help them learn how to treat each other respectfully.

An eye-catching girl named Betsy, wearing black lipstick and purple eye shadow, is reading about India. At one point she says in disbelief that the literacy rate in India is 36 percent. "I say, good God," she says.

Another boy tells her that the literacy rate in Finland is 89 percent. "Why the difference between the two countries?" Chris asks Betsy.

Without hesitation, she answers. "They are poor in India."

It might be worth pursuing this further, to try to get Betsy to think about the correlation between poverty and illiteracy and why it is universally so. But Chris lets it go. There is enough of an edge in Betsy's voice to let Chris know that Betsy is disturbed by this notion. Lesson learned.

Betsy is heading off to a Providence high school next year with hopes of getting into a college to study science. She is bright, gregarious, and charming. One wonders why such a girl had trouble in school in the past or what could have driven her to drop out. One suspects, judging by her makeup and manner, that she has been asked to grow up before her time. And, in fact, she has. Her mother died when she was young. Her father is nowhere to be found. She had been living with her older sister, but the two of them lost their apartment, and later lost their welfare support and food stamps. There were days when they did not have enough to eat. Earlier in the year, the school had set up a food bank in the office for Betsy and her sister. As Chris will tell you, Betsy was an incredibly difficult and obstinate student the previous year. "We fought all the time," Chris says. "It seemed that anything I said would just set her off. But somehow, through our arguing, we managed to work things out—as if that is just the process we had to go through to understand each other better. This year, Betsy has done incredibly well in all her courses. The way she has turned around is amazing." Now Betsy lives with her boyfriend, who drives her to school each morning in his aging Toyota station wagon, the back weighed with stereo speakers the size of large suitcases. You can hear them coming two blocks away. The bass literally shakes the windows of nearby houses. When Betsy gets out of this music-box-on-wheels and saunters across to the school yard, she moves with self-satisfaction and a certain pride.

"Which continent are we on?" Michael asks.

Ryan comes in with a late pass and tells Chris, "I need work." When she hands him a geography sheet, he sighs, drops his shoulders, spins his Chicago Bulls cap around backwards. But Chris, ignoring all this, patiently lays out some options and eventually coaxes him into studying Brazil. Unlike a traditional school, the Urban Collaborative has classes of different lengths. The major classes last an hour and fifteen minutes, which is twenty-five minutes longer than classes in most schools. This allows students to concentrate for a solid block of time on a single subject. There is a conscious plan not to bombard them with a flurry of classes. Instead, the course-load is kept small and the time expanded.

Ryan has arrived late, but there are still forty-five minutes left in the class. Plenty of time to begin a project. He sits down next to another boy, who is doodling on the back of his assignment sheet. The other boy slips on headphones to his cassette player and listens to rock and roll. Ryan tells him to do some work. The other boy says, "Chill out."

The students get quiet, then grow noisy again, like cicadas on a midsummer day, alternately talking and working. If one throws out some comment to the class, the others will join in. There is often a flurry of exchanges:

"Shut up."

"No. You shut up."

"No. *You* shut up."

"I ain't shutting up. Make me shut up."

"I'll make you shut up. You don't think I'll make you shut up?"

Like a good trout fisherman, Chris lets them run with the line but reels them in before they can actually make each other angry. Michael, a handsome, athletic boy, openly defies Chris' request that he stop talking and do some work. She asks him repeatedly, but calmly. In a traditional school, he would likely be on his way to the principal's office by this point, huffing and puffing and bound for a fistful of demerits. But Chris is extremely tolerant. As the librarian, Connie Zeeland, points out, "Yelling and screaming at these kids does no good. People have screamed at them their whole lives. Punishment? Nah. They're mostly abused anyway." Chris is trying to calculate what is going through Michael's mind, and she takes a guess. Michael has already accelerated in math and science but not in social studies. "Come on, Michael," she urges gently, coming over to him. "This isn't too hard for you. Finish this up this week, and you'll be in great shape."

Michael eventually settles down, looks at his sheet, and asks, "Where's Iceland at?"

Betsy wants to know what Chris means when she asks about the religious practices of a country. Before Chris can respond, Maria offers an answer, the correct one, then comes over to help. Chris lets her go.

On the wall is a tribute to Rosa Parks: "You are the spark that started our freedom movement." In the front corner of the room are photographs and short profiles of women who have been among the first women to succeed in fields dominated by men: primatologist Dian Fossey, astronomer Maria Mitchell, biologist Jewel Plummer Cobb, photographer Dorothea Lange, astronaut Judith Resnik, violinist Kyung-Wha Chung, and poets Lola Rodrigues de Tio and Gwendolyn Brooks. Beside this is a small poster given to Chris by a driver's education instructor. It's a photograph of a train that has smashed a tractor-trailer rig into bits at a railroad crossing. Encouragement and warning.

"Is Spain a large city in France?"

"No, Spain is a country south of France."

"And where's France at, anyway?"

Chris came to the Urban Collaborative after teaching for eleven years in relatively risk-free independent schools. She had not worked with at-risk kids or even in a public school until a few years prior to coming to the Urban Collaborative, when she helped Rob with the SPIRIT program. She says she was getting tired of the type of teaching she had been doing and needed a change. The taste of working with inner-city kids at SPIRIT was enough to prompt such a change. "So I jumped ship," she says. Chris recalls attending her fifteenth reunion at Williams College, where she was amazed by the wealth and power of her classmates, most in business or law or medicine. In teaching, that sort of advancement is not possible. Financially, perhaps, there are plenty of incentives to take a school administration job. But Chris, and many good teachers like her, quickly reject that idea because it means giving up what they love best: daily interaction with students in the classroom. "It's ridiculous to think I could give up teaching and move into an office," she says. "I like teaching. It really grabs me."

So where does a teacher go? For Chris, the answer was a new kind of school, a new teaching challenge. The summer she joined the SPIRIT program also convinced her that she could switch to another kind of school and be happy. Almost instantly, her batteries were recharged. "I loved working with those kids," she recalls. "It was just more exciting than what I had been doing. I didn't know how to do it well at the start. But the kids were just so vital and very interesting.

"I also feel that the work is more important," she continues. "That's such a clichéd thing to say, but certainly for me working in the SPIRIT program and here at the Urban Collaborative, I feel as if I'm doing something for people who really need me. And I think, too, that there is a chance here to develop a model for education that might just work. We are doing something here that offers concrete answers to some of the problems that plague our schools. But it's the kids most of all. They are such wonderful kids, most of them, and they have such low expectations. A lot of them say to me something like, 'Oh, I really want to be the first kid from my family to graduate from high school.' In a way, that's sad. But in a way it's great that they have some ambition. It makes helping them seem that much more vital."

To watch Chris teach, one would think it is the easiest thing in the world. But down the hall in John Howard's social studies room, one can learn just how hard this job can be. John holds much of the same beliefs as Chris about the importance of helping children who have not been given a chance, but he'd be the first to admit he is still struggling to find his way. What is surprising is that John is not a young college graduate starting out on his career, but a fifty-two-year-old rookie who has given up a successful banking career to help urban kids learn.

John came to the Urban Collaborative during the school's second year of operation. During the first year, Chris was the sole social studies teacher—the initial (and since abandoned) budget-saving logic was that social studies and science didn't need the same attention as English and math. But trying to run large classes was so overwhelming for Chris, especially with all the students working at their own pace, that the school decided to hire another teacher the second year who could teach two sections of English and two of social studies. John Howard was the lucky candidate.

John is a fit, broad-shouldered man who, with wire-rimmed glasses and an oxford shirt, even unbuttoned at the collar, seems slightly out of his element in an urban middle school. There is something about his manner—at once formal and hopeful, as if in each class he expects a sudden breakthrough—that makes it clear he is not a veteran teacher. John worked for fifteen years at Irving Trust Company in New York, then for another twelve years at State Street Bank in Boston as a senior vice-president for international banking. He was financially well-off and secure in his work. So, one can't help but ask, what is he doing in an urban middle school?

"Years ago I decided that when I retired I didn't want to have done only one thing in life," John says. "I didn't know I would end up teaching. I just started off wanting to do something more immediate, more current, more socially relevant, if you will, than the abstract business of banking. I considered low-income housing development, social work, lots of things that would have been more socially positive. And then I saw that teaching was the thing I really wanted to do. I wanted to teach American History in an urban high school, to try to do what I could to make the urban adolescent more connected to this country. And with all my travels over the years, I knew that I had some experience that could help these kids connect. That was my objective, anyway."

After twenty-seven years of banking, he went back to school (Harvard) and got a master's degree in education. When John heard about the opening at the Urban Collaborative, he drove down from Boston to talk with Rob. Rob, for his part, was impressed with the idea of a former banker who was willing to take a substantial cut in pay coming in to teach.

Talking to John, one can't help but sense his intelligence and his concern for the kids—those two traits that no doubt caught Rob's eye. But John will also admit that teaching at the Urban Collaborative has been one of the most difficult tasks he has ever undertaken. He tacked up a set of rules—"John's Rules"—on the wall earlier this year to try to keep order in the classroom. And though these rules are tested or broken most days, they have helped at least bring a semblance of order to what he thought was pure chaos. "I have to admit that things did not go very well for me last year, and I'm still struggling to get a handle on all this," John says. "I totally, *totally* had a misconception of what this job was all about. There is no preparation whatsoever in graduate school for what one will encounter as an urban teacher in America today. I didn't expect the social issues to be so dramatic. I didn't expect to have to spend so much time dealing with classroom management. I didn't expect so much resistance. I once asked our seminar leader at Harvard about controlling a classroom, and she said, 'Oh, don't worry about control. What do you mean by control, anyway?' as if no one ever had trouble with students. Of course, I could never quite say what I meant because I had never been in the situation. But now I know. To this day, I'm still angry at her."

Things got so bad for John that he actually turned in his resignation a few months after he arrived. "I was teaching two sections of English and two sections of social studies," John recalls. "And I was really flailing. I came at the kids way wrong to begin with, then I was in this huge hole and couldn't get out. The kids were literally running the class. Nothing was happening. I told Rob I couldn't deal with it. I was sorry. I didn't know whether it was me or what, but things were just not working out. So I quit. It was really a hard time in my life, very emotional, but I could see no progress in the kids and I didn't think I was ever going to be able to help them. I quit, and I went home to Boston, and I didn't know what I was going to do."

Rob reluctantly accepted John's resignation, though he felt the problem lay more with John's expectations than with the classroom itself. A few days later, Rob decided to call John and ask if he would come back and teach just the two sections of social studies, since this is what he cared most about. They would find someone else to take over the English classes. From Rob's perspective, John was doing a good job in just getting the kids to come to school each day—something most of the kids had not done in years past. With fewer classes, scaled-down expectations, and some help from the rest of the teaching staff, things would get better. John thought it over, and decided to come back. This was, after all, what he left banking for.

A year-and-a-half later, John is more comfortable with his classes. He is still learning what works and what doesn't, but he feels in control, feels he is, indeed, making a difference in the lives of many of these kids. For one, he has started an explorer's club that organizes monthly weekend adventures for students. They have gone to Block Island, to the woods of Coventry, to Quincy Market in Boston, to a Christmas tree farm to cut down a tree for the school. They've attended dance concerts and baseball games. They've gone camping, once at John's cabin in Vermont, where the kids had to learn to get along without electricity or running water—in the dead of winter. "I think that was the best experience," John says. "They were overwhelmed by the nature of it—no plumbing, no electricity, and *no* TV. They had to build a fire to keep warm and to cook. And they had to divide up tasks so everyone was contributing. They learned a lot about the value of working together." They also went skiing at a nearby mountain and came back claiming it was the best of times.

"For the kids, the biggest problem is getting along with each other, with relating to each other and to adults. And the more we can show them that people, especially adults, are not real threats, then maybe we can improve the situation," John says. "And these outings also help me get closer to these kids. There are a couple of kids with whom I have very good relations because of the club, kids other teachers can't stand for one reason or another. I've gotten to know them. And they've gotten to trust me a little more because we can get off campus, as it were, and laugh about something unconnected to school. We experience things, get beyond the teacher-student relationship. It helps. It's exhausting, but it helps."

John's struggles are not unlike those of teachers stepping into hundreds of urban classroom for the first time each September. But they are compounded in a school like the Urban Collaborative, since the students are by and large the worst of the school system. Given this, and given that the teachers are literally inventing their roles daily, this is no easy place for a rookie, even a fifty-two-year-old rookie with twenty-seven years of business experience, a master's degree from Harvard, and a wealth of knowledge. But already John has invested himself to the point where he says he is not ready to move on. "As long as this school exists, I'm perfectly happy to work in this situation. I'm beginning to think I have some ideas that might help me deal effectively with these kids. And I realize it does take a lot of time. A big difference between me and other teachers, I think, is my reason for teaching. First of all, I'm not interested in a career in education. I don't see this job as a stopping point on my way to becoming a department chairman or principal or anything. I've already done that ladder-climbing crap. And I'm not really in it for the love of history. I went back to Harvard recently to take part in a panel that was considering incoming teacher candidates. As I looked around at those teachers who came back, I realized that most of them were hard-core content people—history, English, math, whatever. But I am not in this because I'm a historian or even a great student of history. I am here because I want to work with these kids. It's not the job, and it's not the subject. Teaching social studies just seems to be the best way to get at what I'm trying to get at—which is helping these kids reconnect with this society."

7

PETER CASE, ONE OF THE URBAN COLLABORATIVE'S TWO MATH teachers, walks out into the hall to look for stragglers to his midmorning class. He finds one blissfully digging his hand into a bag of Fritos and shuffling along as if returning from the concession stand at a less-than-thrilling ball game.

"Pedro," Peter says, gesturing with his arms, "What's the story?"

Pedro smiles, picks up the pace.

Peter is already feeling harried. Normally, he is a paragon of calm, but it's near the end of the year, a warm and pleasant spring day outside, and most of the kids are restless. While he's out of the room, two other boys, Ray and Calvin, start wrestling on top of a table. It begins in jest, but turns serious. Ray has Calvin pinned, but Calvin has gotten his hand on Ray's chin and is pushing so Ray's head is bent back hard, both their faces straining. Their classmates watch with mild interest. A few cheer. One girl tells them to grow up. When Peter returns, he takes one look at the boys and grows flush with anger. This, apparently, isn't their first scuffle.

"Come on, you two," Peter says.

Ray and Calvin pay no attention, both afraid to ease up. They are hot and tense and stuck in this awkward standoff. Peter puts a hand on Ray's shoulder and more or less helps to ease the separation. Peter, who has just turned thirty, is tall and broad-shouldered. One imagines he could easily tuck both boys under his arms and carry them off to a quieter place for reflection and discussion. But he cautiously pries them apart, giving them the opportunity to end this on their own. Finally, Ray lets go and hops off the table with a shout of triumph. More than anything, this annoys Peter, who immediately escorts both kids into the hallway and points them in the direction of the office.

The two boys complain that they were just playing. But Peter holds his ground. "Go," he says.

It is hard for them to argue. Unlike other schools, the students not only know the rules at the Urban Collaborative, they helped write them and enforce them. Once a week at a disciplinary committee meeting, a rotating group of appointed students sits down in judgment of their peers in the educational version of the small claims court (serious violations go directly to the supreme court of Rob and the teachers). It's fairly even-handed, democratic justice, designed to help the students take more responsibility for their own actions. It's also a way of reinforcing the notion that community service should start in one's community. Of course, it doesn't always work. As Ray and Calvin head off down the hall, Calvin gives Ray a shove and gets a good hard shove in return.

"All right," Peter says to the rest of the class. "Show's over."

At that moment, Pauline Hilgers strolls into the class after passing the boys in the hall. She and Peter are team teaching most of the math classes, which are the largest classes in the school. Most days they both arrive promptly, but this time Pauline had been talking in the office with Rob about another disciplinary case.

"What was that all about?" she asks.

"Those clowns were wrestling," Peter says, shaking his head.

"Oh," Pauline replies, adding, "What is it with Ray these days?"

There are any number of things Peter would like to say about Ray, but he lets them go. In another school, this confrontation may have been a big event. But here it's taken in stride. And, besides, Peter and Pauline know that Rob will deal firmly with both Ray and Calvin. Kids are given a great deal of freedom, but there are lines they cannot cross without consequence.

A few students sidle up to Peter's desk looking for pencils. Peter opens a small strong-box, hands out pencils, and takes their money in return. If the school handed out pencils freely, it could end up giving every kid a dozen a day. This way, with the students paying for pencils, they're apt to hang on to them a little longer—though there always seems to be brisk business.

Pauline, meanwhile, starts her rounds, seeing who has work and who needs work. She tries to get them all settled as quickly as possible. It takes more time than she would like, but eventually the kids turn to their assignments, or most of them do.

"I see you've got some work," Pauline says to Vicki.

"I'd rather have my teeth pulled than do math," Vicki says, looking at the geometry before her. Vicki, tall and thin in the extreme, hides behind straight brown hair that falls across her pale face and the page on which she is working.

"It's that bad, huh?"

"Yep."

"I know you can do it, Vicki. Just give it a try."

She exhales frustration. Pauline rubs her shoulder, then moves to a boy named Arlin.

"You haven't answered one of these questions on magnetism, Arlin. Come on. You're falling back into bad habits again."

Arlin chooses not to respond. Pauline bends over and offers him a few pointers. He listens, shoots back a couple of questions, then starts in.

On one wall of the classroom is a nautilus design of the Pythagorean Theorem and various attractive, complex student-drawn tesselations. Some have the quality of an M. C. Escher drawing. A staircase appears to be constantly going up, yet always returns to the starting point—an image with which many Urban Collaborative students may be subconsciously familiar. Another is a humorous hexagon built of funny faces. Along a second wall are bright color photographs of geometric designs in nature: a starfish, a honeycomb, a dandelion flower gone to seed. A small poster on one of the rarely used chalkboards explains how one can calculate baseball batting averages and earned-run averages. Across from this is a poster of a disheveled Albert Einstein posed with a statement of inspiration: "Small is the number of them that see with their own eyes and feel with their own heart."

Peter has moved to the other side of the room and sits across from Mark, a short, feisty Italian boy. Mark has announced that he is ready for his quiz on multiplication, one of the last areas of study he needs to master in order to accelerate a grade.

Peter grins at him. "You sure you are ready for this?"

"I'm ready," Mark says, "I'm ready. Come on, ask away." He slouches in his seat and crosses his arms.

Peter pauses a moment, then asks, "What's 400 times 40?"

Mark stares up at the ceiling, calculating, and replies, "16,000."

"11 times 11?"

"Oh, that's easy. I memorized that one. 121." Apparently, Mark tripped over that on his last attempt at the test.

Peter asks a few more large, but simple, multiplication questions, which Mark handles with ease. "OK," Peter says. "I think you are ready."

Peter asks the official test questions, writing down the equation and Mark's response. These questions get progressively harder, but Mark handles them all confidently, puzzling over a few, but recovering and giving Peter the correct answer. In the end, he gets fifteen out of fifteen correct and pounds his desk in triumph. Immediately, he starts in on a new task. A year ago, he'd just as soon walk out of class as take a test.

Pauline Hilgers, like most of the teachers at the Urban Collaborative, had never taught in a public school before coming here. Unlike the others, however, a school like the Urban Collaborative has always been her dream, the exact sort of school she had been training for since the age of seventeen. To listen to her talk about it, one would think the Urban Collaborative was created just for her.

Pauline is young, blonde, and model-thin. She is also an ultraconservative from St. Louis, Missouri, who voted republican in the last election and who feels less-than-at-home in this more liberal-minded, democratic state. She came to Rhode Island from the Midwest a few years back when her husband enrolled in a math Ph.D. program at Brown University.

At a staff meeting before the start of the first year, when the group was trying to hammer out school policy, Pauline found herself at odds with some of the others about the sort of classroom behavior they would tolerate. Someone suggested that it would be all right to let the kids wear hats and Walkmans and swear in class. Pauline wasn't sure about the hats or Walkmans, but she strenuously objected to swearing. There is never a need for it, she insisted. At this point, trying to interject a little levity into the discussion, Rob DeBlois turned to her and said, "Fuck you, Pauline." Pauline didn't think it was funny, and the incident tainted their relationship for much of the first year. (As it turned out, the staff agreed not to permit swearing, though the response to student violations of the rule has been fairly lenient, considering how often these words surface in the day.)

Still, Pauline will tell you she loves working here and has come to like Rob as well—even if she feels like the odd person out at times. "Since I was seventeen, I always knew I wanted to teach in an inner-city public school," she says in the teachers' room. "I grew up in a bad neighborhood in St. Louis without my father and attended a high school comparable to some of those around here. We had armed guards in the hall and at least one or two stabbings or gun incidents a year. I watched a lot of my friends, who were incredibly bright and talented and gifted people, just go down the tubes because the school was so big and overcrowded. Teachers didn't have time to get to everybody, and most of the teachers were so tired of dealing with problems for so long they just didn't care anymore. I watched a lot of people with a lot of potential either go through the motions or simply drop out. It was then that I knew I wanted to become a teacher and see if I could help out some of these kids."

So she got her master's in math at the University of Missouri; taught college algebra and calculus; taught a few continuing education courses, including courses at an Army base; and then came East with her husband. Waiting for her teaching certification to be approved, Pauline worked as a substitute, helped out at a Pawtucket rehabilitation center for adolescent girls with drug and alcohol problems, and one day opened the paper and saw the advertisement for the Urban Collaborative job.

Despite her training and desire, she admits that coming here took a lot of adjustment. "I'm a very strict teacher. I'm very old-fashioned and traditional. So when I'd tell a kid to do something and they simply said no or gave me one of their flip responses, I was down their throats. As my mom had always been with me, you know." She pauses and smiles. "Of course, this would immediately put them on the defensive, and once you've done that, you've lost them. Not only are you not going to get them to work, but you've disrupted the entire class and you've made an enemy in the process. So basically, you've lost ground, and that certainly doesn't help anyone.

"It took me a long time to figure out that for these kids, given what they have to deal with outside of school, it is ingrained in them never to back down. If you back down, you are weak. If you back down, other people are going to see that weakness, and you are done for. The trick here is giving them a way to do what you are asking without making it look as if they've succumbed. Give them a chance to respond in a positive way without losing face with the whole class. This means that when a kid goes off on you, instead of getting on his case, you have to switch your tone of voice in the opposite way, make it quieter and softer and more gentle, and say more pleases instead of less. And never *ever* talk down to them. And, boy, was this tough for me at first."

Much of what Pauline has to say is surprising, since she now seems so comfortable with the system, moving among the students with ease. If one of them swears in class, as they often do, she quickly reminds them that this is not acceptable, but does so gently, without the threat of punishment. Of course, they also know that if they keep it up, she will gently assign them to after-school detention.

Tran, a lithe, quiet boy asks Pauline about a trinomial equation that has him stumped. She points out that he has to find the factors to simplify the equation, then circles one of the factors to give him a hint. Tran nods his head in understanding and starts rewriting the equation. Stops. Puzzles over it. Tries it again. Gets it right.

She turns to another student, a boy named Malcolm, who is sitting with his arms crossed, staring off into space.

"Are you going to work?" she asks politely.

He says he is tired of working.

"It's up to you," she says. "If you work, you get credit. If you don't, fine. Just make sure you leave everyone else alone so they can work."

A bright-eyed girl, wearing a gold chain with a gold heart, asks another girl to quiz her in geometry. Surprisingly, she can define an equilateral and isosceles triangle with ease, but forgets the definition of a right angle. She looks at the book, then throws back her head as if to say, "Of course."

Mela, a Southeast Asian refugee, asks Pauline to give her a geometry test. She says she is ready, but the first question—How do you find the area of a triangle?—trips her up. How do you find the perimeter of a triangle? Add up all the sides. Can you draw a trapezoid? At first she looks puzzled, but does it correctly. An equilateral triangle? Gets it. Scalene triangle? Can't do it. Rhombus? Can't do it. An isosceles triangle?

Pauline is patient with her. But the rule here is that you can only miss four out of fifteen in order to pass a test. Students must have something close to mastery of a subject before going on. Mela misses five out of the first ten. Pauline sends her back to study. "You can do it, Mela," she says.

Pauline was a straight-A student throughout most of her time in school. She was very good at playing the academic game, as she puts it, sitting quietly, taking notes, and doing all the things her teachers told her to do. But she admits that she hated much of school, hated especially having to listen to teachers lecture day after day, "talking at you, not to you." She realized that if a good student hated it, kids like these are going to hate it even worse. "Instead of listening, or not listening, to somebody talk about math, these kids are engaged the whole time with real math problems," Pauline points out. "They are on task more time than a kid in a regular school. And when they hit a snag they can get immediate help."

Playing the role of coach wasn't easy for Pauline. "It was a hard adjustment," she says. "In this situation I don't have as much control anymore. They have control over what they will study, how fast they will study it, and when they will turn in their work. A kid can study percents before doing whole number division. It goes against everything I was taught in college. It means I have to let go of the wheel, stand back, and let them tackle it all in their own way. I admit, I also miss lecturing. It is fun to stand up and present an idea to a bunch of students and see if any light bulbs come on. You work up a nice presentation and draw nice graphs, and it makes you feel good."

Accelerated learning, which at the Urban Collaborative means letting students tackle each subject at their own pace (there are other interpretations of the term in the world of education), may require Pauline to ease up on the reins a bit, and for her and Peter to spend hours preparing numerous, multilevel exercises to challenge students at their various levels of knowledge, but she is still a happy convert to this method of teaching. It's especially valuable, she says, when working with children who never warmed up to the standard methods of teaching. "What motivation are you going to offer these kids to stay in school?" she asks rhetorically. "They've had a lot of hard knocks; they are behind their peers; school work has never come easy to them. What can you offer them as a reason to stay in school? You could try saying, 'Oh, to get a better job in the future.' But these kids aren't oriented toward the future. Most of them really can't see past the end of the week. So offering them the chance to make up for lost time is a big carrot. It gives them something to focus on, and offers them the motivation to push themselves.

"Some of these kids take to it instantly," she continues. "We had a girl who arrived in the middle of the year last year. The first day, she came up to me and asked me for all sorts of work. From experience, I didn't expect to see any of it coming back, but I handed it to her anyway. The very next day, she walked in and put it all down on my desk, completed. Then she asked for more. In two weeks she finished the entire seventh-grade math curriculum. It was amazing. This was a girl who couldn't even get herself to school before coming here. Not all kids catch on like this, but many of them do."

Peter Case has worked his way around the classroom and finally settles in with a few students who are working on new tessellations. It is, he readily admits, one of his favorite things to do. It's the one place in the curriculum where math becomes beautifully visual. Judging by the quality of the other student-drawn geometric designs on the classroom walls, Peter is also very good at coaching students through these projects. They are complex, patiently rendered, and attractive. Math in motion.

Peter talks briefly with two boys who have just returned to the classroom after spending time upstairs at Community Prep. The boys had been tutoring a group of fourth-grade math students. He thanks them for helping out, then directs them to get some new work of their own. Another boy asks if he can go to the library to work on his essay about Copernicus. Peter sends him on his way.

In many respects, Peter is the polar opposite of Pauline. He's as casual as she is formal. Tall and athletic, he wears his hair long, brushed back and falling in brown curls well below his shirt collar. Some days he'll put on a tie and oxford shirt. But he is equally inclined to slip on blue jeans and a T-shirt. She's a Midwestern conservative. He's a Cambridge-bred liberal. She's pro-life. He's pro-choice. She's devoutly religious. He's, as he puts it, "agnostic at best." And they fought like street cats the entire first year.

Peter laughs about it now. He came to the Urban Collaborative from a private school in Brazil, a job he took more or less for the experience of another culture right after he finished his master's degree in education at Harvard. Like Pauline, however, he had always wanted to teach in the inner city. "That's my idealism showing through," he says. "By coming here, I thought I would be saving the world. What I got instead that first year was the most stressful year of my life."

Like Pauline, Peter also expressed an interest in team teaching when he arrived. So after Rob hired them—Peter in part because he spoke fluent Portuguese, the preferred language of nearly one quarter of the school's parents—he granted both their wishes and threw them together. What Peter never expected was that he'd end up with someone with a completely different value system. "We basically came from opposite ends of the planet," he says. "And it was extremely difficult at first. Here we were being bombarded by all these zooey kids and dealing with their outrageous behavior, and we had to work out our differences as well."

Pauline tells a similar tale. "It's true, I always wanted to team teach. But when I met Peter, I thought, Oh, boy, who's this Looney Tune, and why did Rob hire me to work with him? We fought most of the first year, drove each other up a wall. We'd both go home each night furious at the other."

To their credit, they both stuck it out and eventually began to see the value of their differences, so much so that when in the second year they faced the prospect of splitting up a large group and teaching individually, they opted for keeping the group together—so they could be together.

"I get an incredible amount of support from Pauline," Peter admits. "Just to have another adult in the room when the shit hits the fan, someone you can make eye contact with, is wonderful. I owe my survival in the first year to Pauline. I think I would have cracked. I really do. It was almost as if the incredible adversity of the class itself forced us to bridge our differences.

"But then it is also great for the kids," he continues. "If a kid is really lost, I can sit down with him and spend as much time with him as he needs. I know Pauline is there to help out the rest of the group. Or vice versa. You know you have someone backing you up. We're like a pair of math cops. One person goes in and the other covers."

Pauline agrees, and runs down the list of the value of team teaching. "Because of our personality differences, it turns out that Peter often gets along better with certain kids than I do, and vice versa. Peter is also better at artistic stuff than I am. He's got a real gift for that and I don't. I realized early on that if it were only me in the classroom, kids wouldn't get to do much of this, and that would be a shame. If something blows up in the classroom, one of us can deal with the problem while the other keeps the class going. Or if I get really frustrated and feel as if I'm going to freak out, I can look at Peter to let him know I need a break.

"Knowing there is someone in the room who thinks you are human makes all the difference," she adds. "The kids can be so hard sometimes. They'll let you know that your shirt doesn't match your pants, or that those shoes went out of style two years ago, or that your hair doesn't look right, or that you've got a pimple on your forehead. It's hard to take that day after day after day. The class can be so chaotic some days, too, that I'm ready to scream, and all I have to do is look across the room at Peter and remember there is another person here who respects me and understands what I'm going through, that I'm not alone and everything is going to be OK."

Yesterday, Peter's birthday, Pauline brought a small cake to their classroom during a free period, shut the door, and served up two thick slices. The two of them sat quietly at their shared desk eating and enjoying the momentary peace.

Near the end of class, a girl named True saunters up to Peter and announces that she is ready for her math vocabulary test. She is wearing a flowing, tie-dyed dress, heavy bracelet-like earrings that tug at her earlobes, and a smaller gold ring through her nose. She is brash, bold, energetic, and about as confident as a sixteen-year-old can be. When she first arrived, everyone at the school thought she wouldn't make it through the year. "This girl was essentially at the bottom of the barrel," Peter recalls. "Her family life was a mess and she'd come in here and be totally disruptive, go completely off the handle at the slightest provocation. But we've worked with her on literally everything, starting with the way she lost her temper and on ways she could learn to control her anger and frustration. And eventually, she turned things around."

True's anger is not hard to trace. She has grown up without a father, and until recently lived in poverty with her mother, two sisters, and a brother, who is on probation for breaking and entering. True's mother is a cocaine addict. For a good part of the previous year, the school found out later, True's mother took off and True and her siblings lived by their wits, without electricity and scrounging up whatever food they could. This year, True's mother is spending time in jail for possession of crack, and True has moved in with the family of another student. In the early grades, she had been in the gifted program. But later she was kicked out for confronting a teacher and saying, "Fuck you." The irony of this is not lost on True, who quipped to Rob once, "One 'fuck' and it seems you're no longer gifted." Her test scores have fluctuated wildly depending on her feelings on the day of the test. In the fifth and sixth grade, she scored in the 90th percentile on her MATs. In the seventh grade, she dropped to 50th percentile, and ended up repeating the year. At the Urban Collaborative, she has scored both in the 90th percentile and the 50th percentile again. What the staff knows is that True is immensely talented and intelligent. What they hope is that they can keep her on an even keel and that she'll make it to college.

When True completes her test, she strolls confidently to Peter again and waits as he runs down the list quickly. Eventually, he looks at her and says, "Very good, True. Eighty-seven."

She smiles. "Hah," she exclaims, "I'm a bad wammer-jammer." And does a little victory dance back to her seat.

"How are skills learned? By experience," writes Ted Sizer, one of the nation's leading educational reformers. "How are skills taught? By coaching."

8

WHEN JIM SNEAD AND MAUREEN FARRELL, THE SCHOOL'S TWO science teachers, arrive with a group of students at the Moshassuck River in the town of Lincoln, ten minutes north of Providence, Jim hurries the group over to the riverbank. Here the river is narrow and flowing steadily beneath a canopy of trees.

"What do you notice about the water today?" he asks, his voice booming above the springtime giddiness of teenagers.

"Its color," one boy says.

"What about its color?"

"It's ugly," one girl says.

"It's different. It's darker, a rusty golden color, sort of," says another.

"What else do you notice?"

No response.

"What about the speed of the water?"

"It's flowing more slowly."

"Good. Why?"

"Because the water level is lower."

"What else do you notice?"

"Foam."

"Good. What does it mean?"

"Pollution?"

"Maybe," Jim says. "Could it be caused by anything else?"

No one hazards a guess. Instead of telling them the answer, Jim lets this last question hang in the air for the time being.

"Okay, let's get to work," he says.

The science classes have been studying the Moshassuck River (as well as the West River, a tributary to the Moshassuck) all year, taking samples from two locations ten miles apart. One location is in rural Lincoln, in the backyard of a woman named Elizabeth Parker, who kindly gave the class permission to work behind a converted mill where she has lived for forty years. The other location is in downtown Providence near where the Moshassuck and Woonasquatucket Rivers converge and flow humbly and quite exhaustedly into Narragansett Bay. The difference between the two locations is startling: one is sparkling with life, the other is murky and choked with industrial pollution. Earlier this year, after collecting data and recording observations, the students presented their findings to the Rhode Island Rivers Congress where, with students from other schools, they attended workshops about water and water pollution. The students continue to monitor the river and to learn more about river life and seasonal fluctuations. Someday, the school hopes, the data may be used to help clean up the rivers around Providence. The program has been such a success that both Jim and Maureen have decided to continue monitoring the rivers with their classes next year. The data they gather now will be useful not only for the current students but as a basis of comparison for future studies. At the same time, studying the rivers, Jim says, helps the students realize the application of "schoolwork" to life in their communities.

The equipment for the river project has been funded by the Toyota Corporation. For his work with the students on the Moshassuck, Jim received a 1992 Tapestry Award for excellence in science education, again from Toyota. In addition, Toyota sent a photographer to the river one afternoon to photograph the class in action. The following summer, the company used the photographs in an advertisement in a variety of national magazines, including *Forbes* and *Newsweek*. The connection with Toyota might smell of commercialism, but that's just fine with the Urban Collaborative. Without Toyota none of this would have happened. And for the kids, the notion of affecting change in their community (not to mention appearing on the pages of *Newsweek*) is particularly exciting. It's one of those things, Jim points out, that they will remember with pride for the rest of their lives.

While Jim helps two students don waders to take samples from the river, Maureen assists others as they collect river data.

"Come on, guys," she says, echoing Jim, "We haven't got all day."

Maureen is a compact, feisty woman. One could easily imagine her zipping through the paces of a tough aerobics class without difficulty. She has an unmistakable Irish edge, from her short straw-blonde hair and crowd of freckles to her strong chin and borderline hyperactivity. She wears wire-rimmed glasses that seem always to sit low on her thin nose, and, this day, large hoop earrings, sneakers, shorts, and an oversized sweatshirt. Her considerable collection of keys, a variation on the coach's whistle, hangs on a string around her neck. She wears no makeup.

Earlier in the year Maureen handed her resignation to Rob. She has been working part-time at the Urban Collaborative and part-time as a nutritionist elsewhere. Her desire, however, has always been to be a full-time biology teacher. So when a full-time position opened up at an East Providence Junior High School—a large, sprawling school tucked among shopping centers and car dealerships on the outskirts of the city—she grabbed it. But after two weeks in her cramped East Providence room, she realized she had made a mistake. That afternoon, she returned to the Urban Collaborative and asked Rob if he had handed her resignation to the board yet. When he said no, she asked if she could withdraw it, and he readily agreed.

"I thought I'd be happy teaching science full-time," Maureen says. "But the classes were so big and I felt I got absolutely no support from the administration. Nine of the twenty-five kids in one class were recently mainstreamed from special education classes. I just couldn't deal with that. Here I have smaller classes, support from the administration, and a good rapport with the kids. This is how education should be."

Maureen hands out a data sheet on a clipboard to a tall boy named Terence and runs through the checklist with him. "What's the water's appearance?" she asks.

"Clear," Terence says, then qualifies that. "Well, not exactly clear. It's sort of rusty looking."

"Put that down," she instructs. "What about the smell?"

"No smell," he says.

Tran, one of the school's top students, steps closer to the river, scoops a handful of water, sniffs, and says it smells musty. "Why is it like this, Maureen?"

She points out the pollen on the surface of the water and suggests that the smell may be caused by this, or some other form of natural decay. "Note the pollen," she says to Terence.

Maureen takes out a measuring tape and sends Luis, in waders, across the shallow river with one end of the tape. Betsy, also in waders and insisting that she feels foolish, takes the other end of the tape. Because of the river's width, they pull the tape to its full twenty-foot extension, a measure that is just short of the river's true width. They try to extend the tape further, tug it, tug each other off balance. But it's still short. Then they find they can't get the tape to rewind. Maureen, who had spun away from them momentarily, turns back and points out that the spot they're supposed to measure is a few yards north of where they're standing. They look at each other, smile, then shuffle upstream, moving awkwardly like overdressed astronauts. They stop and measure again. Here the river is just less than twenty feet. Luis calls out the width, then tries again to get the tape to retract. When it won't, he folds up the broken tape measure and drops it on the shore. But Maureen sends them back into the center of the river with the broken tape and an apple. They take three measurements of the speed of the river's current by timing how fast the bobbing apple travels six feet downstream. Each measurement is slightly different, but they decide to take the average. Terence records the times and does the math. "Maureen, got any more apples? I'm hungry," he says, flashing her a smile.

Afterward, Betsy collects water samples from the river. Back at school, they will take titrations, measuring the pH balance and percentage of oxygen in the water.

A boy named Cal watches as if for the first time. He turns to Maureen and asks, "Is it bad?"

"Is what bad?"

"Is it bad to have oxygen in the water?"

Maureen holds in her surprise at this elemental question. One thing you never do with these kids, she says later, is mock them. True moves in next to Maureen and watches as Betsy collects a water sample. Maureen looks at her and asks, "Is oxygen good or bad?"

"Good," True says, rather distantly, as if she is thinking about something else and barely hears Maureen.

"What's it good for?" Cal asks.

At this, True turns to him and smiles. "For breathing," she says. "Even fish need to breathe."

Maureen looks intently at True. "What happened to you?" she asks.

True's left eye is dark and puffy. She laughs nervously. "I got into a fight with some bitch girl."

"Are you OK?"

"Yeah, yeah. I'm fine."

"You sure?"

"Yeah." She stares down at the river. "I've got to stop doing this. You keep fighting and your face won't be pretty no more."

If the other kids are concerned about True, they don't show it. Cal's attention is already elsewhere, and one wonders if he will remember whether or not oxygen is important for aquatic life. Some of the kids dutifully watch. But some are easily distracted by the outdoors. One girl, Tina, seems pale and uneasy among so much nature. She has snuck back into the school van and has shut the door and windows. She tries to hide behind her full head of frizzy hair. When Jim notices her, he tells her to get out, but she doesn't listen. He is too busy at the moment to pursue the matter. Tina sits. Other kids have started wandering off down river toward an open yard. Maureen calls them back. They turn as a group and shuffle back slowly.

"It's one of those days," Maureen says to Jim.

Jim gets them all back at the spot by the river. Then he notices Tina still in the van and in his booming voice calls her out. She moves to the edge of the group and crosses her arms, defiant, unhappy, hating the proliferation of flying insects that have come out since their last visit to this site.

A boy named Gilbert continues to fool around, picking up a branch and pretending to use it as a sword, so Jim recruits him to put on the last pair of waders and help take samples from the water.

"Me?" Gilbert asks incredulously.

"Yes, you, Gilbert. You haven't done this yet, and I think you can learn something from it."

"Why me? I don't want to put this on."

"Put it on, Gilbert. You're wasting our time."

Jim Snead, forty-one, is by anyone's measurements a large man. Standing a few inches over six feet, he weighs easily in the range of three hundred pounds. In college at the University of Rhode Island, he was a star football player. Afterward, the New England Patriots invited him to try out for the team. With his strength and size, it's hard to imagine him not making the team. But he says he decided that playing professional football wasn't right for him. As he puts it, "I just wasn't in the mood to take directions from coaches anymore. I didn't like the way they operated, and I didn't need them to tell me what to do. It was no longer the same game I loved in college."

Jim did hook up with a semi-pro team and stayed with them for fifteen years, playing football around New England the way he always enjoyed it, for fun and the immediacy of competition. Meanwhile, he started working toward his degree in science education, a move that eventually led him to the Urban Collaborative.

One of only two full-time minorities on the staff, Jim applied for the job at the Urban Collaborative during its first year of operation, shortly after the original science teacher quit in utter disillusionment. Rob remembers being greatly impressed with Jim, but by law he had to choose another candidate who had the proper certification in biology (Jim was certified only in general science at the time). Fortunately for the Urban Collaborative, the science teacher didn't sign on for the second year, and Rob hired Jim as the full-time science teacher and Maureen as a part-time biology teacher. Because the average age of the students dropped the second year, there was more call for general science anyway, and less for biology. Meanwhile, Jim is pursuing his certification in biology at night.

Prior to the Urban Collaborative, Jim had taught science and physical education for a few years at a school for juvenile delinquents and had worked in a program that provided physical education in Rhode Island's Catholic schools. What he may have lacked in teaching experience, he easily made up for in life experience. Jim's physical size notwithstanding, he is larger than life, with patience, dedication, and an understanding of how it feels to be on the academic fringe. He has been there himself.

Jim grew up in Providence in neighborhoods much like the one surrounding the Urban Collaborative. In fact, he still lives in the area, three-quarters of a mile from the school. Most of the other teachers commute each day from comfortable suburbs or upscale areas of the city.

"When I was young," Jim says later that day, "a lot of the minority kids were thrown into what they called 'ungraded rooms.' These were supposedly places for kids with learning problems, dyslexia or whatever. You'd think we'd get more attention in these rooms, but we got less. Once there, we didn't learn much of anything. Still they promoted us along just to make it seem as if we were learning." He talks slowly, staring at the ceiling as if trying to conjure the feelings of those days. "It was just the way things were back then. But when I think about it now, I can't believe what they were doing. They were taking all these minority kids and essentially shoving them aside. And what happened was that many of these kids eventually ended up in the Adult Correction Institute. Some, like me, actually made it through to college. But for most, there was no place to go, so they got involved in crime of one sort or another. Small stuff mostly, but enough to ruin their lives."

When his parents moved to North Providence, Jim made it out of the ungraded room and into a regular fifth-grade class. At first, he was nervous about it, but in time he found he could do as well as anybody.

His own experience has helped him deal with students at the Urban Collaborative in ways that perhaps no other teacher can. He understands firsthand what life is like for the inner-city poor. He understands how, growing up as minorities in the city, kids can lose sight of the future. "These kids need to grab onto a dream and believe they are going to become somebody someday," he says. "But that is hard in an environment where they see most people failing to get anywhere. It's hard for them to believe that they can do it, so they quit. They think: What makes them any different? You know? When I was a kid I didn't believe in anything. I didn't have a clue where I was going or what life was all about."

What helped Jim was football. When he realized he was good at it, he began to dream, like so many kids, of being a professional. So football became his motivation to work in school. He knew that if he didn't do well, he couldn't go to college and couldn't play professionally. As with so many children who succeed, what also helped Jim was a family who convinced him that he could excel both in the classroom and on the field. In the end, it was the classroom that saved him.

He mentions by way of contrast Joe, a boy who is struggling to keep his spirits up at the Urban Collaborative. Joe is ready to quit school, sees no reason to keep working. The problem is that what Joe does in school draws little praise at home. His father died early in the year. Joe was devastated by this, but managed to come back and get some work done. In the winter he joined Jim's wrestling team, vented some of his frustrations, and in the process discovered that he was a pretty good wrestler. In fact, he went on to become one of the best wrestlers in the state and was awarded the team's most valuable player trophy. But his mother didn't come to the award ceremony, and when he brought home his shiny new trophy, the first ever in his household, his mother showed no interest. "That would tear your heart apart," Jim says. "After something like that, it's understandable a kid would give up and say, 'what's the use?' And there are a lot of kids here who go through similar experiences."

Jim mentions Joe in part because Joe has been struggling of late, refusing to do work and talking about dropping out. Earlier in the day, Joe was called into Rob DeBlois' office over a minor confrontation with another boy that Rob feared would escalate into a real battle if he didn't stop it. In Rob's office, however, it quickly became clear that Joe's anger had little to do with the other boy and everything to do with his family. Rob, as is his way with discipline, was tough on Joe, telling him he didn't want Joe to be sent to the office for any reason for the rest of the year. Joe, a slight boy with unruly black hair, sloping shoulders, and the swagger of someone twice his size, nodded each time Rob said, "Do you understand?" But he wasn't thinking much about the current problem. Eventually, playing with the brim of his Pirates hat, he said to Rob, "I'm sick of doing the right thing."

"What do you mean, Joe?" Rob asked, still with an edge of the disciplinarian.

"I'm tired of doing whatever my mother asks. I'm sick of her. I'm moving out." He glanced up at Rob briefly, then looked back down.

Rob softened. "I know things have been hard on you this year, Joe. You lost your father. You should try to remember, too, that your mother lost her husband."

Joe nodded. "I don't go out no more. I don't do nothing. My mother is always trying to get me to go out. But ever since my father died, I don't want to go out no more. I don't see anybody. I don't have any friends."

Rob waited him out.

"I've ended up like my father," Joe continued. "He never cared about anything; now I don't care about anything. He didn't want to be around people; I don't like to hang around people. I have an attitude now."

"Did you like the way you were before better?"

"I used to go out a lot more," Joe said. "But the neighborhood changed. Jumbo died. He was an old, friendly guy. He was funny. We used to clown around with him. But he died, and Cisco is going a little crazy. He used to go around collecting cans. But the guy had money. He bought his daughter a Porsche a few years ago. But he's crazy now. Everybody in the neighborhood is . . . is losing. Jack got caught dealing, and he's going to be doing time. There ain't no winning in my neighborhood. Everybody's disappearing."

Rob points out that Joe isn't losing. He has done well at the Urban Collaborative and has gotten into a good high school program for next year. Still, Rob knows that Joe is confused, feeling despair and hope at once, the former gaining the upper hand. He suggests that Joe talk to Al Lemos.

"I don't care no more. Why should I talk with Al? I don't like to talk to people about this. I just want to be alone," Joe said. Then he added, "I'm sick of Rhode Island. I'd love to move out of this state. I'd love to get lost for once. Just for once. I'd love it. I've spent my whole life here, and I never get lost. I can't get lost in Rhode Island."

Joe headed back to class, but a short while later, Rob rounded up Al and Jim to sit down with Joe. He knew that Joe was clearly in emotional pain and he knew that for most of the Urban Collaborative kids, being in such a state can be dangerous. It can manifest itself in destructive ways. Joe might provoke a fight with another student. He might skip out of school. He might curse out a teacher. He might, as he threatened to do, give up on school entirely with only two weeks to go.

Al is good at helping the kids see their way through tough situations. But this time it was Jim who got Joe back on track. Jim knows Joe well from wrestling. Jim also knows the pressures that drive a kid to drop out, ironically, at the time when he needs school the most. Jim sat down across from Joe and began talking about wrestling and all that Joe had done during the year. He pointed out that only two months ago, Joe had vowed to revenge a loss to another top Rhode Island wrestler the next year. "You can't do it if you are not in school," Jim pointed out.

"I'm tired of school."

"Everyone gets tired of school at some point. But it's all you've got."

"I don't need it."

"If you didn't come here this year, you never would have wrestled. If you didn't wrestle, you never would have gone to the state meet, and you never would have won that trophy. You need school. Everyone does. The big problems start when you leave school."

"Who cares?"

"You do," Jim said. "That's why it hurts so much now. You care, and you wish other people cared as much. And I'm telling you that there are people here who care. And I'm sure your mom cares. She's just going through a hard time, like you. You've done a lot this year, Joe. You've done well in school. You've accelerated in all your subjects. You're one of the best wrestlers. You've got to remember these things. You can't always think about what's wrong with your life."

Joe nodded. "I don't even go fishing anymore. I used to always go fishing."

"You will go fishing again some time," Jim said. "Nothing is permanent. You're just going through a hard time now. If you hang on, things will get better. And we'll help you all we can—if you try."

Joe nodded again. It was a tentative agreement, but it was an agreement nevertheless. Yes, he believed things would get better. Yes, he really did want to wrestle next year. Yes, it had been a tough year, but he had managed to accomplish something. And yes, he was still here—and that was something. You could see it in his eyes. You could feel it in his deep sigh, as if he were psyching himself up to get back into the game, try a little harder.

Jim tries to help his students find motivation in any way possible both in and out of class. He started the school's wrestling team (Jim also wrestled in college) and has encouraged Urban Collaborative students to join a local football team he coaches. In class, like the other teachers, he offers small incentives—including taking students out to lunch at the local pasta restaurant for perfect attendance each month.

One of the greatest motivators, however, has been a science curriculum that allows the kids to explore the world around them. Jim received a grant to take a group of students to Niagara Falls, where they studied the effects of toxic waste on the river and in the community. They visited Love

Canal, and he showed the kids the houses that were still condemned because of toxic fumes that had seeped in over the years. They talked to residents in the area, toured some of the companies along the river, and interviewed chemical company representatives about their plans to clean up the leaking toxic waste. The kids, he said, were amazed by what they saw. "This was big time education," Jim insists. "I mean, colleges don't do some of the stuff we did.

"They were also a bit shocked by the community's willingness to put up with all the pollution. Some of our kids wanted to organize a protest right then and there. But they decided we needed more information first." Jim adds that he'd like to take a group back to Niagara Falls soon to study the problem of containing spilled chemicals and perhaps to offer the companies a solution. "What I want these kids to realize is that they should know what is going on in their own communities and that they can affect change."

His desire to get the kids out of the classroom also led to the Whole Rivers Project on the Moshassuck. The previous year, most of the science curriculum was confined to the classroom. Jim wanted to change this, so he wrote a grant to study the river and then took part in a seminar on how to direct students in such a study. He came back and taught Maureen what he had learned, and the two have been working with the kids all year. The river project has even spilled over into other classes. The students designed calendars that featured things they had learned from the project, complete with illustrations and poems. Social studies classes also added a unit on the history of rivers and commerce. "I love taking them to a place they may know, such as this river, but have never really looked at carefully before," Jim says. "It blows their minds. They love it. I brought them to this stinky old river in Providence, and they seemed unimpressed. But when we started finding all these creatures that live there, they were amazed. I got them to write letters to people asking for permission to study the river on their property. And I've gotten them to talk with people who run businesses along the river and to visit the companies. And they do it. I think there are a million lessons in all this. They learn quite a bit about science; it's a great civics lesson; they practice their writing skills, their speech; and they learn that they can accomplish things they set out to accomplish, that they are able students."

Jim wades into the river in his sneakers. He hands a long-handled net to Gilbert and instructs Luis to stand upstream of the net. Then, timing it very carefully, he instructs Luis to pick up stones from the river bottom and rub them together to knock loose various macroinvertebrates. Jim encourages them to work quickly. Gilbert stays close to Luis, pressing the net against the river bottom with the handle pointed skyward.

"Come on, Luis," Jim coaches, "faster."

Luis, wearing rubber gloves, works quickly, scouring a small section, then moving a foot to his right. In precisely two minutes they stop, Luis dropping the last two rocks and putting his hands on his hips like a competitive athlete.

The net is brought ashore, where Jim instructs another group of students to start picking out the macroinvertebrates with tweezers. Most of them hold the tweezers gingerly and pick at the river creatures with a mix of disgust and fear, then quickly drop the specimens in a plastic bag. Jim pokes his head over their shoulders, pointing out the various life forms in this sample: salamanders, hellgrammites, caddis flies, dragonfly nymphs. "Great stuff," Jim says. "Great stuff."

Maureen wanders off with a group to a second spot fifty yards down river beyond Mrs. Parker's garden of lilies. They cross a sunlit stretch of lawn and are suddenly surrounded by dragonflies patrolling the area. Maureen points them out excitedly, explaining how good they are about controlling mosquitoes. Most of the kids start ducking and swatting at the air. Maureen laughs and leads them down to the water where the river is more narrow and the water gurgles swiftly over rounded rocks. She sets them to work here, repeating the same steps—detailed observation and carefully collected samples. Soon, Jim and the others join them.

Besides continuing the river project, Jim and Maureen are also planning to add a unit on genetics next year. Maureen will attend a workshop at Providence College and bring back equipment that students can use to learn about DNA fingerprinting and how to break down DNA with enzymes. She is also planning field trips to a Boston University medical lab and a company that specializes in cutting-edge genetic technology.

"I think the Urban Collaborative is serving them well," Jim says. "Once kids catch on to the system here, they can learn just about anything. Most important, I think they find the motivation to learn, to continue to learn. If they attack the rest of high school the way they've attacked work here, most of them can succeed." He relays a story about one boy named Billy who just accelerated in science—that is, completed his science requirements in less than a year. That one taste of success has given him the boost he needs. Now Billy is pushing hard to accelerate in all subjects before summer. "For most of the year, Billy just plodded along not doing much of anything. Then his aunt called me and asked what she could do. I told her, very specifically, to turn off the TV, sit him down, and work through the science book with him one page at a time. And she followed every word I said. Eventually, he learned that if he stayed with it he could understand this stuff. It was hard, but he could understand it. Step by step, piece by piece. You know? Now he's all excited and trying harder than ever. Hopefully he'll be able to sustain this."

The group finishes taking data and collecting samples and hurries back to the van. They are late for the last period of the day. But before they take off, Jim stops and sticks his hand into the second sample bag. "Look at this, guys. Look at this." He pulls out a large hellgrammite, the largest he says he's seen on this river. "We've hit the jackpot."

"Disgusting," one boy says. "Looks like something from *Aliens*." But he stares at it with curiosity nevertheless. Most of them do, even Tina. And one gets the feeling that they'll remember this for a long time: this spot in the river, hellgrammites, how industrialization can choke the life out of a river. They'll remember the feel of the current around their legs, the smell of the water late in spring, the swarm of dragonflies, and the kindness of the woman who let them use her backyard. And they'll remember that there are lessons to learn outside the classroom, even from a narrow, "stinky old river" that has silently wound through their lives all these years.

9

"I MAY BE VERY WRONG ABOUT THIS," SAYS LYNNE ABBOTT,
the school's only full-time English teacher, "but I have a theory that the
best and the brightest in this country aren't graduating from Yale or the
University of Michigan this spring. The luckiest are, for sure. But I think
many of our best and our brightest are withering away on our urban
streets. The talent and potential that we are losing every year is frightening.
And very sad."

Why are we losing them?

Lynne shrugs. "Oh, God, If I could answer that. . . ." She continues,
"It's a multiple of reasons, from family to society to schools themselves.
They are all interconnected." What she *can* say with clarity is that she is
very glad to be able to work with at-risk kids, some of whom she most
definitely considers among the nation's best and brightest.

Lynne, in her mid-forties, is one of the older full-time members of the
teaching staff at the Urban Collaborative. And she is one of the few who had
actually worked with at-risk kids before coming here. "I think the kids are
such a vital bunch," she says, "and I enjoy working with them immensely."

An Ohio native who came to Rhode Island via New York, Lynne
worked in two other Rhode Island programs that targeted dropouts or
at-risk students before she took the job at the Urban Collaborative. One
she describes as a mentoring program in which she'd keep tabs on a group
of troubled kids, monitoring their attendance and performance in class,
meeting with them and their parents often, encouraging them, offering
advice and academic guidance. The other was an in-school program for
the most difficult kids in the Central Falls High School.

What brought her to the Urban Collaborative was the attractiveness of working in a school designed entirely for the at-risk population. "In specialized programs within larger schools, you tend to be very isolated," Lynne points out. "You tend to be looked down upon by the staff and even by the students. Because the at-risk kids are looked down upon, by some crazy logic their teachers are, too. The other problem is that it gets very discouraging to work with kids when you know they'll never make it in high school. When you know that the school is just waiting for the day it can throw them out. In one school I know, the kids were put into a special program not to get them back in the mainstream, but just to put them some place for a while, get them out of everyone else's hair. So I was really excited by the prospect of working for a school that was geared for and truly interested in at-risk kids."

Lynne's class is currently reading a book called *Are You in the House Alone?* by Richard Peck. It is one of many young adult works of fiction written specifically for teenagers. Lynne often teaches more traditional works of fiction—*The Old Man and the Sea, Of Mice and Men*—but she likes many of the young adult books, especially for this group of students. The writing is simple, and the stories usually deal with issues close to their lives. In this case, *Are You in the House Alone?* tells the story of a sixteen-year-old girl who moves with her family from New York City to a rural Connecticut town, where she is raped by a top student-athlete who is the son of the town's leading family. Since there are no witnesses to the rape, there is little the girl can do about it. If she presses charges, it will become a matter of her word against his, the word of the newcomer against the word of the establishment, the word of the poor against the word of the rich, the word of a girl who deliberately lives on the edge of society against the word of Mr. All-the-Right-Moves.

Lynne, sitting comfortably at one end of the large table, reads a chapter to the group. She is a tall, thin woman, with dark hair that's turning gray. Today she is wearing a gold turtleneck sweater and large gold earrings. At ease in the classroom setting, she stares down at the page through an oversized pair of glasses and reads slowly and with rich inflection.

The small group sits around the table. Each student has a copy of the novel, but only half of them have the book open and follow along while Lynne reads. Some quietly preen. Others slump in their seats and seem to let their thoughts drift to who knows what painful memories or secret hopes.

The class period began only a couple minutes earlier. Lynne, who has little tolerance for nonsense or wasted time, jumped into reading, even before all the kids arrived. When one boy knocks at the door, she doesn't pause the story or look up. The boy is late—one of a handful who are late this day—and this is her way of impressing upon them that she expects them here on time, expects them to be ready for English class the minute the period starts. At this juncture in the year, one imagines that the teachers might relax a bit more before summer break, but Lynne presses on, knowing that many of the kids need to finish this book and the accompanying assignments in order to accelerate a grade. It's the nature of this school that the end of a term can be the most critical time. Some have already made it. Some have given up. But there are a good number of them who could benefit from hard work now. In one week, a student can accomplish much here, if he or she tries. It's the nature of this group, however, that few would try unless pushed.

A girl lets the late boy in. He quickly gets a book and takes a seat at the table, his soft steps offering an apology. Three other boys slip in quickly behind him, but they are more inclined to interrupt.

"Awh, we reading again?" Cal asks incredulously. "I'm already reading a book. You mean I have to read *two* books?"

Lynne pauses to glare at him over her glasses. "Take a book," she says. Then she's reading again, telling the story of the narrator and her views of this Connecticut town.

One of the boys, Irving, is not quick to settle down. He walks over to the sink in the corner of the classroom and washes his hands slowly, as if preparing for surgery. Lynne glances at him, reads on. Irving gets himself a drink of water, then dries his hands, ever so thoroughly. Irving, a handsome young boy with a high forehead and bright eyes, is one of the school's failures. He is undoubtedly smart. And he can bring a whole class to laughter with his antics and one-liners. Yet, for whatever reason, he cannot make the commitment to school. One wonders what gets him here each morning. He is leaving the Urban Collaborative for good at the end of the year, having failed to advance in any of his classes. In the yearbook is a picture of Irving asleep on a couch. The caption reads, "Laziest"—a moniker arrived at by his peers. He has in many ways succumbed to the role of class clown, playing a part that is as old as the moon.

Irving sits. He and another boy inspect each other's shoes. Irving has black Fila high-tops. The other has Saucony running shoes.

"Are you going to continue to be rude?" Lynne asks suddenly.

"What are you looking at me for?" Irving says.

"Open your book to page twenty."

Irving huffs, opens his book, and stares out the window.

Lynne's classroom is one of the neater rooms in the building. On one wall is the ubiquitous poster of Michael Jordan with his considerable arms outstretched, a basketball held firmly in his right hand as if caught in a hawk's talon. The poster is entitled "Wings." Beneath the photograph is a line from William Blake: "No bird soars too high / if he soars with his own wings." Echoes of the Einstein poster across the hall—hopeful advice designed to encourage these students to find their own paths to happier lives.

On one chalkboard is a definition of personification in perfect Palmer penmanship. Nearby is a poster of famous African-American writers and another of famous African-American leaders. On another wall is a series of posters from Shakespearean plays. Beneath them is a note about the rhyme scheme of *Romeo and Juliet*, with an example of iambic pentameter. Earlier in the spring, the class performed a dramatic reading of *Romeo and Juliet* and loved it.

Given the struggles these kids have had with school, it is surprising to learn that Shakespeare is a part of the curriculum. But Lynne readily defends it. "I'm very committed to doing Shakespeare," Lynne says later, "because most of these kids when they get to high school, if they are not on the college prep track, will never read Shakespeare. More important, they like it. The group expected to hate it, but I think they really loved the story of forbidden love and desire. And they were very proud of themselves. They were doing big stuff, you know. Shakespeare. They read it out loud, each kid with a part, and had a great time."

Lynne tried to approach the play from as many different angles as possible. Besides the dramatic reading, the kids watched the Zeffirelli film of *Romeo and Juliet* and discussed the differences between the two versions—how in the movie the fight scenes are drawn out, some of the speeches are dropped or shortened, and Romeo doesn't even kill Paris in the end. One of their favorite scenes was when Juliet drew the anger of her father by refusing to marry Paris, her prearranged husband. "It's such a vital scene to them," Lynne says, "because they understand Juliet's passion and how unfair life can be for the young." So Lynne had them rewrite that scene in modern, inner-city language to demonstrate the universality of such a conflict. When she worked with them on iambic pentameter, a number of kids found rap songs that were written in this meter. The Shakespeare unit was also supported by the social studies class in which the kids studied Elizabethan England ("They had no idea at first what a queen was all about," laughs Chris Cuthbertson).

If such a unit is successful—and Lynne thinks it was—it has a three-fold purpose. First, it exposes students to a great piece of literature that also touches on themes close to their own lives. Second, tackling a "hard" book boosts their self-esteem and confidence. And third, a good narrative has a way of reaching students, subtly teaching lessons or values the way no lecture can. "A lot of people ask me why I don't teach these kids a unit on filling out forms," Lynne says, shaking her head. "You'd be amazed. There are a lot of curricula out there for low-level students or at-risk students on how to fill out social security forms and employment forms. But I think that's absurd and really insulting to the kids. It's insulting to *me*. It's more important to build up their confidence in their ability to use language and to offer them something of substance."

Lynne has another rule about reading. "First and foremost, it must be an enjoyable experience," she insists. "I will cut off any lofty discussion if I feel that it is going to ruin the general experience. I don't care what the current pedagogical logic is, I think it is much more important for these kids to have a good reading experience than to be taught, for instance, imagery. Who cares about imagery? I might because I'm an English teacher, but these kids aren't ready for that. They want to get caught up in the story."

In part, this explains Lynne's choice of *Are You in the House Alone?* as a follow up to Shakespeare. Peck's story is in some ways a modern-day variation on *Romeo and Juliet* with easier language and portrayals of romance and sex that touch closer to home. In particular, the novel exposes the inequalities in our society that are born of wealth and poverty, and it raises questions about whether the law protects the criminal or the victim.

Aileen, a heavy-set girl, interrupts Lynne's reading near the end of a long passage describing the protagonist's feelings about moving to rural Connecticut. During this passage, the plot does not advance, and Aileen, for one, has grown restless. "Lynne, what's this story about, anyway?"

Lynn doesn't answer. She looks around at the others. Nobody offers an answer at first. Then Carole speaks up, saying rather darkly, "It's about a girl being followed by a creep."

"That girl's gonna get killed. I know it," Aileen retorts.

"Shut up, you don't know nothing." This from Irving. He flashes her a smile.

"You shut up."

"Both of you stop it," Lynne says gently, then elaborates on Carole's remarks.

Carole is one of the school's shining successes. In one year she has completed nearly two years of school by working steadily. Born in Monrovia, Liberia, Carole emigrated to America with her father two years earlier, leaving her mother behind, because her parents feared for Carole's safety during Liberia's recent civil war. Unlike most other students, she has always studied in school. She stayed back a year not because of laziness or illness but because the civil war had shut down her school. For Carole, just being allowed to attend school now is a privilege.

Lynne finishes the passage then hands out worksheets with the instruction to answer in complete sentences. "You don't get any credit if you don't answer in complete sentences."

First, however, she opens the floor for discussion of the setting.

"Where does the book take place?" Lynne asks.

"In Connecticut."

"What town?"

"Old something."

"Oldfield."

"Oldfield Village. Right? And what sort of town is it?" Lynne asks.

"What do you mean?"

"What does Gail think of it?"

"She doesn't like it much."

"And why not?"

"I don't know. It's not too friendly."

"People there are messed up."

"In what way?"

"Well, it's like she says. They aren't too friendly."

"Some of the people that have been there a while don't like the new people like Gail."

"Exactly," says Lynne.

"And the rich people don't like the poor."

"Good."

"Like my shoes?" Irving says to Aileen.

"Irving, there is no one here who needs a special project more than you," Lynne says, then gets up and opens the window. It's stuffy in the room.

Aileen slaps viciously at Irving's hand while Lynne is at the window.

"What about the Laver family?" Lynne asks, returning.

"They're rich and stuck up. What's that word? Considerate," says Carole.

"Considerate?"

"You mean conceited," says Penny, a pale, shy girl with thick glasses and teased dirty-blonde hair.

"Right, conceited."

A few laugh at the mistake.

Lynne explains the difference between the two words, then says, "All right. Get writing." They have practically been fed the answer. Most write.

Others stare desperately at the pages. Irving simply doesn't bother. In his mind he has already started summer vacation. He has already shut the door on the school. The happy future they work toward is some well-kept garden on the other side of town where, he believes, he'll never be admitted. For Irving, such fatalism is a self-fulfilling prophecy.

The other questions require simple analysis of characters. Who are they? What are they like? What do they want?

It's now raining outside. The kids seem to lack energy. Lynne senses this and draws the class to a close a few minutes early. She passes around a plastic basket to collect the books, asking students not to throw them. Then she hands out lottery tickets to those who participated. The lottery tickets are new this week, a not-so-subtle attempt to keep the kids working through the end of the year. One of the problems with accelerated learning is that once kids accelerate a grade they tend to sit back and bide their time. Near the end of the year, especially, when there is not enough time to accelerate another grade and only time to earn partial credit, the school needs a way to keep kids focused. There are no final exams to hold over their heads, so the librarian, Connie Zeeland, introduced the lottery. Kids get tickets for working in each class. The tickets are thrown into a box, and a random drawing is held at the end of the week. The winners get their choice of prizes, everything from backpacks to movie tickets to makeup kits. Lynne passes them out fairly liberally.

"Hey, what about me?" Irving asks.

"You? What did you do?"

"Come on, Lynne. I worked today."

She turns and gives some to other kids.

"I'll buy some from you," Irving offers.

Lynne turns to him and smiles. "Here, Irving. But if you want more you are going to have to work harder."

"Thanks, Lynne," he says, genuinely excited. Then he asks, "Where do we put this at?" Apparently it's the first one he has received.

Unlike the math classes, the English class can handle a few group projects a year. They are called Special Projects, and students must complete some of these in order to advance to the next grade. The rest of the time, the students more or less work on their own, as in math, honing their knowledge of grammar and the elements of good writing. Skill work, Lynne calls it, as opposed to the study of content. The students have to tackle grammar and vocabulary, work on their library skills, study logic and reasoning and paragraph development, and read both in and out of class. The criteria are essentially the same for each grade, though Lynne—and Kate Carbone, who teaches English part-time across the hall—has higher expectations for those in the upper grades. In other alternative schools, such a class might be run more as a writing workshop, with the kids sitting down to scratch out their thoughts and feelings on various subjects each day. But Lynne and Kate feel the need to balance things out. In particular, they want to make sure these kids learn grammar.

"When I first started teaching, kids didn't get any grammar in elementary school, and they didn't know top from bottom," Lynne says. "This bothered me. So I always advocate the teaching of grammar. I know a lot of people think it's a waste of time, that kids are just supposed to pick up grammar through osmosis or by imitation or something. But the thing is, kids don't get it. I think if they know grammar, they are empowered by it, because now they can look at their own writing and see what's missing. I would probably feel better if I knew how my car worked. I mean, if something goes wrong, I am at the mercy of some mechanic, because, while I can drive just fine, I haven't a clue what is going on under the hood. These kids don't become great grammarians. But at least they have an idea of how words fit together."

A week later, Lynne's class is finishing up *Are You in the House Alone?* The day is brighter and the class is a bit more lively, though Irving has his head down on the desk, eyes closed.

Aileen takes advantage of a break in the reading to tell Lynne, "This book is boring."

"That's because you weren't here the past few days and you don't know what is going on," Lynne says matter-of-factly.

Betsy, at Lynne's request, summarizes the plot for Aileen. It's a quick, cursory summary.

"Are you listening, Aileen?" Lynne asks.

"Yeah. Why she scared for?"

Carole pipes in. "She's been getting those obscene phone calls and letters that say, 'you know you want it' and stuff like that. She knows someone is watching her."

"What does she look like?" Lynne asks.

"A whore. A rich whore." Katrina says with a surprising amount of spite.

"No."

"Eccentric," says Terence, who is wearing a Reebok hat emblazoned with the name *Dave*. "She's like some artist type."

"Yes, with velvet bellbottoms and lemon yellow shoes with three-inch heels," Lynne adds.

Kane walks in late for class. Lynne stops to tape a sign on his back that reads, "I will not swear." Kane has grown too fond of four-letter words, and even though it is late in the year, Lynne is hoping to break him of the habit. He mouths the word *shit* and sits down.

"What is squash?" Rosa asks.

"Squash? I saw that once on 'Miami Vice,' " Kane says.

"No, dummy, that's jai alai."

"What's squash?" Lynne asks the group. "Anyone know?"

No one knows. Lynne admits that she doesn't really know much about squash either. "It's like an indoor tennis game played off a wall. What's important," she notes, "is that it is a game associated with the rich."

Lynne jumps to another question. "What about Gail's relationship with Steve? Is it OK for her to be doing this, to be having sex with him?"

"Oh sure," says Liza, a petite girl with straight, thick brown hair. "She's sixteen. She's using protection. She'll be fine."

Lynne looks around. "Everyone agree with that?"

One suspects that Lynne is hoping for a different view. But there are no dissenters.

Lynne asks them to write briefly about Gail's character. Who is she? What does she do? What is different about her? Then she goes on with the reading, the crucial scene in which Gail is raped by the squash-playing Phil Laver. He has come, he says, to teach the slut a lesson. In actuality, he is jealous and too used to getting his own way. Six students are reading along, Irving sleeps, and Mela stares at her feet, listening intently.

Afterward, Terence asks, "Is she brain damaged?" Phil had hit Gail across the head with a fireplace poker when she tried to resist.

"No," Lynne says. "Let's read on."

There is one chapter left, the denouement, and she wants to get to it so they can discuss what has transpired.

The author offers some fairly explicit descriptions of tests Gail submits to after the rape to prove sexual intercourse had occurred. But when Gail implicates Phil Laver as the rapist, she receives only looks of incredulity from the doctors, the police, and even her parents. She is interrogated by an arrogant police officer, or, rather, intimidated by him. And finally, holding to her story, she is warned by the family lawyer what could happen if she presses charges. The lawyer says he'll press charges if she wants to, but feels it is his obligation to first present her with a daunting list of considerations. The bottom line: Phil Laver is untouchable.

"Why do people act funny when Gail says it was Phil Laver?" Lynne stops and asks.

"Because he's rich and they can't do nothing about rich people," says Liza.

The cop who questions Gail is deliberately obnoxious and threatening. This draws an unsolicited response from Aileen, "I hate that cop."

Terence says, "They should make a movie out of this."

They talk about Gail's chances in court. The odds are against Gail because there are no witnesses and no evidence of rape, just sexual intercourse.

"Anything else?"

"His family is too important in the community."

The message to Gail, the group agrees, is simple and cold-hearted: take care of yourself because society doesn't favor women in such situations. Keep your guard up at all times and don't allow yourself to get into that situation.

Irving is awake now. He adjusts and readjusts the cuffs of his pants. Like most of the boys, he wears his pants very low on his hips so they are baggy in the crotch and show off a few inches of his underwear.

"What do you think will happen to Phil?"

"The bastard will go to jail," Kane says.

"No. Not likely."

"Nothing will happen to him. He'll get away with it because of who he is," says Carole.

"Why does the law protect the rapist instead of the victim?"

"The law is crazy. Always has been."

"Would the real law take this more seriously?"

"No," says the class, nearly in unison.

But Carole isn't so sure. She feels that in real life Gail would have pressed charges. "She should press charges. She might not win, but at least then she might stop the bastard from doing it again."

"Good point," says Lynne.

But this is followed by an awkward silence. No one seems to know what to say next.

10

LYNNE ABBOTT, LIKE THE OTHER TEACHERS IN THE URBAN Collaborative, is happy about the accelerated learning system and thinks that the school is definitely helping most of the students—a welcomed change from programs that she worked with in the past. But Lynne has her reservations. "I think the big question is always going to be, 'How many of these kids will ever really make it when they return to their regular high schools?' " she says. "I think that we can make them successful here, and I think this is actually happening. But I don't know whether this translates into success in traditional high schools."

Jim Snead voices a similar concern about the program because it takes students only as far as tenth grade. "I'd like to see us make it possible to help these kids straight through high school. I've seen a number who, after a long struggle, have done well here. And then they return to the mainstream school, fall back into old patterns, and eventually drop out. Some of them have gotten their GEDs, but it would be better if they stayed in school. If there were a program like this through the twelfth grade, they could have made it. I know it."

Adds Chris Cuthbertson, "Sometimes I feel as if we are throwing them out to fend for themselves. Many of them go from here to Central High School where there are a million kids, mostly older kids, and our students are just plain scared."

Ask any of the students currently enrolled in the Urban Collaborative and the majority will tell you the same. They would love to get their diploma from the Urban Collaborative. And why not? Most of them have found a home here. For the first time in their lives, they are succeeding in school. Most have managed to keep pace or accelerate their learning. And most of them are enjoying school in ways they never did before, never imagined they could. In short, they are happy here. Why leave just when things are getting good?

Shayla, a student who by her own admission has not done as well as she could have at the Urban Collaborative, is nevertheless a staunch defender of the school and is among those who wish the program could be extended through high school. "As I was telling Rob," she says, "this definitely should be more than a two-year program. We should definitely be able to graduate from here. No question. The other schools can't handle all the kids who are already out there. Now they are going to have to try to fit all of us in. It's not going to be much fun." Shayla has been accepted to Central High School's cosmetology program for the fall. She is, on one hand, excited about it and certainly glad she was accepted to the program. Her current ambition is to finish high school, get a job in a Providence salon, and perhaps open her own salon some day. The cosmetology program allows her to get her high school diploma and cosmetology license at the same time. But Shayla is also extremely leery about returning to a system she was determined to quit two years ago. "I think they need a whole bunch of these schools around here," she says, referring to the Urban Collaborative. "Really. A few for high school. A few for junior high. A few for elementary. Well, maybe not elementary. That was easy. Anyone can do that. But they need more of them starting in junior high. We *need* them. Those other schools, they just don't have the time or space for people like us."

Shayla says the Urban Collaborative has helped her immensely. For the entire first year and most of the second, she resisted. She had dug in her heels, crossed her arms, and practically dared the staff to teach her. As a result, she found more than her share of trouble. At the beginning of this year, a series of events seemed to spell doom. Without a driver's license, and certainly without permission, Shayla drove her mother's car around the neighborhood, took a corner too fast, and swerved head-on into a telephone pole, shattering her leg and totaling the vehicle. Later, after she recovered and returned to school, she was suspended for a violent outburst in an elective course. When she came back from suspension, Rob was so disappointed with her attitude that he sent her home again. "I'm hardheaded," she readily admits. "It's just the way I am." While this is a trait she never expects to abandon, she says the school has helped her temper her anger. "Believe me. A few months ago, I didn't do anything. I had this attitude, you know, like just leave me alone. But they kept after me and after me and after me. And finally, I got sick of it. You know? I'm too old to get yelled at. I'm seventeen. I'll be eighteen soon. And it sort of got embarrassing having them yell at me, especially in front of all the younger kids here.

"And it's nice now—now that I'm trying a little harder. They're always congratulating me, saying 'Shayla, you look so pretty when you're not mean.' Stuff like that. It's nice. They give you a lot of pep talks and they give you lots of chances. I never got any of that in my other school." She says she likes the size of the school and the attention each student receives. In particular, she likes how students can call the teachers by their first names. "That's pie," she says with a smile. "That's the most pie. I love that about this school. It might seem silly, but you get closer to them if you can talk to them by their first names. I feel that we are on the same level or something. But next year it's back to Mr. This and Mrs. That. I don't get it and I don't like it. They don't call me Ms. Jackson.

"Next year," she concludes, shaking her head, "next year is going to be hard. I've been dying to be a cosmetologist, and I know that when you want something that bad you'll do the work. But it'll be hard." Then she laughs. "Rob told us to call him Mr. DeBlois for the rest of the year so we'd get used to it. He's not Mr. DeBlois. He's Rob. And he's a pain sometimes."

Would she recommend the Urban Collaborative to others?

"Yeah, definitely, if they need it. The only messed up part is that you are only here for two years. It would be great if we could stay."

An evaluation of the Urban Collaborative by the Rhode Island Department of Elementary and Secondary Education has reached a similar conclusion. In a 1992 report, the state department evaluated seven dropout-prevention programs prior to distributing state funds to the schools. The Urban Collaborative fared well in the study, getting high scores for nearly all elements of its program, particularly the school's curriculum in which "student progress is judged by a record of performance outcomes" rather than the time a student spends "in seat"—the measure of most schools. But the report also raised questions about the value of a "pull-out" program such as the Urban Collaborative, in which students are taken out of mainstream schools for one or two years, then fed back into the system. "Our observations lead us to have doubts about the general wisdom of pull-out projects," the report concludes. "These doubts apply even to otherwise exemplary projects such as [the Urban Collaborative]. Delivering services in this way creates re-entry problems for the students and discontinuity for the project." In essence, such programs are designed to get kids *to* high school, but not necessarily *through* high school.

Even though the Urban Collaborative received its thirty thousand dollars from the state department, Rob couldn't help but argue against this notion. "I think you need to weigh the wisdom of each program and not just challenge their general wisdom," he says. "To tell the truth, I think it is a very positive thing for most of the kids who come to us. For one, the kids don't feel stigmatized as they would if segregated into a remedial program in a regular school. And that is very important if we are to build their self-esteem. At the Urban Collaborative, all students are on an equal footing. As far as the transition is concerned, what's important is how it is made. The first year, I'll admit, we didn't really have a system in place to get these kids into the proper high school programs and follow up on their progress. And maybe that's what the department bases its concerns on. But now we have two counselors keeping tabs on these kids. They know a great deal about every student. They know what the students want and what they need. They know the students' talents and the program for which they are best suited. And they know the other public schools and the school counselors well so that they can help the kids get on track and stay there. All year long, they are visiting former Urban Collaborative students, encouraging them and helping them, and I think things are generally working out well for these kids."

This said, Rob recognizes that the transition back into traditional schools is difficult. And he agrees that it might be best for most of his students to stay in a program like the Urban Collaborative straight through high school, though not at the Urban Collaborative itself, which is designed strictly for the middle school ages. "For one, I don't want the school to become too large because we then face the possibility of losing our close relationship with the students. I also don't think it is a good idea to have such a broad range of ages in a school like this. Once you take on eighteen- and nineteen-year-olds you face a whole new set of problems." All along, he has hoped that the Urban Collaborative would not only help a particular population of students but that it would also serve as a model for other schools, or at least offer the public school system a new way of instructing students. The problem, as he sees it, lies not with the Urban Collaborative but with the system to which students return. "Most students like the Urban Collaborative and express dissatisfaction with the mediocrity of the programs they are returning to," he says. "Does it make sense to penalize our program for raising their expectations in school?"

Money is also a consideration. Even if Rob wanted to extend the Urban Collaborative or create a high school program based on the same principles, the Providence School Board—and, Rob points out, most school boards in the country—would likely veto the plan. Already, in each of the past three years, the Providence School Board has cut the program out of its budget. And each year Rob has had to give all his teachers layoff notices with only the slimmest of assurances that the school's funding would be restored. The problem is part economic. Rhode Island's slumping economy of the late 1980s and early 1990s has inevitably led to reduced funding for all sorts of services, including education. But the problem is also part attitude and perspective. Even though the Urban Collaborative, dollar for dollar, is more effective in educating Providence students than the mainstream schools, the political climate does not favor such alternative programs. This has a great deal to do with the fact that the Urban Collaborative is a small program with a nonunionized staff. But it is also born of a certain suspicion of "new" and "alternative" programs—little maverick satellites orbiting the monolith of traditional American public education.

So, for now at least, the Urban Collaborative has had to make do with what it has—a two-year program serving 105 students who eventually will have to sink or swim in the area's large high schools. Rob, however, will continue to challenge the notion that Urban Collaborative graduates can't make it in traditional high schools. Currently, he points out, more than 80 percent of those who graduate from the Urban Collaborative go on to finish high school. Part of the reason for this, he feels, is that the kids are better equipped to handle school after leaving the Urban Collaborative. In addition, he has done everything he can to make the transition as easy as possible for the students by hiring the two part-time counselors, Sylvia Blackman and Steve West. In essence, they are the school's air-traffic controllers, guiding kids in and out, recruiting them from middle schools and keeping tabs on them through their high school years.

Sylvia Blackman, a retired Providence public school counselor, came to the Urban Collaborative during its second year. When Rob asked for her help, she did not hesitate to come out of retirement, she says, because "this job is an answer to a counselor's prayers." Sylvia, a sixty-something, gray-haired bundle of energy, wisdom, and compassion, with a trace of a Brooklyn accent that belies her past, is the first to admit that counselors in public schools are so overburdened with students and so weighed down with paperwork and regulations that they can't help as many kids as they would like. "It's sad. In the regular school system, there is one counselor for every 300 or 350 students. That is way too much. On top of that, the priority for these counselors has always been for legally mandated counseling of special education kids. It's great that the special education kids get attention. But there are so many others—like the kids who come to the Urban Collaborative—who could use a counselor's help and for various reasons never get it. Here, the kids are my priority, period. I'm zeroed in on them. And Rob makes sure I can stay zeroed in. For one, there aren't as many of them to keep track of, so I get to know them all well. And I have much more freedom to do my job as I see fit than I had in a traditional public school. I can't tell you how wonderful it feels to be able to work this way, to really be able to make a difference in the lives of these kids, to be able to advise them all and give them the opportunity to succeed."

Sylvia's job is to work with the Urban Collaborative students who attend high schools in Providence. (Steve West helps students in East Providence and Pawtucket.) She spends part of her time recruiting new students for the Urban Collaborative, talking with counselors, meeting kids, finding out who can benefit from such a program.

"We end up talking to hundreds of kids," Sylvia says. "The parameters are huge. We are looking for kids who are at least one year behind and who have the academic ability to accelerate in grade. We also look for a kid with some sort of spark, a kid who still seems interested in trying and who has not become a major discipline problem. You'd be amazed how many kids fit this profile." From the various public schools in the three cities, she and Steve have found 160 kids for the 40 openings at the Urban Collaborative next year. Some will eventually back out, but in the end Rob and Al Lemos, with the advice of Sylvia and Steve, will have to make the tough choice of who comes and who doesn't.

Because she has worked in traditional public schools and because she has seen the number of kids who need help, Sylvia is a vigorous advocate of the Urban Collaborative. "There is clearly a desperate need for this school. And I've seen firsthand that it can do wonderful things for these kids. Certainly many of them would have dropped out of school if not for the Urban Collaborative. In particular, I think there is a great need for kids to learn about taking responsibility for their own actions and education and to learn some solid values. They need to learn how best to treat themselves and others—how to care. And I think that while they are getting a good academic education here, they are also learning these other things, a moral code of living, if you will, that will help them lead better lives." At the Urban Collaborative, she adds, they learn about compassion, caring, and security—those things they should have gotten at home but, for various reasons, did not. Here, they find adults who will listen, and therefore the kids are more willing to open up, to ask "those big questions that no one lets them ask, to talk about elements of life no one lets them talk about." As an example, Sylvia mentions a day she spoke to a group of middle school students. Instead of lecturing them, she asked them what they would most like to talk about, and the majority said sex. They were shy, but extremely curious. So Sylvia asked them to write down anonymous questions. "You wouldn't believe how little they knew," Sylvia says. "And reading the questions, I realized that these were the sort of questions they couldn't ask their parents because parents would probably misinterpret them, or, at least, this is what the kids feared." The point of her story is simple: kids need adults they can talk with freely. They need adults who have the time, who care, who will listen, and who will help guide them. If this is not happening at home, then it must happen in school; if not in a traditional school, then in a place like the Urban Collaborative. "This experience," she concludes, "is invaluable."

Because she feels so strongly about the program, Sylvia also works tirelessly with those who are leaving the Urban Collaborative and heading back into traditional programs. As Rob told the state education department, Sylvia spends most of her time getting to know the kids, finding out what interests they have, then trying to find out the best place to send them. Her experience working in the other schools has helped tremendously. She knows the schools, knows the programs, and knows the counselors well.

This day she is particularly excited because she has just learned that five students—the only five who applied—have been accepted to the Hope Essential School for the following year. When she receives the news, she runs off to tell Al. The Hope Essential School is an alternative program situated within one of Providence's large high schools. It is one of many such "essential school" programs across the country that follow the educational ideas of Ted Sizer, one of the nation's leading educational reformers, whose office, ironically, is only a mile from the Urban Collaborative. Sylvia returns from Al's office still beaming. She says this is good news for these five students because most of them have done very well at the Urban Collaborative and have high hopes for the future. Enrolling in the Hope Essential School should provide them with the greatest opportunity of getting to college in a few years.

Steve West likes to say he "served twenty years in the Pawtucket Police Department," as if his job, like a military service, was an obligation he needed to fulfill. The first ten years he worked the night shift, 7:00 P.M. to 3:00 A.M., six days a week, walking a beat. Eventually, he earned the rank of detective and was assigned to the juvenile division—a position that opened his eyes to the troubles of urban youth. "Part of the time I worked on child abuse cases, which is an area of law enforcement known for its high burnout rate," Steve says. "The frustration is awful, especially when you are dealing with kids who aren't old enough to understand what has happened or aren't old enough to explain what has happened to them.

There is so much despair. It got to the point where I would even end up changing diapers on patrol. I'd go to a house and the mother would be high on drugs or drunk and the kid would be lying there crying for attention." Instead of leading Steve to burnout, working with kids prompted him to take a post as an inspector in charge of juvenile prosecution in the Rhode Island Family Court, a post he kept for six years. "I wanted to do something that might help kids," he recalls. "But I realized two things. First, that the school system was failing these kids in a lot of respects. And, second, that many of the programs designed to deal with family court problems weren't solving the problems at all. The court would, for instance, place a troubled kid in a wilderness program to straighten him out. While he is there, things might go well. But he still comes back to the same house, the same street, the same neighborhood, the same school, and he falls right back into his old habits."

Weighing his own role in helping urban youth, Steve finally decided to turn in his badge at forty-three and become a teacher. "It's the place I thought I could make the biggest impact," he says. He received his master's in education from Providence College, student-taught in an urban middle school, then, not finding a full-time job, accepted an offer from the Urban Collaborative to work part-time as a counselor to some of the school's graduates. He also helps out as a substitute teacher and runs the afterschool detention program, a thankless job that nevertheless gives him an opportunity to get to know the students better.

"I'm impressed that the school cares enough to have two counselors looking after its graduates," Steve says. "I can't imagine any other public middle school doing this. And the thing is, these kids really need us. They have such a hard time looking out for themselves, especially at the beginning of the year. Even the good students. A small thing like a change in schedule can throw them off." On a typical day, Steve heads out to one of eight high schools, most of them in Pawtucket and East Providence, to check up on students. If nothing else, he just likes to talk to them, to find out how things are going in school and in their personal lives. He often takes them out to breakfast, or if they do well in school he will reward them with dinner at a nearby restaurant. But quite often he finds students with one problem or another. "The transition from the Urban Collaborative to a regular high school can be real tough on these kids," Steve says. "Unlike here, they have to take care of their books, carry the right ones to class. They have bells. They have new schedules. The buildings are very large. There are hundreds of kids. They have to get up an hour or so earlier to catch the bus. At East Providence, for instance, they have to be in school at 7:30 A.M. Here, school doesn't start until 9:00 A.M. These may seem like little things, but they are enough to sink a kid. At the beginning of the year, one boy was having all sorts of problems in school, and it turns out it was all because he couldn't get into his locker, couldn't get his books. And he never asked anyone for help. He just got into trouble and fell behind in his work. All he had to do was ask the janitor to fix the locker. A very simple task."

Sometimes the problems are large ones, however. "I went to one school recently and found out one of our students had quit. I tried to track her down, but her family had moved," Steve says. "By talking to other kids I found where she moved to and went to see her. Basically, she says she wants to work for J. C. Penney instead of going to school. She's a bright kid and could do well in school. I tried to explain to her that she can make more money if she has an education. That she can get promoted faster and all that. I don't know what will happen. She agreed to go back for a while. If she quits, I could try lecturing her again, but I don't like to do that, and I don't think it works."

Some of them just won't make the adjustments, even with his and Sylvia's help. But most days Steve realizes the value of his work, playing part-time parent and counselor to young teenagers, many of whom, he believes, would get lost without his help.

Sylvia agrees. "It is so exciting to work here, because it really does feel as if we are making a difference," she says, sitting down to see what other good news might have come in the day's mail. "There is a lot of hope that these kids will get beyond the poverty and disarray of their present lives. I feel it more here than I did in traditional schools. No question about it. And other counselors in other schools are aware of this, too. The ones I talk to are very happy the Urban Collaborative exists to help those kids they would like to help, but, because of time and other constraints, can't help. To them, we are the salvation."

11

AL LEMOS WALKS BRISKLY TO THE REFRIGERATOR IN THE crowded teachers' room, takes a pear out of a brown paper bag, bites off the top, and spits out the stem. He eyes his lunch—fragrant broccoli pie, a Rhode Island specialty—but decides it's too early to dig into it. Instead, he flips open the *Providence Journal* to the sports section and reads through the bad news about the Red Sox, who have lost their third game in a row.

"What's with these prima donnas?" he says to no one in particular and takes another bite of his pear.

Peter Case, who is heading out to class, stops, smiles. "They're a bunch of overpaid bums who can't run. What do you expect?"

Al admits there is some truth to this, but he is more inclined to take first-year coach Butch Hobson to task. It's early in the season, but the year has generally been a bust for the Sox so far. Toronto is pulling steadily away. At one point, only the Cleveland Indians prevent them from hitting bottom.

Al was born and raised in Cumberland, a town just north of Pawtucket, where he still lives. And like many a Rhode Islander he has been a Red Sox fan since the time he was old enough to follow baseball. He is not about to abandon the Red Sox now. For better or worse, they are his team. Over his desk in his office is a photograph of a crowded Fenway Park with the inscription: "There's no place like home." Next week, he's planning a trip to Fenway with Peter Case for a night game against Oakland. It's one of the ways, he admits, he keeps his sanity.

"This place could drive you crazy if you are not careful," he says, smiling.

113

If anyone knows about keeping one's sanity, Al does. At thirty-seven, he is the school's only full-time counselor and has been with the school from its tumultuous start. A graduate of Rhode Island College, where he received his bachelor's and master's in Social Work, Al came to the Urban Collaborative after working in the Central Falls school system for twelve years as a counselor and coordinator of an alternative educational program.

His job at the Urban Collaborative, basically, is to keep the students in line, counsel them, advise them, discipline them, praise them, encourage them, guide them. In short, he plays parent to 105 students. No easy task even with average kids. But this group consists mostly of troubled, poor children from dysfunctional homes, all with bad academic track records and an aversion to taking directions. Each year, he does his share of crisis intervention, as well. This year alone he has worked with five students who have either thought about committing suicide or who have "gestured," as he puts it, by taking pills. With these kids, he does some initial counseling, then makes sure they get in touch with the right agency. He also does some group counseling with students, "just to get the kids to learn how to work together in groups, to cooperate with each other, and simply to get to know one another better." Although they live in fairly crowded cities, most of these kids lead isolated lives, never getting close to anybody. Al tries to open them up, get them to realize they are not alone, that others care, that others suffer, and that they can help each other. "I think the latter is a particularly important lesson for these kids to learn," he says. "They are in desperate need of belonging."

Throughout the year, he organizes programs for parents to address questions and problems of raising inner-city teenagers. During the summer, Al spends a good part of his time meeting the families of new students, learning their social histories, explaining the school a bit more, and getting a better sense of the students and their home life: how they behave, how they interact with their parents, and vice versa. Ask him about this part of his job, and he'll shake his head. It is the key for him, but it can be hard. "Some of the kids live in the projects in Providence," he says. "The projects are really sad places. A couple of summers ago I went to a home there. The family lived on the third floor. It was the middle of July and it must have been ninety-something degrees with humidity that would melt your mind. This family didn't have a fan. They barely had a stick of furniture. I remember sitting at the kitchen table with the mother. She was kind of staring off into space, answering my questions vaguely. The windows were open, but it was stifling. Nothing was stirring. And I was sitting there literally perspiring onto my notes, which were all smudged so I could barely read them. And I just sat there thinking to myself, 'How can a kid survive an environment like this? How could anybody?' But the funny thing is, that kid came here and he's doing pretty well. He's cheerful and friendly and is trying pretty hard." He pauses. "Kids. You know? They're amazingly resilient. Just amazing."

What one notices first about Al is that he is full of life, quick to banter with both students and faculty, quick to take kids to task for slacking off, and quick to offer compassion when they are in need. He is constantly measuring the emotional pulse of the students and, to a lesser degree, the faculty. He's a man of medium height and medium build with dark hair going gray, bright blue eyes, and a healthy dose of self-confidence. He speaks fluent Portuguese and passable Spanish, a talent that helps him cope with a number of students and parents who speak no English. And, as Rob will tell you, he is utterly invaluable to the school.

After tossing the core of his pear across the room into the trash, Al decides to head out in one of the school vans to pick up a student who didn't make it to school this day. In fact, she has missed the last two days. It's Wednesday, and Al is hoping to help the girl, Tonya, salvage the rest of the week. Tonya is one of a handful of kids who needs to complete a lot of work to accelerate in grade before the end of the school year. At the moment, things don't look good. But Al isn't giving up. He knows she is prone to outbursts, knows she has a tendency to fight with words or with fists, whatever is needed. He knows she'll give up school easily. He also knows she is basically a good kid, bright and talented, but troubled.

Tonya has missed many days of school recently because a police officer pressed charges alleging that she bit him on the arm. That case, however, has been settled, and Al isn't sure what is keeping her away now. He called this morning, and she said she missed the bus. She says she hasn't been feeling well, but Al knows better. He gives her a call back and says he's coming to pick her up.

On the ride over, he talks about Tonya. "Like most of the kids here, she has a hard life," he says. "She's sixteen. She lives with her mother in a tenement in Pawtucket. Her father is long gone. She has a terrible record in school in the past. She has gotten into fights in the past. But I know part of her really cares, really would like to succeed. Basically, I think all her frustration starts at home."

Al navigates the back streets of South Providence to the highway, then heads north through the capital city to Pawtucket, ten minutes away. Pawtucket is Rhode Island's equivalent of the Bronx: part industrial, part suburban, and mostly poor. It is home to Hasbro, one of the nation's largest toy manufacturers, and the Pawtucket Red Sox, a triple-A farm team that holds the distinction of playing the longest game in history, a pitchers' duel against the Rochester Red Wings in 1981, which the Red Sox won 3–2 in thirty-three innings. Recession aside, things haven't gone well for this city in recent years. In 1991, the mayor of Pawtucket, with members of his administration, was convicted of running an extortion ring in which he received kickbacks for accepting high bids from city vendors. Not long after, the city's water system had to be shut down due to excessively high counts of fecal chloroform. It's the sort of city where poor immigrants tend to take shelter and where low-paying jobs keep them going at the subsistence level.

"I've come here quite often to pick up Tonya," Al says. "Once I came here and I didn't know exactly what was going on, but Tonya and her mother were not getting along well. I think her mother was forcing her to go to school when Tonya wanted only to stay home or hang out with some friends. I don't know what it was. But I arrived and Tonya was sitting outside with her notebook and didn't move. So I said, 'Come on, Tonya, let's go.' And she still didn't move. Then her mother started screaming at her, 'Tonya, you have to go, you have to go.' You know? Just frantic and full of anger. And all of a sudden, Tonya stood up, turned to her mother, screamed, 'Fuck you,' then took her notebook and threw it into the next yard, paper flying everywhere. I waited her out. Then tried to talk to her about it. But she just stormed off down the street.

"It's hard to blame her," Al continues. "I mean, her life is so confusing. I used to counsel her brother in Central Falls. He was going through some really difficult times, too. Apparently there was a history of physical abuse in the family, and the brother ended up dealing drugs and getting into all kinds of trouble. Their father, from what I understand, has thirty-four children. *Thirty-four.* Apparently, back in Cape Verde he was a very strong political figure before there was all kinds of turmoil and he had to leave. I guess it was a big thing in Cape Verde that men just have one female conquest after another. Now the father will have nothing to do with Tonya's family. Once, her mother was really struggling and asked Tonya's father for money, but he refused to help, refused even to acknowledge their existence."

Tonya is not the only student Al has picked up in the morning. Early in the year he made many stops, as he has since the school began three years ago. Kids who enroll at the Urban Collaborative are often reluctant to go the first week. Some of them are afraid. It's a new school. Everyone is expecting great things of them. It's just too much. They would rather stay home than to go to school and fail once more. Or at least that's how they perceive it. So Al rouses them, almost literally, packs them in the van and gets them off to school. Eventually, they find their own motivation to get up each morning. But some, like Tonya, have been year-long projects.

"Part of the problem with Tonya, with a lot of these kids, is that they have no positive adult role models," Al conjectures, "and they just don't think adults care. They are around people with broken dreams, people who drink, who do drugs, who can't get good jobs, people who have never had role models themselves and don't really know how to deal with children, people who abuse them and abandon them. So these kids, they grow up not trusting adults. They've been screwed so many times. And schools really haven't been much better for them. Because they are troubled kids, they end up mouthing off to teachers, or they simply turn teachers off and just use their time in class to let the world go by. And the regular schools aren't really equipped to deal with them. Most schools want to keep order, indeed need to keep order given their size. So they end up being short-tempered with the Tonya's of the world, giving them detention or suspending them—doing just about everything these kids don't need. At the Urban Collaborative, we are far more tolerant. I mean, I have kids who come up to me and scream 'Fuck you' in my face. In other schools, they'd be long gone. But we try to work with them, try to teach them to control their anger. Practically every day some kid has to publicly apologize for his behavior." He turns off the highway and heads down a narrow road flanked by old brick factories. Some are occupied, some abandoned. One has been turned into an impressive senior citizen center. But generally the area is showing the effects of the recession of the early 1990s. Unemployment in Pawtucket is high. The signs of the promised recovery are hard to find.

"It takes a long time to gain their trust," Al adds. "For most of the kids, though, I think it really helps when I come out to get them like this. It's just another example of the school going above and beyond what traditional schools would do, and I think the kids appreciate it. Most do end up coming on a regular basis. Most of them learn that we really care about them, that someone in the world gives a shit enough to come all the way to their homes, wake them up, and actually drive them to school. It might not seem like much, but for kids who have a profound distrust of adults and of schools, this can mean the difference between them staying in school and dropping out."

Al maneuvers through a series of turns, then finally bears right onto Hope Street, a short side street crowded with three-story tenement buildings. The sidewalks are cracked and heaved in places, the buildings and sparse greenery in need of attention. Trash and broken glass are scattered about like the calling cards of poverty. Cars, many of them one or two trips away from the junk yard, huddle along the curbs. Al pulls up in front of Tonya's home and honks his horn. It takes a while for her to come out.

Al waits patiently, as if he is picking her up for a day at the beach. And when Tonya arrives, she arrives smiling and neatly dressed in jeans and a white shirt. She's a pretty African-American girl with large, look-away eyes and short stylish hair. Beautiful, actually. To see her, one would never guess there is so much anger and fear inside her. One could imagine her strolling happily along a college campus, an honor-roll student. Though it's not hard to imagine things going the other way, either, with her numbly serving up hamburgers in the night. The edge she walks on is that sharp.

"Good morning, Tonya," Al says.

"Morning," she responds, and readily hops in back.

"You've been sick, Tonya?"

"In court," she says, changing her story.

"What's it this time?"

"My mother had to go for something." Obviously, she doesn't want to talk about it. So Al lets it go.

"It's a beautiful day," Al says. "A great day for learning."

"Yeah, I suppose."

"You follow the Red Sox, Tonya?"

She laughs a little. "No. I don't care much for baseball. Basketball's all right, but baseball is boring."

"Just as well," he says. "They'll break your heart, these guys."

Back at school in his office, the most private place in the building, Al talks some more about the kids at the Urban Collaborative, about gaining their trust. On one wall is a poster that is designed for the edification of adults, but is perhaps a reminder to Al when things get tough. "If a child lives with criticism," it reads, "he learns to condemn. If a child lives with praise, he learns to appreciate." It goes on down the list: hostility leads to violence, tolerance leads to patience; ridicule leads to shyness, encouragement leads to confidence, shame leads to guilt, approval leads to confidence; with acceptance and friendship one learns to find love in the world.

"I think the key is being open and honest with them," Al says. "We don't patronize them. We don't talk down to them. We try to listen to them as we would to another adult, and we try to be fair with them. In addition to that, the whole staff goes out of its way to do things for them. Jim took a group up to Niagara Falls during vacation to study water pollution. He has also been working with them on this Whole Rivers Project, which has been great. John has taken a group to his cabin in Vermont and elsewhere as part of his explorer's club. Peter coaches the basketball team. Pauline coaches cheerleading. Jim coaches wrestling. Rob is constantly calling their homes to keep parents informed, keep them involved. Each month, kids who have perfect attendance go out to lunch. The team of students with the best academic record are going to the beach for a day. Just a few weeks ago we took a group to New York City and spent the day there, on a Saturday. We had forty-one people, students, parents, staff, and we went to the Statue of Liberty and Rockefeller Plaza, where everyone got to go their separate ways for a few hours. It was excellent. All kids were assigned to a parent, and if a parent couldn't go, we assigned him or her to a staff member. We left school at 6:30 A.M. and got back at 11:30 P.M. What other public school does this sort of thing?"

What brought Al to the Urban Collaborative was this energy and commitment on the part of the staff. He says he enjoyed his work in Central Falls at a school with more than seven hundred kids, but he also felt stifled by the school and its layer-upon-layer of regulations. There's a rigidity to the regular public school system that eventually works against itself, he says. "I started looking around and seeing the people who had been in the school for fifteen or twenty years," he recalls, "and it was clear that many of them were just going through the motions. Classic cases of burnout. They had just resigned themselves to the fact that they couldn't change anything, so why try. This is the way it has always been, and this is the way it always will be. You know what I mean? The dropout rate has remained steady or has gotten worse. Trying to counsel troubled kids, trying to find ways to help them stay in school gets tiring when you see the system fail them year after year. So counselors stop trying. And I really became afraid that this was going to happen to me, too. I've always had a lot of energy, and I was constantly locking horns with the administration about how we should deal with individual kids, constantly fighting to keep them in school when the administration wanted them out. Anyway, I heard that this school was starting up, so I decided to come take a look, and I really liked the idea of it. I thought it was just the sort of place these kids needed, first of all. And I thought it was just the sort of place I could work happily and really help kids. It was a good opportunity all around."

Al has never regretted the switch and thinks the Urban Collaborative is working amazingly well. One of the big surprises for him, however, was how intense the work has been. He says he thought his work at Central Falls was difficult. He counseled special education students and did a great deal of crisis intervention and group counseling. Ironically, however, he finds the work he does at the Urban Collaborative, with only one hundred and five kids, far more challenging. "What happens here is that you get to know all the kids very well," he says, "and so you end up caring about them all. With seven hundred kids, you just kind of get numb. And here we take it more or less as a self-imposed mandate to stay with these kids for as long as we can."

Al has to excuse himself because a crisis has come up with a student. For the next few hours, this is the focus of his work. Afterward, he manages to wolf down his broccoli pie and hurry off to a class for students on probation. This group consists of ten kids who are near the end of their ropes. They have failed to do much of anything all year. Or if they have worked, they've worked in spurts and have not managed to complete any of their courses. The probation class is a new experiment, a last-ditch effort to see if the school can get them to earn some credit or produce some work that would warrant keeping them another year. "If they don't make it," Al says, "they go back to their sending schools."

He meets them at the door and takes a deep breath, as if preparing to dive into a turbulent sea.

"All right," he says, clapping his hands. "Let's not waste time here. Sit down and get out some work."

The students readily find a place to sit, clustering in three groups. But none of them gets right to work. They are generally grumpy about being here.

"Come on," Al says, raising his voice. He walks around to each of them and asks them what they are working on. Those who are behind him chatter away about anything but their work. One girl hisses to another, "This school sucks." Those Al talks with make a weak effort at getting some work started. One boy has arrived without a book, notes, or assignments. Al sends him scurrying back to his teacher to get something to do. Then Al turns to the group and makes a general announcement.

"When you come down here, bring work with you. How do you expect to accelerate if you don't do your work?"

This appears to be one of those thankless jobs: monitoring those who don't want to be here and don't take kindly to monitoring. But Al takes it in stride.

A boy named Ryan enters class late. He has on a Chicago Bulls hat turned backwards. He shuffles slowly across the room, not looking at anyone, but letting them all know he is not about to be hurried. His face, dark and set, says, "just don't ask anything of me." He sits down next to Michaela and asks her something. She answers briefly, then turns to her work. Ryan keeps talking to her in a low voice. Al walks over to him and asks him to move to an empty table. Ryan doesn't move.

"Come on Ryan. Move over here and do some work."

Ryan looks up at Al with pure hatred, it seems.

"Move, so Michaela can get some work done."

Ryan slams his book, and looks ready to take a swing at Al. This would be enough to get him sent to the office. But Al just talks to him calmly. "Ryan, I'm only trying to help you. If you don't do some work, things aren't going to be easy for you next year."

"I don't give a shit," Ryan says.

"Well, then just sit over here and let everyone else work."

Ryan stands up and starts toward the free table, mumbling to himself and staring daggers at Al's back. He starts to sit down, but then thinks better of it and storms out.

Al turns when he hears the door slam. If all this is disturbing to him, he doesn't show it.

Another boy, Cal, is joking with two girls, Liza and Shawna.

Al turns to Cal suddenly and says, "Cal, move or go to the office."

Perhaps Al is angry.

Cal, a soft-faced smiling boy with a flat-top and an earring, tries to imitate Ryan's anger. He mumbles a curse, slams his book down. But he moves to the next table, looks bitterly at Al, then smiles at the girls.

Eventually they all settle down, ten minutes into the period, and start working on projects or, at least, start looking at their assignments. But soon their minds are wandering again. Shawna and Liza are drinking Cokes and sharing a bag of popcorn. They keep their heads down, but eye each other in collusion. One of them rustles the Smart Food bag and looks at Al. The other makes a small noise. They are playing the ancient game of seeing how far they can go before they get the teacher's attention. Soon they are both tapping the ends of their pencils, looking at their work and smiling knowingly.

Al walks over to Shawna. "I'd hate to see you have to leave here, Shawna. You have three weeks left of school. You can do a whole lot of work if you want."

"It don't matter to me," Shawna says, looking not at Al but at Liza. But she does turn her attention back to her work.

Cal, meanwhile, is constantly monitoring everyone else's behavior. Every time Al turns his attention away, Cal flirts long-distance with Liza. And Liza, for her part, seems to think this is just fine.

"Sometimes," Al says later, "There is not much we can do. A few of the kids on probation are trying. Others have given up. They let things go too long and now they don't think they have a chance." He talks about Ryan. When Ryan came to the Urban Collaborative, Al knew he was a huge risk. First of all, he is older than most of the kids. At seventeen, coming here was more or less a last-ditch effort for Ryan. But halfway through the year, Ryan more or less gave up. Sometimes these kids reach a point when they can't try anymore. "It's often too painful for such a kid to be presented with another chance," Al says. "They have tried and they have failed and they have tried again. But Ryan couldn't open up once more, couldn't take another chance. It's too painful for him." Ryan is smart and physically very strong. And both these qualities are a problem in school. On the one hand, being bigger and older than most of these kids in school is a source of embarrassment for him. On the other hand, both these qualities make him, in some ways, an ideal street kid.

Despite the failings of the students in the probation class, Al sees the school as successful. "I think the program is extremely successful, especially when you compare it with other programs," he says. "Academics aside, I think the kids leave here feeling a whole lot better about themselves than when they arrived. And that's a tribute to the staff. Because these kids are treated with respect and fairness, they learn to believe in themselves—and this is something that they'll carry with them the rest of their lives. Having confidence is so important. Many of these kids come from families that have been on public assistance for years and years and years. And they see people who pick up a check every two weeks then sit around all day doing nothing and feeling depressed. A lot of the kids who come here have already resigned themselves to joining the welfare rolls some day. They don't like it, but they think, 'Why bust my hump when I'm only going to end up like that anyway?' Our challenge is to get them to realize they can lead better lives if they work at it."

After school, Al heads to the parking lot to keep an eye on the students as they wait for their buses. He leans up against the fence and talks with Rob about the Red Sox game. It's a glorious June day, hot and sunny. A perfect day for a beer and hotdogs in Fenway. A good night to berate José Canseco and Ricky Henderson of the Oakland A's. Al makes no bones about needing to get away from the Urban Collaborative for a night out. "With a population of kids like these," he says, "I know we need to go above and beyond other schools. But I know my limits. This was a difficult thing for me the first year. And I think it was difficult for the rest of the staff. Where do you draw the line? The first year I more or less tried to keep up with Rob," he adds. "And it was as if I were trying to commit suicide. I couldn't do it. This guy's amazing. He's got endless amounts of energy. No one can keep up with him. It took me awhile to figure that out. But now that I have, I'm a lot happier."

The bus arrives. Lucia, a petite, dark-haired girl, heads toward the bus. Rob realizes she is supposed to stay for detention after school. He calls her over. She doesn't respond. "Lucia, I'm telling you, you are making a mistake," he says. "You will regret this." She hesitates, starts back toward school, then turns and hurries onto the bus. After she leaves, Rob turns to Al, "What can you do when a student truly doesn't give a shit?"

But Al isn't buying this line of logic. "She cares," he says. "You can tell by the way she hesitated. She was squirming. She was listening to you. Maybe next time she'll turn back."

12

A GROUP OF STUDENTS STAND IN A CIRCLE IN THE MIDDLE of a classroom. A minute earlier, they had pushed the tables against the walls to give themselves a wide, open space. Their teacher, Valerie Tutson—a professional storyteller, occasional actress, and recent graduate of Brown University's theater arts program—stands among them. She is a young, fit, African-American woman in her mid-twenties, dressed casually today in fitted blue jeans torn at the knees, cowboy boots, and a simple, button-down shirt. She is equally as likely to appear in a beautiful multicolored African dress—wearing her heritage proudly.

"OK," Valerie tells them, her voice strong and playful, "shake your hands over your head." She demonstrates and they mimic, smiling and giggling. "Now stretch in a circle." Valerie demonstrates again, showing off a limberness that most cannot match.

"Touch the floor," she instructs in a playful voice, "twist at the hips. Come on, you can do it. Come on, Pedro. Come on, Karen."

The group is relaxed, in good humor, willing to do as told. Valerie doesn't explain why they are doing these exercises. She doesn't have to. At this point in the year, they are used to all the odd exercise routines she puts them through. This is, after all, drama class. They are supposed to do things with their bodies. And their voices. "I stress to them that an actor has voice and body," Valerie says later. "Those are your instruments. You need to know how to use them."

In the classroom, certainly, she uses hers. "OK, OK," Valerie says, straightening up. "We're going to sing 'Old MacDonald.'" Instant groans and smiles. "No, no. This'll be fun," she insists. "We're going to first do

124

it the original way and then see how we can change it." Then she adds, "Just keep it clean."

At her lead, they start singing "Old MacDonald," and before they have gotten through a single verse, some of the boys—hats spun backwards, baggy pants riding low—have transformed it into a rap song. One boy cups his hands over his mouth to make the percussion sound of rap. Valerie lets them go for a while, then stops them. She wants each one to try singing it differently, taking turns around the circle. Pedro goes first. He hesitates, seeming shy about it, then does a rap version. The group picks up on his cue and starts rap dancing, clapping and moving with abandon. Then Valerie cuts off the song and suggests that the next version be different. "Use your imagination," she says. "Come on. There's more to life than rap."

Liza goes next. She starts, stops, laughs. Then she tries singing with a British accent. Her accent is a poor imitation, but Valerie praises her. Liza is trying something different, and in this class such creative efforts earn high marks.

"OK, next. John," she says. One boy is laughing and saying something on the side to another. "Marvin," Valerie turns on him firmly, "focus on what we're doing here." Then she turns back to John. He delivers the song in a quick, flat monotone. Valerie nods her approval, then moves to the next student, and the next, prodding them to be spontaneous and uninhibited. And, for the most part, they are.

"It's just to loosen them up," Valerie says after class. "I also want them to have a real basic comfort with theater skills and theater activities and group building. I try to do a lot of exercises because kids at this age really have difficulty in terms of touching and being comfortable with their bodies. So I try to do a lot of stuff that gets them moving, that gets them touching and trusting each other, and listening. Listening is really important—and very difficult for this group."

After "Old MacDonald," Valerie has each member of the group make up a sound, any sound. "Just say whatever comes to mind. We'll say them real fast. And keep it clean." The kids twist and groan, look at the ceiling, think. One whoops. The next says, "Bombada." This is followed by "zing" and "come on" and "goddamit." Nonsense words, telling phrases—most of which prove Valerie's assessment of them. On one hand, they are shy and uncertain of themselves. On the other hand, they are surprisingly game and focused on the class in ways they never were in years past. They do the exercise again, quicker this time, so the words flow together in a string of discordant sound.

After the warm-up, Valerie has them work on improvisation. At this point in the year it is too late to start on a major drama project, so she decides to run the class much like a college acting class in which the students practice some of those skills that make for good acting. The first exercise involves using a single prop, a bright blue feathery boa, to suggest something else. "I want a sense of who you are or what you are. I want to know character, place, and age," Valerie instructs, then sits cross-legged on top of a table.

The first boy wraps the boa around his shoulders and mimics a singer. It is clear he is a singer, and probably a woman. But no one guesses who. "I'm *Diana Ross*," he finally tells them, angry and disappointed they couldn't guess. Another wraps the boa around his neck and lets it hang to his knees. He swaggers across the room, shoulders erect, lower lip turned down slightly. The class guesses easily that he is a pimp. Another goes through a singing routine, and when no one guesses, he tells them he's a gay rap singer. Valerie encourages them to think more creatively. "Don't depend on what you already know or the expected." A girl pretends the wrap is a leash and she is walking an undisciplined dog that almost pulls her off her feet. "Good," Valerie says. "Good. Now that's different." For others the boa becomes a tie, a mustache, a hangman's noose, a headband, a tail, a shoelace, a lasso. And afterward, Valerie offers her own invention: floppy blue dog ears. Her expressiveness and abandon, one realizes, helps give this group courage.

She talks to them briefly about this exercise but doesn't push too hard with theory. She is happy enough that they are all engaged, and she doesn't want to lose momentum. Next, the group improvises scenes without words. The first two actors, Pedro and Marvin, huddle to one side. They gesture animatedly, laugh, offer ideas. Finally, they step outside the classroom and return as if onto a stage. The rest of the class watches anxiously as one of them wears a backpack and climbs cautiously onto a table as if it is a forbidden and dangerous place. The other looks back as if worried someone may be watching, then joins his friend on the table. They both stare over the edge of the table at the floor, as if they are perched at some great height. The first boy is extremely unsure of himself, the second more at ease. They pretend to debate some point. The first boy gestures toward leaving, but his friend urges him to stay. Convinced, the first boy takes something out of the backpack and leans cautiously over the edge in an attempt to perform some chore. It gradually becomes clear that what he holds is a can of spray paint and that he is attempting to write on the wall of a high structure, a bridge perhaps. But he is deathly afraid. The other doesn't offer to do the painting, but he does offer to help hold his friend so he can lean out farther and get a better angle for painting. The pantomime becomes an exercise in fear and trust. Will the first boy trust the second with his life while he paints? What is also clear is that the act of spray painting one's name is extremely important to both of them. In the inner-city culture—at least the one portrayed here—it is a rite of passage. The second boy has probably passed his test. Now he is helping his friend.

The class picks up on this right away. One student tells them, "It's dope, man. It's dope"—which means the illusion is good.

And it is—until Marvin jokingly lets Pedro slide onto the floor and says, "Oh, sorry, man. I guess you're dead."

Valerie Tutson has been working with students at the Urban Collaborative since it opened in 1989. Prior to that, while a sophomore at Brown, she worked for the SPIRIT summer program when Rob was director. Valerie has her own career as a storyteller (mostly traditional African, Caribbean, and African-American tales), traveling to schools and festivals. But teaching at the Urban Collaborative is equally important to her. "I love teaching here," she says. "And I don't want to give it up. I find the staff very supportive. They value what I do. And that's really important to me because so many schools look at drama differently, like, 'oh, it's just drama,' as if it is not important or not central to their lives. I like the kids a lot, too. They are smart, and they are fun to work with. I love to see them stretch and try things and surprise themselves. It's a wonderful process for them."

Because the core of the academic program at the Urban Collaborative is still traditional schooling—English, math, social studies, science—the staff decided in the first year that it needed an elective program to give students a chance to show off talents that would not otherwise arise in the school day. Every quarter, students must choose two electives, each of which meets twice a week. To keep students interested (in addition to hiring superb teachers), the elective courses offer a variety of choices every quarter. To date, students have had an opportunity to partake in drama, sex education, art, African-American history, African storytelling, mask making, calligraphy, Spanish, basket making, bowling, sign language, swimming, basketball, martial arts, billiards, aerobics, computers, video, jewelry making, choir, cosmetology, animal studies at the Roger Williams Zoo, and community service.

Most students enjoy these courses, and some even find the joy of learning here. As one student told Rob recently, "Thank God for the electives. They make all the other classes more interesting." There are some, however, who view many of the electives as "boring" or "stupid." Among this group, most of them show a preference for one elective but feel that the others are not worth their time. And herein lies a problem for the school. The Urban Collaborative's emphasis on acceleration has gotten the school into a bind with electives because students know they can accelerate in school while failing electives. Laggards have a built-in excuse for blowing off these classes. The school tries to counter this by giving quarter credits for electives, which simply means that when students go to high school they need to complete fewer credits in order to graduate. Fortunately, those who work hard in regular classes also respond well to electives.

It is clear from watching Valerie's class at work that she considers drama not a diversion but an essential component of the students' education. "I think that any sort of activity like drama that involves group building and real cooperation, that develops listening skills and verbal skills and personal-presentation skills helps in every aspect of school and of their lives," Valerie says. "It builds confidence. If these kids can get up in front of their peers and deliver a monologue or act out a scene from a play, then certainly they can stand up in English class and give a brief report. That's basic. I also try to tie the drama class into the curriculum in other classes, too, because this helps them remember it that much better. You perform a play about what you are reading in English, and it makes it real. You remember it that much better because it's in your words and in your bones. It's not just a book anymore. I don't care what anybody says, when you get out of school, whether it's high school or college, you remember the plays you were in. A lot of kids have an interest in drama, but in most schools there is no opportunity to pursue it. One high school in Providence, for instance, has no drama program at all. Hundreds of kids and no drama program. Kids need drama. They like it. And it can help them in everything they do in life." Providence might counter Valerie's point by noting that it has an entire magnet school dedicated to the arts, but this would miss Valerie's point—that *all* students could benefit by drama and by other courses too often considered extraneous.

Earlier in the year, her class worked out scenes from *Romeo and Juliet*, which they were reading in English class. In light of the Rodney King verdict in Los Angeles, an event that touched every student in the school, Valerie also had students create a short play based on the general response to the verdict. "It was very powerful," Valerie says, "for me and for them. For them, because they were responding to something that was happening right then, and they were doing it creatively." The scene opens a year before the verdict with an inter-racial group of boys at play. A white girl happens by and the boys start picking on her for no particular reason—

because she is a single girl, perhaps, and an easy target. She is stung by this, and runs off to tell her father. In the next scene, the girl's father storms out cursing the "niggers" and warns the white kids that he is going to tell their parents they've been hanging around with "a bunch of niggers." The next scene jumps to 1992. Same group, only now one of the African-American boys is dating the white girl surreptitiously. Then the verdict is announced over the radio. In anger, another African-American boy produces a gun and announces he wants to shoot somebody. Running quickly through the lists of potential targets, he remembers the white girl's father who had belittled them a year earlier. But before acting upon this impulse, the boy watches as an innocent white man walking down the street gets jumped and beaten up by a group of African Americans. Upon seeing this, the boy decides to give up his plan. He realizes then that the innocent white man, in different circumstances, could be one of his friends and that such violence won't solve the problems. This leads into a rap song the students wrote about how two wrongs don't make a right. The fact that white police officers viciously beat an African-American man—or, more important, that racism against African Americans still exists in this nation—is not left unacknowledged, however. The class's rap, while advocating peaceful solutions, also chastises society for the Rodney King verdict, asking the question, "How many Kings will it take 'til they see?"[1]

"They came up with this whole thing by themselves," Valerie says. "I facilitated it, but they hardly needed me. They stayed after school to rehearse for a presentation they were giving one night. And I was trying to direct them. But they kind of got angry at my intrusion and said, 'Val, just let us do this, OK?' So I said fine, this is wonderful. I sat back and let them go. I only told them when I couldn't hear them well, but that was about all. They did the rest themselves. And it turned out to be very, very good." One suspects that Valerie is being modest here—that her role in directing and providing structure was far greater. But it's also clear that she was touched and impressed by how much initiative these students can take when given a reason.

Another drama class led to a discussion and improvisation about an eighth-grade boy who had been shot and killed. "They know about guns. They know about being in the wrong place at the wrong time," Valerie says. "This story happened to be about a real-life incident involving some-

---

[1] Later, students at the Urban Collaborative would also become engaged in the O. J. Simpson criminal trial, cheering loudly when the verdict of innocent was announced. Most of the students felt it was very possible that the police framed Simpson—and they held firmly to the belief that the justice system does not treat people of color justly.

body's little brother who was going to make his eighth-grade graduation speech. He was a good student with a promising future, and he ended up getting shot over a dumb thing, a fight over a girl. It was a very powerful and sobering event for them."

One of the glaring misconceptions about dropouts and potential dropouts is that they are not intelligent people. Everyone at the Urban Collaborative will refute this, but none as strongly as the elective teachers. "With improv, which I use a lot, I can see how quickly they think on their feet," Valerie says. "I put them in situations where they have to react quickly: listen, think, create. And when they do this, I can see they are pulling from a wide variety of sources, from personal experience, from books, from life. Their skills may not be as good in traditional classes, but I can still see how quickly their minds work. And I love how open and willing they are to learn. Many of them are so happy because this is the first time they've really been allowed to show off their talents or express themselves in school."

Gloria Merchant, the art teacher, is equally glad to be teaching at the Urban Collaborative, and equally impressed with the students she teaches. Prior to coming here, she had taught art for five years in the Warwick, Rhode Island, school system and for four years in the town of Situate. She holds a bachelor's in art from Simmons College and an master's in art education from New York University. She is an artist herself, an active member of the Arts Center of Northwestern Rhode Island, but her "focus," as she puts it, is on art education. Along with her classes at the Urban Collaborative, she teaches courses at Rhode Island College and Rhode Island School of Design. If you ask her if her experience at the Urban Collaborative is different from her experience teaching other places, she'll laugh. "It is totally different. The students who were considered the exceptions in other schools—the troublemakers—are the rule here," she points out. "This alone makes things different, and quite interesting."

What one notices first about Gloria, a mother of two teenaged boys, is that teaching here is not just a job. She truly enjoys working with these students, loves their energy, and loves how eager many of them are to be working with their hands and their imaginations. "The most difficult thing about teaching here," she says, "is that you have to find all new ways of teaching if you want to succeed. Until you realize this, life can be pretty rough. The traditional methods simply don't work here. And those things you are taught in school don't really work, either." For Gloria, dealing effectively with these students required her to abandon her lesson plans and techniques that worked well for her in other schools for nine years. "The funny thing is, if I taught in a traditional school the way I teach here, I would be reprimanded by the administration. But here, it's the only way I know that works," she says.

What's the difference?

"I discovered that most of these kids don't learn sequentially. Instead, they are very good intuitive learners. For art, this means that I don't need to explain much. The more I talk the more impatient they get. I need simply to get the materials into their hands and let them go, let them explore, experiment, and when they have questions or want help, then I come to their rescue. I've discovered the hard way that they won't listen to the answers until *they* ask the questions."

Like the other teachers, Gloria doesn't teach group lessons. Nor is there a sequence to learning in her classes. Instead, she mixes materials, lets the kids choose, and teaches particular skills on demand. "It's hard. It's definitely hard," she notes, "because there are so many things going on at once. But when I realized that the kids were doing fine, and that I was the only one in the classroom going crazy, I knew everything was all right."

Gloria is quick to praise Rob and the rest of the staff for their attitude about electives. In most schools electives seem primarily designed to give the regular teachers a free period. The full-time teachers generally don't pay attention to what goes on in elective classes and don't offer much support when such classes are threatened at budget-cutting time. "The opposite is true at the Urban Collaborative," Gloria says, which is why she prefers teaching here to any other school with which she has been associated.

Equally important are the students themselves. "I'm just nuts about these kids," she says. "While I would never pretend that they're incapable of being royal pains in the butt—they can set the pace in that department— once you manage to get past all that, they're wonderful to work with. They're energetic, ambitious, full of ideas, and they definitely have a lot of nerve. That last quality is essential in an art student, and in an artist, as far as I'm concerned. These kids blitz past the elementary stuff into doing their own best work really fast. And I like that."

One of the electives—sex education—is actually mislabeled, since it is not an elective at all, but a requirement for every student during at least one marking period of their stay at the Urban Collaborative. "A required elective," Rob says. "One of the Urban Collaborative's oxymorons." During the first year, with a number of the students literally showing up at the school's doorstep with babies of their own and others getting pregnant during the school year—not to mention the threat of HIV infection—the staff realized the school had to make sex education a priority. The first year, the school offered a series of compulsory programs taught by an outside agency. Before the start of the second year, a year-round program was developed based on suggestions from Deoshore Haig and Jen Borman, the two women who conducted the earlier program and who agreed to teach the more in-depth course as well.

At this time of the year, most of the work in the sex education class has been completed. Deoshore Haig returns tests to her students, letting them know they did very well and that all passed the course. But there are some points worth reiterating. So she drags in a video monitor and shows the class two short videos. The first, reviewing an earlier discussion, is an explanation of the human immune system, how it works, and how it fails to work in the case of sexually transmitted diseases. It's hard to tell how the class reacts. One boy, for whatever reason, chooses to face away from the screen. The others stare silently. The second video, however, strikes home. It's about teenagers infected with HIV, some of them with full-blown AIDS. These teenagers are by and large average kids, some still looking quite healthy, others in hospital beds, gaunt and close to death. They tell their own stories and don't shy away from the camera. All of them say the same thing: "I did not think this could happen to me." And all of these ill teenagers, the students understand, could easily be students at the Urban Collaborative. Afterward, Deoshore turns on the lights and asks for reactions.

"I don't want to talk about it," one boy says. "It's too depressing."

Another says inexplicably, "It would be messed up having HIV and passing it on to a baby."

A number of students blurt out surprisingly disparate comments. Deoshore lets them go, then turns the lesson toward its central issue. "Does it matter how you got HIV? Is that the issue?"

"No," another girl says. "It can happen to anyone."

"What do you do to avoid getting HIV?"

"You protect yourself."

"Who's in control of your behavior? Who's in control of your life? Do you trust your life in anyone else's hands?"

Two boys laugh about something privately.

Deoshore, who is kind but deadly serious about this topic, turns on them. "This is not a joke. You've got to know the risks. You've got to know that you are in charge of your bodies and your lives. Sex is easy. Biologically it couldn't be easier. You don't have to tell your body what to do. The tough part is thinking about the ramifications of having sex. Your lives may depend on it."

Lesson over.

Deoshore, a stocky, no nonsense African-American woman, a native of the Bronx, is the assistant director of the Family AIDS Center for Treatment and Support, a nonprofit organization helping families with HIV-infected members. Currently, the organization is working with ninety families in Rhode Island and some in neighboring Massachusetts, offering broad-based support. (Jen Brown, the other teacher of sex education at the Urban Collaborative, is from Planned Parenthood.) As Deoshore puts it, "the HIV infection of mothers and children is just the tip of the iceberg." These families have to deal with a whole slew of problems. The heart of the program is education, counseling, helping these families obtain legal services, and helping them work with state offices that can offer further assistance. The organization also runs a residential nursery program and a play-therapy group for children infected with HIV, and it owns two apartments that it offers temporarily to families. "Basically," Deoshore says, "we want to teach skills that will help these people be successful in their communities. We want to enhance the quality of their lives."

Such concern makes her a natural teacher for students at the Urban Collaborative. "The first thing I try to teach these kids is that sex and sexuality are very normal parts of life. I also want them to know, however, that when it comes to sex, it is physically very easy. It's the mental and emotional aspects that are hard. We discuss biology and sexual anatomy so they can be comfortable with themselves and understand that the changes they are going through physically and emotionally are normal. But we also look at relationships, commitment, and the importance of building one's self-esteem and thinking for oneself.

"Ultimately," she continues, "I would like to see them delay having sex until they are older. But the reality is that some won't. And that is all right, as long as they understand what they are getting into, understand that they have choices. If they want to have sex, they must understand, on one hand, the risks, and, on the other, what it means to be a responsible adult. Society bombards these kids with messages that encourage sexual activity. Just look at television and the movies, listen to the popular music, look at clothing advertisements. They all see this. They are all attracted to it. Then they hear people tell them that sex at their age is taboo. This is so confusing to teenagers."

There is another element to it, too. "Every four seconds in this country, a woman is abused by her partner," Deoshore points out. "*Every four seconds.* I think it is important for girls to know this, to be aware of the problem. And the boys, too. They need to know that it happens, why it happens, and how to avoid it. They need to know if someone tells you he or she loves you, then hits you, that this is wrong. So in class, I put a lot of emphasis on the self and on the relationship. I want them to be clear about their values, those things that we stand by and exercise in our daily behavior. There is so much pressure on these kids. So many of them come into this class simply wanting to know about sex. But they come out with an understanding of why adults want them to wait a few years before having sex. It doesn't help much when adults tell them simply to abstain, that they are too young, when their bodies are telling them the exact opposite. They need to know the facts. But they also need to be aware of the emotional implications of a sexual relationship—which, as adults know, can be intensely difficult at times."

Deoshore recites more daunting statistics: one million teenage girls get pregnant every year in the United States. One in five American adolescents will contract a sexually transmitted disease by age twenty. The majority of those with HIV infection contracted the disease during adolescence. The most seriously at-risk group of adolescents lives in the inner city. There is a great deal for these kids to consider, and Deoshore makes sure they are armed with as much knowledge as they can absorb in a few months.

"One in four girls is sexually abused. One in six boys," she continues. "This is a serious problem. And, unfortunately, a lot of the girls still continue to believe in Cinderella and Sleeping Beauty, believe that someone will come along and rescue them. I tell them that they will never be happy until they realize that only they can rescue themselves. In short, we discuss the messages in society that encourage sex but don't explain the reality of a sexual relationship in terms of its emotional complexity. We discuss adolescence itself, the physical and emotional elements. We discuss sexually transmitted diseases. We discuss peer pressure and the social ills that drive sexual and physical abuse. We discuss sexism, the pressures on girls to sleep with boys, the pressure on boys to be conquerors. We get real gender specific. And I think it really helps them. It not only helps them with their knowledge of what is happening to them physically, but it helps them build their self-esteem. And, God knows, they really need this."

Earlier in the year, a nationally broadcast television program, *The Health Quarterly*, produced a show on the AIDS epidemic and concluded with a segment on the Urban Collaborative. In 1987, the somber narrator told viewers, 2,400 American teenagers were infected with the AIDS virus. In 1991, that number increased dramatically to 9,000. A survey of teenagers reported that most of those surveyed admitted to having had sexual relations. This segment, the narrator said, "gives us a glimpse into a world most of us have not entered. A world where students have tough lives and teachers talk straight." The camera cut to a view of South Providence. The narrator explained the economic woes that have beset the region, then focused on the youth and the fact that nearly one out of two students in this section of the city drops out each year. These kids are highly likely to find themselves in trouble. Many end up using drugs or getting pregnant or prostituting themselves. And many are extremely vulnerable to AIDS.

The camera switched to the Urban Collaborative and to what the narrator called the school's "straight talk" on matters of sexuality. The focus was on Deoshore's class and how she is educating students about basic anatomy and human sexuality. In the segment, Deoshore talked about contraceptives. "What do we know about the pill?" she asked. One boy said, "you swallow it." This is followed by nervous laughter. What we learn next is that a girl in the class, who is pregnant, knows absolutely nothing about the pill, how it works, how one takes it, or even where one can get it.

Perhaps what is so striking about all this is not that the Urban Collaborative is offering a sex education course of this caliber but, as Deoshore pointed out, that it is the only school in Rhode Island that provides such information in as much depth. The need for such education is obvious. But the point of the television program is not that there is a school with a good sex education program. The point is that the Urban Collaborative is trying to educate these forgotten children, keep them in school, help them build their self-esteem, help them care enough about themselves so they will *want* to protect themselves and *want* to lead better lives.

As one student told the reporter, "You respect yourself so much more when you come to this school. I tell my baby sister and my middle sister, don't let nobody put you down . . . . There is no one like you. You're *you*. And if you have self-esteem, you won't let yourself go down." She smiles at the camera as if this is the first time she has articulated these thoughts. Then she said, "Yeah, that's it."

The narrator concluded: "So what does the fate of one school have to do with protecting America's young people from AIDS? In a way, programs like this are an AIDS vaccine because accomplishment, self-esteem, and responsibility can give a child immunity medical science has spent a decade trying to find."

13

JACILYN, AS ROB DEBLOIS DESCRIBES HER, IS A WISE AND SAVVY street kid, and one of a dozen teenagers at the Urban Collaborative whom he has felt particularly close to during the past three years. A handsome, sixteen-year-old African American, she enrolled in the Urban Collaborative in the fall of 1989, full of anger and hope.

Early on she found her share of trouble because, like many kids here, she had spent most of her life backed up against a wall. But she was also thoughtful and reflective. In time, she confided in Rob. In November of 1989, Rob had been invited to speak to a group of educators in downtown Providence. Thinking it would be good for them to hear from students as well, he asked the teachers to suggest someone who might represent the school well. A few suggested Jacilyn. Rob didn't know her well at the time, but he trusted the teachers, who said she was intelligent and articulate.

When he asked Jacilyn, she readily agreed to speak. In truth, Rob says he didn't know what to expect. She could stand him up, become too shy to talk, or get angry at educators who had not helped her over the years.

As it turned out, she rose magnificently to the occasion.

"What I remember most was seeing her walk into that place," Rob recalls. "She had gone to the trouble to get all dressed up, which I had not asked her to do, and looked for all the world like a young woman on a job interview rather than a struggling city kid of sixteen. She was out of her element, nervous and unsure of herself. But she was ready and willing to help us out as best she could. I was suddenly struck by her grace, her good will, and her desire to make something of her difficult life. She did a great job."

136

Jacilyn, indeed, did have a great desire to improve her life. She spoke intelligently and honestly to the educators, explaining her past trouble with school and how glad she was to be at the Urban Collaborative because it offered her another chance. And for the rest of the year, she more or less kept herself on track. But sometimes life is overwhelming. Things fell apart quickly for Jacilyn during the second year, and by the end of October Rob had to expel her for threatening another student with a knife.

There are few hard and fast rules at the Urban Collaborative. Two of those considered sacrosanct, however, are no violence and no weapons. These kids come from a violent world, one getting worse every day. All of them can tell a story or two involving weapons and death. The Urban Collaborative decided that to the best of its ability the school would be a safe place for these kids. And generally it is safe. An independent survey of teachers and students in the Providence public schools indicates that students and teachers at the Urban Collaborative feel safe in school, safer than their counterparts in other city schools. Despite the school's efforts, however, each year someone gets expelled for injuring someone else. When Jacilyn pulled out a knife, Rob had no choice but to make it her last bold act as an Urban Collaborative student.

"Jacilyn lived with an adoptive mother during the first year she was here," Rob recalls. "She had repeated the third, fifth, *and* seventh grades, and she was clearly bound to drop out if something didn't change in her life and change soon. And for a while it actually looked as if she would be one of our star students."

What set Jacilyn apart was her desire to take charge. She was a born mediator and loved to coordinate activities for her friends both in and out of school. There was something about her that commanded respect, and other students readily deferred to her leadership. In many ways, this characteristic was a double-edged sword. At times, people appreciated her desire to help. At other times, it was plain meddlesome. But most of the staff appreciated her involvement in numerous school activities, and how, on her better days, she'd readily express her opinion in class. She wasn't afraid to take a stance even if it ran counter to the position of her peers. One day, a girl not enrolled in the school came onto the school grounds wielding a knife and calling out to a particular student. Although Jacilyn didn't know the vistor, she approached her, calmed her down, and got the knife away from her.

Jacilyn's ability to mediate is interesting in light of the fact that Jacilyn's life has basically been a series of crises from birth. Shortly before she was born, her father died in a fire while he was an inmate at the state training school in Cranston. Her mother, a drug addict, was beaten, scalded with boiling water, and thrown out a window to her death. Even before her mother's death, Jacilyn had been placed in a variety of homes and eventually was adopted by Hattie Brown, a woman who already had two adopted children and three foster children to care for.

It's hard to say what changed between Jacilyn's first and second years at the Urban Collaborative, but things definitely changed. By the second year, around the time of what would have been her mother's birthday, Jacilyn's life fell apart. First, in a fit of despair, she swallowed a handful of sleeping pills and had to have her stomach pumped. Then she stopped going to school. Because of her truancy, she had a bitter fight with Hattie, left home, and ended up living at various locations around the state, staying with whoever would take her in. She became desperate, confused, hungry, bitter, and broke. In October she tried returning to school, but it was not the same place for her, and she was not the same girl. She was hard to talk to, hard to motivate, hard to keep in line. She shut people out, snapped at both adults and students. Then, late in October, shaking with some pent-up fury, Jacilyn pulled a butcher's knife on a girl in the hallway during a morning class change. The cause of the confrontation between them, as in most cases, will never be clear. What *was* clear, however, was that Jacilyn had pulled a knife and threatened another human being's life.

After she got kicked out of the Urban Collaborative, Rob recalls, by law she could not return to public school for ninety days. During this time, according to Jacilyn, she was raped and impregnated and eventually decided to have an abortion. After this, she came to Rob for help. "I don't think she was far from death at the time," Rob says. "She looked like hell. She said she had been drinking heavily. She may also have had a problem with drugs. I don't know. What impressed me was that she did come to me. That she did reach out. I helped her get into a different public school with a sworn promise that she would give it her best shot and not act violently. As of now, she is still in school and doing fairly well." He pauses and shakes his head again. "I hope she makes it. But things are very very tough for her. Since last March, she has lived in three different homes. It's hard to say what will become of her."

In actuality, Rob is doing more than hoping. Even though he had to expel Jacilyn, he has kept in close contact with her. Jacilyn has spent several nights at his house and has come often for dinner and even a night at the movies. Rob has bought her clothes for school, Christmas presents, and food. At the moment, he is the one overseeing Jacilyn's education. They are so close, in fact, that Jacilyn often refers to Rob as her father.

Rob tells the story of Jacilyn in part to point out her resiliency and in part because she epitomizes the sort of child he was hoping to help when he first envisioned the school. She is a capable student with admirable qualities. Give her a stable life and she will succeed. Take that away, and suddenly she needs a school that is wise enough to understand the trouble in her life, flexible enough to tolerate her headstrong ways, and persistent enough to get her pointed in the right direction. Jacilyn is also a clear example of how far a school can go for any one student, and what the limits of those efforts can be.

True, the student Jacilyn had attacked, has many of the same qualities and circumstances as Jacilyn. She has lived in poverty without a father. Her mother is addicted to cocaine and has spent time in jail for possession of sizable amounts of crack. In past years, True had performed well in school, but eventually she'd bring her personal troubles to class and get herself often suspended, for violent outbursts. Despite accepting her into the program, the staff at the Urban Collaborative knew it would be difficult for True to make it through the program. From the beginning, she was a high-risk student. Immediately after the incident with Jacilyn, True spun out of control, screaming, swearing, and verbally threatening everyone in school, including Rob. Rob, despite immense tolerance for emotional outbursts, ended up calling in the police to deal with the situation because it had gotten beyond his control. The police, as it turns out, knew Jacilyn and True well.

The difference between Jacilyn and True, however, is that True had always managed to stop short of violence and had always managed to bounce back. She stayed in school, found a moderately stable home with a classmate, got involved in drama and other extracurricular activities, and eventually learned that the adults in this school were willing to go the extra distance with her. It paid off. She curbed her anger, began to work harder, and accelerated in most classes. At key times she would step forward and take charge, as she did in the filming of the *Health Quarterly* report. Next year she is heading to Central High School's Law and Government Program. If she can hold her course, Rob believes, she has the talent to do well professionally in either law or government.

The tale of these two girls is important because it points out one more truth about troubled youth. On one hand, their troubled lives and frustrations can—and often do—get the best of them. On the other hand, you never know when they might come around. Rob is as aware of this as anyone, and for him this is reason enough to work tirelessly for these kids, even when all efforts seem hopeless. You just never know. So you don't give up.

"How could one not get attached to Jacilyn or True?" he asks. "How could one not want to help both of them get a real education and find a way to live a better life? They are wonderful people living the toughest of lives."

Unfortunately, the mainstream American public education system is not designed to help children like these. And very few people are trying to change this.

Nothing gets Rob going quicker than a discussion of urban education. To learn how he feels, all one needs to do is ask the right questions and sit back.

"The problems of children at the Urban Collaborative," he says, "are the problems of inner-city America. The crisis of youth in the greater Providence area—the crisis that is leading so many to failure in school, to drug abuse, to violence, to crime, to teenage pregnancy, to a sort of modern-day nihilism and hopelessness—is the crisis of poor, troubled youth in every city in the nation. For every True who finds her way to a better life, there are many urban children taken down by the struggle. One can't look at the kids in this school as they confront the utter confusion of their day, and not fear for their future. And one can't look at this nation's attitude toward such youth and not fear for its future as well."

Not surprisingly, the correlation between failure in school and troubled, unfulfilled lives is strong. A study by the National Survey Center for Statistics noted that 36 percent of high school dropouts were not employed and that those who were working were in the lowest-paying jobs. The U.S. Department of Justice found that, of the inmates in local jails, a full 63 percent of the blacks and 50 percent of the whites were dropouts. Harold Hodgkinson, an educational researcher, puts that figure higher. In a recently published report, he notes that of the 1.1 million prisoners in this country, a full 82 percent are high school dropouts. With the national dropout rate hovering around 25 percent (and higher in urban areas), and with these dropouts not finding a happy or useful role in society, it is clear—on a purely economic level—that the country is doing itself a disservice by accepting an educational system that sets up so many for failure. To put it bluntly, dropping out—and the inflexible educational system that leads so many to drop out—costs more than we care to think. In addition to the expense of law enforcement, incarceration, and social services, reports indicate that dropouts cost America nearly $75 billion in welfare funds each year and approximately $7 billion in unrealized revenues.

Given the realities of the educational system and the detrimental effects on the country's economy and psyche, it's hard to understand the resistance to change and the resistance to increasing our investment in education. By any measurement, it's clear that Americans are not investing enough in their children, particularly urban children. The question is: Why is the nation so unwilling to invest more? If this country is to continue as a stable and vital democracy, if it is to continue as an economic force in the world, then Americans have no choice but to increase their investment in education, as well as in other social programs aimed at helping youth. The children, plain and simple, are the future, and right now a high percentage of our children is getting lost. As psychologist Urie Bronfenbrenner puts it, schools are "one of the most potent breeding grounds of alienation in American society." One would hope this is not our intention. School is supposed to provide a nurturing environment that transforms young people into adults with more confidence and self-esteem, teaches them the skills needed for today's work force, and prepares them to become active citizens.

There is a great deal of lip service paid to improving education these days. And the gap between rhetoric and reality is growing each year. In the same week, politicians express ambitious and laudable goals for education and then vote to cut funding for critical programs. It is fairly easy to make grand pronouncements, as former President Bush's America 2000 panel had done.[1] But in light of the reality (for inner-city schools in particular), such pronouncements seem utterly ludicrous—and way beyond reach without a substantial increase in the financial support for education. By the year 2000, the panel declared, *all* children in America will start school ready to learn; the high school graduation rate in *all* communities will increase to at least 90 percent; U.S. students will be first in the world in science and mathematics; *every* adult will be literate; and *every* school in America will be free of drugs and violence.

Most people would like nothing more than to see these goals realized. But there is reason to be skeptical. Around the same time that America 2000 made these proclamations, the Children's Defense Fund reported some sobering statistics—statistics that Rob prominently displays on his office wall. On any given day in America, 7,742 teenagers will become sexually active, 2,795 teenage girls will get pregnant; 1,295 will give birth. On the

---

[1] Bill Clinton's Goals 2000 program is basically a modified extension of the Bush administration's educational goals in both word and spirit. What is interesting about Goals 2000 is that it has gotten beyond rhetoric to real debate over national standards, and it is pushing the states to act on these issues. It's not clear, however, that any of this will have a real or lasting impact on education in America.

same day, 135,000 children will bring guns to school; 40 will get shot, 10 of whom will die of their wounds. And on the same day, 1,849 children will be abused or neglected by their parents; 3,288 will run away from home; 211 will be arrested for drug abuse; 437 will be arrested for drinking or drunken driving; 1,629 will end up in adult jails.

The pronouncements are easy. But currently there is no political will to ask for sacrifices in the name of education that will allow any of these pronouncements to be remotely possible. Unless the changes are massive, the children will continue to suffer—as will the nation. To make matters worse, the current system, as Jonathan Kozol so clearly points out in his sobering book *Savage Inequalities*, is patently unjust, favoring the children of wealthy communities over those in poor, urban districts. Wealthier communities, for the most part, can make do because much of the funding for education comes from local property taxes. A state is considered progressive if *only* 50 percent of its educational funding comes from local property taxes. This funding formula results in the wealthy communities, where there are far fewer social and developmental problems to begin with, having greater resources and much better schools than poor communities. Students from wealthy communities perform well on tests, relatively speaking, while students from poor communities perform poorly. Along with whatever other reforms are necessary to improve public education in general, it is absolutely vital that we work toward a more equitable system. And the answer lies not in taking money or resources away from the wealthy school districts, as some fear school reform might do. At the very least, the answer lies in finding a way to bring schools in poor communities up to the wealthy communities' level of quality.

In Rhode Island, the disparity between urban and suburban education is clear when you compare the Providence system to that of well-to-do East Greenwich. In 1991, for every child in East Greenwich, the town had $405,547 worth of property to tax. Providence had only $143,634 worth of property to tax for each child.[2] Obviously, to simplify the funding formula somewhat, this means that with the same tax rate, East Greenwich gets the better school. If Providence were to raise its schools to the same standard as East Greenwich, according to Jean Rosiello and Michelle Seiter of the Rhode Island Campaign to Eliminate Childhood Poverty, it would have to tax its residents at *three times* the rate of the affluent in East Greenwich. "The key here," Rosiello and Seiter write, "is not that some families are richer than others (that is undeniable), but that government deliberately compounds the inequity by giving more and better educational

---

[2] The numbers are slightly different today, though the ratio is basically the same.

opportunities to those who already start out with the greatest privileges. What we have, contrary to every political principle we profess to hold, is an educational caste system, orchestrated and enforced by our own elected representatives." Couple this with the fact that inner-city poor already pay a greater percentage of their incomes for housing than the wealthy pay—and struggle with a host of other problems, including high unemployment, low paying jobs, dwindling social services and government support—and one can begin to see how the odds are stacked against urban children.

As Horace Mann suggested some 150 years ago, education is supposed to be "the great equalizer." But it certainly hasn't turned out that way. And it won't until major changes have taken place in the way the nation conducts its system of public education—the education available to even the poorest members of society. Without better and more equal education, the poor have few opportunities to improve their incomes and lives. Without better and more equal education, the poor will remain embittered and society will remain divisive. Without better and more equal education, this nation will continue to move closer to creating a permanent underclass that will pass from one generation to the next a legacy of poverty, personal alienation, crime, and family instability.

Part of the problem is that the American system of education hasn't changed significantly in the past seventy years, while society has. Students are coming to school with greater needs, especially in urban areas, and the schools—without additional funding—are being asked to deal with these needs. Harold Hodgkinson points out that "the top 15 percent of America's students are truly world class on any set of indicators" but the "lowest 35 percent are truly awful, due to factors that were present when they first knocked on the kindergarten door." These factors include poverty, fetal drug exposure, poor health, hunger, bad housing, and inadequate parenting. Schools were originally developed to teach reading, writing, and arithmetic and not much else. Today's schools still need to hold to these fundamentals while adding a wide spectrum of courses designed to train young people for a modern, increasingly complex and competitive society. Although schools don't currently serve as centers for the delivery of social services, there is clearly a need—and also an unstated directive—for schools to take a more active role in providing such services as health care, counseling, substance-abuse treatment, day care for the children of working parents, day care for the children of students, you name it. And schools just don't have the money and resources to do this.

In short, everyone expects a great deal from our schools, but the nation is not yet willing to provide the support these schools need. In the war against Iraq, Rob points out, America demonstrated unequivocally that it can accomplish its goals with amazing efficiency. It also demonstrated that when it decides something is critical for national security, it will find the resources and make the sacrifices to do it. Whether one was for or against our military invasion of Iraq, most people would agree that George Bush showed leadership in undertaking Desert Storm, as he called the war. He defined his objective to the American people, then he made clear, unmistakable, and swift progress in achieving it. The problem with education is not a lack of resources, as has been suggested. America was spending $1 billion a day on Desert Storm. The problem with education is, plain and simple, a lack of will.[3]

All of this is not to suggest that Americans haven't tried to reform their educational system over the years. They have, and they still do. There are perhaps more alternative programs than ever being tried today. But these programs tend to remain as alternative, experimental projects and, even if brilliantly successful, rarely get beyond the fringes of mainstream American education. In the past six years alone, there have been hundreds of studies of education, some by very powerful groups. But here again very few changes have resulted—mostly because they all require money and enough desire to effect lasting change.

"On a human level, " Rob concludes, "it is our moral imperative to improve the educational system for all. This will not only help the nation's economy, it will help promote greater opportunity, more equality, less bitterness, and less poverty in the cities. There are days at the Urban Collaborative when we get so overwhelmed by the problems facing our kids that I can't help but turn around and face society and the unequal public education system this society has created and say, 'How could we let these children get this way? Why wouldn't we try harder to make a better world for them?' Sometimes I think if everyone spent a day in a traditional inner-city public school—or a day here—then they'd find the means to make the necessary changes."

---

[3] There is a darker view that suggests the division between the haves and have-nots is more than a lack of will—that there is something in America that prefers this unjust system of winners and losers to a more equitable system, that a leisure class needs and demands a poor class for whatever strange fulfillment it brings to their lives. One has to wonder. Certainly the mood in Congress of late, with its seeming desire to punish the poor with regressive welfare reform policies, suggests a country full of confused motives.

14

IN TIMES OF FISCAL AUSTERITY, MOST ALTERNATIVE SCHOOLS
are viewed as expendable, luxury items serving only a small number of
students. The Urban Collaborative is no exception. Since the day Rob
DeBlois proposed the idea of the Urban Collaborative, the school has been
in a constant struggle for public funding. In the school's first three years,
East Providence and Pawtucket have paid their share willingly. But each
year, the Providence School Department, which funds most of the Urban
Collaborative's operating expenses, has initially cut the school out of its
budget. Each year, Rob has had to give his teachers lay-off notices. And
each year he has had to fight vigorously to get the city's funding reinstated.
From Providence's perspective, the Urban Collaborative is a fine school
doing a good job helping at-risk kids. But the city is in a financial bind.
The school department's budget has been reduced substantially in recent
years, and the Urban Collaborative—the newest and smallest program—is .
the easiest target for cuts. Providence has more than twenty thousand
students; only about seventy-five of them attend the Urban Collaborative.

Rick Richards, a program evaluator for the Rhode Island Department
of Elementary and Secondary Education, points out another part of the
problem. "To give Providence its due," he says, "the city really is in a
desperate funding struggle. Its base of revenue is shrinking. Meanwhile,
the student population is expanding, and the nature of that population is
changing in ways that make more demands on the system." But the problem
goes beyond the financial crisis. "There are kids who do well in the
traditional public school curriculum as it is, and there are kids who don't
do well, almost regardless of who teaches. The question is: With limited

funds, who are you committed to in that system? Who do you pay attention to? Do you fund something for those who drop out? Do their parents pay a lot of taxes? Are they going to be productive citizens? Are they even going to vote? By being a dropout, you are almost, by definition, a member of a dispossessed class. You are economically and politically powerless. And I think that plays a part in why the Urban Collaborative struggles for funding. You look at who pulls the strings in Providence or who pulls the strings in the state house. It is not the parents of the dropouts."

Without a doubt, the Urban Collaborative's struggle for public funding is one of the most powerful challenges facing the school. With the urban revenue base shrinking and the school consisting of an unrepresented constituency, this problem is not likely to change in the near future. The irony in all this is that, while the city struggles with its responsibility for at-risk students, Rob has had little trouble raising additional money from private sources as a means of augmenting the basic education of Urban Collaborative students. As the fight for public funds continues, many private foundations readily understand the value of helping a school like the Urban Collaborative. The private sector is unlikely to provide for the general operating costs of the school—especially in a small state like Rhode Island. Nor would Rob allow this. But additional money is another matter. The first year, the school raised $67,000 from private sources. For this third year, the school has raised $112,000 from 20 foundations and companies, which amounts to a little more than 10 percent of the school's budget. Next year, the school hopes to raise $114,000. The increase in private funding—again, during difficult economic times—suggests that the private sector sees a great deal of merit in a program like this.

The money raised from private sources makes a huge difference in the quality of the school's program. In the first two years, this money has been used for the purchase of a school van, student and office computers, a photocopier, desks, chairs, audiovisual equipment, art and music equip-ment, library books, and reading material for slow readers. These funds have also paid for staff stipends for summer in-service programs, student orientations, field trips, substance-abuse programs, sex education, an explorer's club, a part-time curriculum coordinator, counselors to ease the student transition to traditional high school, a public relations program, a summer program for students, community service projects, art workshops, family outreach programs, parent programs, and special counseling services. Money has been used for the purchase of clothes, medicine, and medical treatment for students in need. In addition, the school created a variety of incentive programs designed to encourage good attendance, effort, academic achieve-ment, and behavior. In the first two years, all those students with perfect attendance for a month were eligible to win $100 savings bonds. The school also takes students out to breakfast or lunch periodically and offers special field trips as rewards for good behavior. Recently, a group of students who accelerated in the final two months of school were taken to the beach. And all students (except the few who have been serving in-school suspensions) were treated to a day at Rocky Point Amusement Park.

The breakfast and lunch program is particularly valuable, Rob says, "because this kind of reward not only makes the students feel special and feel as if they have achieved something, but it also gives the teachers a chance to get together with students in a comfortable setting away from school. Anything we can do to get students and teachers together outside of class is money well spent."

Barbara Cervone, of the philanthropic Rhode Island Foundation, is among those who pushed her board to support the Urban Collaborative. "What I told my board, and what I would tell anyone now, is that the Urban Collaborative has really homed in on the notion of what public education should be about and what real school reform consists of—which is that you need different kinds of curriculum than the lock-step curriculum that most schools offer. And that teachers need to be mentors as well as teachers." In her own past experience working for the Alternative Learning Program, an alternative high school program in Providence, Cervone says she has learned that the relationship between students and adults in the learning environment is the most important element of a school. "That's one of the key foundations for learning," she says. "And it's something I see working very well at the Urban Collaborative and not at other schools.

"Then there is the curriculum itself," she adds. "I think the school has been doing some wonderful things in how it approaches a simple subject like math. The staff acknowledges that kids proceed at different speeds and arrive at different levels and that you need to provide an individualized curriculum. In my graduate school work, I took a historical look at education and all those proclamations—that we should have *this* emphasis in education, or *that* emphasis—and how they never really filtered down to the classroom. People have been talking about individualized instruction for years. You can read great treatises on it from the 1890s, and again in 1910, and so on up to the present. But these things rarely ever find their way into the classroom. At the Urban Collaborative, they have."

At first, the foundation's board was reluctant to give money to the Urban Collaborative on the grounds that the school was a public school and, therefore, the public's responsibility. But Cervone argued that the foundation needed to do more than pay lip service to dropout prevention and educational reform. And this is finally what sold the board. "I saw this as an opportunity to help a good alternative educational program," she says. "The trustees liked the idea that it was a dropout prevention program helping kids stay in school." Cervone also made the argument that while most of the money for the school comes from public sources, this group of kids has greater needs, or more-difficult-to-fill needs than typical students. It only makes sense that it would cost more to educate them than it would to educate average students. Essentially, the private sector's role is to help the Urban Collaborative level the playing field for these kids.

To date, the foundation has given the school $44,000, with another $10,000 promised for the following year. If Cervone gets her way, the Rhode Island Foundation, which in 1991 made 810 grants worth a total of $5.5 million, will invest more in education in future years. "As a foundation," she says, "we are ready to serve the general good of the whole state, whether it be a request to repair a lighthouse or support a battered-women's shelter. It runs the whole gamut. But I personally feel the foundation should be investing a lot more in education because, in truth, what we really want is to create a better society, more equality, less poverty, and so on. An awful lot of the grants we make here, almost two-thirds of them, fall into the social service realm. And of those, two-thirds are going to provide services for people who already have problems, who are already drug-dependent or homeless or whatever. Very few of the grants actually go to prevention. For some reason, we'd rather spend two thousand dollars on the treatment of a child with some awful health problem that could have been prevented with a two dollar pill."

Another supporter of the school, providing both time and money, is Jan C. G. van Hemert, the Dutch-born general manager of Patriot Metals Company, an expansive scrap-metal yard located by the state pier in South Providence. Van Hemert, who got involved with the Urban Collaborative through the Adopt-A-School Program, will admit there is a self-serving reason for helping: public relations. His scrapyard, set on twenty-four acres among oil storage tanks and the city's water treatment plant, is not the most physically appealing business. "Rather than having people look at us as a nuisance to the community with dirty-looking scrap metal all over the place," van Hemert says, "I was hoping we could gain some respect by showing our support for the community." Personally, he adds, he also wanted to get involved in education because he feels the school system needs a great deal of help—for the sake of the students, the community, and the society at large. "I was born and raised in Holland and went to school there," he says. "If I compare my schooling to what I see around here, the schools here are rather pathetic. It's not the fault of the kids.

The schools fall considerably short of my experience. Coming out of high school, for instance, everyone in Holland can speak four languages. Here, language is optional, even—it sometimes seems—English. So whatever can be done to improve education all around is worth doing," he continues. "The few years you go to school are a real investment in your own future. This time lifts the rest of your life up considerably. If you finish high school or get a college education, your level of income for the rest of your life is considerably higher than if you drop out. And to see so many kids in Providence dropping out is really sad. That's why I think it is important to help a school like the Urban Collaborative. They are not only helping potential dropouts stay in school, but they are helping them make up for lost time. What an excellent idea."

It's important for private companies to invest in public education, van Hemert continues, "because we all benefit from a better system, and because the public sector has not yet made it the sort of priority I think it should be. Take, for instance, the Urban Collaborative's funding struggle. This is a highly successful and innovative school with a very dedicated staff. They shouldn't have to suffer through this every year. That is an absolutely terrible situation. One of the first areas where cutbacks occur in the public sector is always in the schools. That should be the last place, as far as I'm concerned, especially at a school like this."

In each of the Urban Collaborative's first two years of operation, Patriot Metals has given grants of twenty thousand dollars, in part for the purchase of computer equipment. This year, the company gave an additional five thousand dollars.

The Urban Collaborative's funding struggle is made that much more puzzling by the fact that most people in the private sector and in public education are firm supporters of the school. Henry S. Woodbridge, Jr., the former CEO of Hospital Trust, a leading Rhode Island bank, left his post in 1987 to work on a program called Workforce 2000. Currently Woodbridge is the president of the Rhode Island Anti-Drug Coalition. He also serves as president of the advisory board of the Providence Dropout Collaborative, an organization that promotes a stronger connection between schools and the community at large.

As the director of Workforce 2000, Woodbridge studied the entire spectrum of employment and training programs in Rhode Island, assessing the systems to see if they were responsive to the needs of the state's future. In particular, he began looking at the educational system. "It was clear right from the beginning," he says, "that there wasn't much point having good training programs if so many students were dropping out of high school and if the majority of those graduating from high school had difficulty performing simple tasks. So rather than putting money into restructuring existing training programs, I began steering a lot of money into programs that were designed to influence and improve public education." In the process, Woodbridge eventually met Rob DeBlois, accepted an invitation to visit the Urban Collaborative, and came away impressed. "I should say, first, that I am greatly impressed with what Rob has done personally to get the school going, given his physical condition, never mind the other barriers," Woodbridge says. "I don't know how to measure what Rob is doing against new and creative educational ideas in other cities. But for Rhode Island, what he is doing is really fantastic—taking students who are a year or two behind and very much in danger of dropping out, and creating an entity where teachers have the flexibility to be responsive to the needs of those students in a more personal, caring way. I think that's important in education. Touring other schools, I get the impression of frustration, a desire for change, dissatisfaction with the system. Some people are pleased that some progress is being made. I happen to believe that we need a revolution in public school education at the elementary and secondary level. And the Urban Collaborative could be one hell of an example for revolutionary change."

Joe Maguire, principal of the Roger Williams Middle School, one of six Providence middle schools that send students to the Urban Collaborative each year, is particularly impressed with the program. "I'm very happy the school exists," he says. "I have seen amazing growth in kids we've sent there. They come back here each year and put on presentations for our kids. And to see these kids, some of whom were my main nemeses over the years, coming back in a very adult-like fashion and serving as models for other kids—it just blew me away."

Joe Maguire readily admits there are students whose needs really cannot be met in the traditional public schools. With seven hundred or so students, the Roger Williams Middle School requires—or so conventional wisdom argues—a great deal of order and discipline. Most classes are taught in the traditional manner with the teacher standing in front lecturing or trying to engage the group in "class discussion." What one notices, observing these classes, is that about half of each class responds fairly well to this system, readily answering questions posed to the entire group. Many of the teachers are intelligent, energetic, and concerned. But the other half of the class, at best, sits passively or fidgets uneasily, disengaged from the activity. When asked a question, they stumble, blush, stare at the floor; the teacher then moves on to someone who can answer the question, in order to keep the pace of the class—"the lesson"—moving smoothly. Day by day, hour by hour, class by class, many of these students are sliding slowly toward failure, toward that sad moment when they'll believe it is better to drop out.

Academics aside, many larger schools unwittingly lose students through their need to keep order. In Roger Williams' cavernous lunch room, for instance, kids are expected to respond to a series of whistles and to the amplified orders of the vice principal. Sit at this table. Wait in this line. Be quiet. Clear your table. Stand in this line until your teacher comes and collects you. It's too eerily prison-like. All day long they are supposed to follow a rigid set of rules, enter through the proper door, climb up one set of stairs and down another, get a pass to use the bathroom, and so on. The school has some ninety teachers and a complex system of classes, with students changing classrooms six times a day. In the student handbook one finds the following "guideline": "Shorts result in exposure to splinters, insect bites, etc. They can also distract and create a relaxed mood that makes full attention to schoolwork more difficult. For these reasons, shorts, although they are allowed, are not recommended. No hats are allowed in school." The surprising word here is "relaxed," as if the school really believes that students learn best when constantly on edge. Many kids become frustrated—and, unfortunately, there is no room to work out such frustrations. Somewhere along the line they fall out of step, and the system doesn't wait up for them.

"I'm sure part of the problem is that we are just so big and imper-sonal," says Maguire, a thoughtful, kind, and concerned man. "But there is nothing we can do about the size of the school. This is the reality of urban education today. These are the facilities we've inherited, and we try to do the best we can with them." He also echoes what others say: that there is not enough money. That, despite its size, there is not enough room in the school. Some classes at the Roger Williams Middle School, for instance, are held in sections of corridors that have been partitioned off. At the same time, the needs of the student body have gotten far more complex. "I was here in 1968 when the first Hispanic student came into this school. That seems like three lifetimes ago now. Today we are close to 50 percent Hispanic. I look at the failure rate in some of those classes and it's shocking," he says. "Teachers keep coming to me and complaining that kids are changing, that they don't care anymore. And I tell them that the kids do care. It's just a different world they live in, a tougher world, and *we've* got to care three times more."

Like many public schools around the country, Roger Williams Middle School is experimenting with new ways of educating today's students. One teacher attended a workshop on cooperative learning and came back with ideas that Maguire says "have worked minor miracles" with some students. In cooperative learning, the teachers act more or less as facilitators while students work in groups, explore ideas together, quiz one another—help themselves, in effect, by helping others. But it remains to be seen if any of these experiments will make it into the mainstream curriculum—that is, if any will effect desperately needed change. In the meantime, Maguire and his colleagues are thankful for the Urban Collaborative, and they are greatly impressed by the success of some of their more recalcitrant students. "What is really nice about the school is that its reputation is growing each year. Kids hear about it. I've had kids who I didn't think cared at all about their education come in and ask me if they could go to the Urban Collaborative. The way they look at it, they have fallen behind here. They are not doing anything of value. Some of them are nine-feet tall and starting to grow beards. They don't want to be in the eighth grade any more, but they don't want to drop out either. They hear that the Urban Collaborative is a good place where they can make up a couple of years of work quickly. Of course, for those kids, you'll try to do anything to help them." To Joe Maguire, the Urban Collaborative is not a luxury but a necessity. "I believe in it," he says. "And I think I can speak for my colleagues in the other middle schools. They all believe in it. We're the ones who deal with these kids on a day-to-day basis. We know what our limitations are. I think if you want to know about the Urban Collaborative, the right thing to do is to talk to the principals of these so-called traditional schools, then see Rob's place in action."

Steve Raffa is a young, energetic lawyer with Blish & Cavanagh, a small Providence firm that specializes in litigation. Raffa occupies a corner office in the stately Commerce Building directly across from Kennedy Plaza, the city's central square. His window overlooks the construction site of the city's new convention center, rising out of the rubble of the old bus station. Raffa doesn't have much to say about the city's efforts at self-improvement through construction, but he talks passionately about the city's need to improve the quality of life for its poorer residents.

"I will always be appreciative of the Urban Collaborative for waking me up to the realities of the world," Raffa says. "I'm just a middle-class kid from middle-class white America. I was no social activist growing up. I did teach school for a year in Nicaragua between college and law school. But things like that I always did on a whim." Raffa went to Georgetown and to the University of Pennsylvania law school, came to work at a large Providence law firm. "I worked hard all the time, and I went on a couple of real nice vacations," Raffa says. "I had turned into a real yuppie type."

Three years later, looking for something with more social relevance, he quit his job at the large firm, moved to Blish & Cavanagh, signed up with the Junior Achievement Program, and found himself spending one morning a week at the Urban Collaborative teaching economics and current events. His first impression was that the kids were hostile and uncooperative. But he stuck with it, and after a couple months he asked Rob DeBlois if he could take some kids out to get to know them more personally. "Around Christmas that first year, my boss gave me some tickets to a Providence College game, so I invited three kids along. I'm not usually scared of anything. I rarely have more than two dollars on me. But I was scared when I went to their housing project to pick them up. This may sound stupid, but I saw where they live and I suddenly started to think, well, maybe this is why these kids aren't paying attention in class. Look at this dive where they live."

Raffa took students on three or four more outings that year. When the school year ended, Rob asked him if he would keep in touch with a couple of students. Raffa said he would. He also returned to the Urban Collaborative the second and third year. He taught classes and took students on more field trips—to his law firm to see how things operate or to a restaurant to watch big-screen sporting events. In the meantime, he kept in close contact with one student from the first year, a half-black, half-Hispanic boy named Michael.

Michael made it through the first year at the Urban Collaborative, then went on to Providence's Hope High School. For a while, Raffa would meet with Michael once a month, take him out to eat Chinese food or to Celtic games, all along believing that things were going well. One day during his sophomore year, however, Michael called Raffa with two bits of bad news: he had gotten himself thrown out of school for showing up drunk and threatening the principal. And he had gotten his girlfriend pregnant. He was sixteen.

"I got pretty involved in his life," Raffa says. "I took Michael under my wing. I thought I would see this kid every day for one or two weeks and I'd knock him into shape—as if it were that simple. He asked if he could live with me, and I agreed. He stayed for the summer. It was just incredible. Every day for the first week he would tell me something new. One day he told me he used to sell drugs. I asked why, and he said, 'How do you think I fed myself, Steve? How do you think I bought my clothes? How do you think my mother pays the rent?'"

During that time, Michael went to summer high school at Brown University and did well. Raffa got him a job stocking shelves in a supermarket. Everything looked good. But eventually Michael started getting into trouble again. He was arrested three times in August and September. Once he was implicated in a robbery, which, it turned out, his cousin committed. Another time he beat up a man who had been harassing Michael's brother. And the third time he was with a friend who had stolen a six-pack of beer. Eventually, he started selling drugs again. Raffa later found him with a sawed-off shotgun in the apartment and kicked him out. "We still keep in touch," Raffa says. "Over time, Michael improves and slips back. But basically I think he has made a lot of progress. He has learned a lot. And I've learned a ton.

"I can't believe there are so many kids like Michael," he continues. "And the problems just make you sad. I think most white professionals just look at them and say, 'these no-good kids.' But they end up doing the things they do just to survive. It's really horrible. Michael's dad is a junky. The last time he saw his dad, the first thing his dad asked for was a joint. He has a stepfather who beat him for several years, just beat him for no reason. His mother never once called to see how Michael was doing when he lived with me. Hopefully Michael will make it in the world. But he may not. And that's the sad reality."

Raffa, who has given Michael's family money over the years to help pay bills, has also learned that society doesn't make anything easier for kids like Michael.

"I try to get these kids jobs after school in banks and law firms and accounting firms," he says. "And it's real interesting. You have all these people who are allegedly concerned. But getting them to hire one or two black kids is incredibly difficult. I think it would be easier for me to run a four-minute mile than to get a lot of these kids a job. Part of my mission is to get a lot more people involved with these kids. But given the sort of attitude most people have around here, it is going to take a lot of time."

Once, he went Christmas shopping with Michael and Michael's girl-friend, Denise. They went to a department store at a mall. Michael was buying pillows and blankets for his family. Denise was buying other house-hold items. "The check-out woman didn't realize we were together," Raffa recalls. "Michael put his stuff on the counter. I was not really paying attention. Ten or fifteen minutes later, Michael was still standing there. So I asked him, 'What's going on?' He said they were doing a price check. I said, 'You are buying things without prices on them?' He said, 'No, they have prices. The woman is just checking on them.' They wanted to make sure he didn't switch price tags. It happens a lot, Michael explained. So I started to think he has done something wrong. I started to get mad. Here I was, taking him out, and now he was switching prices. But everything came back and the prices were fine. I went through next and they didn't check any of the items. Denise went through and they did the same thing to her as they did to Michael. I was standing off to the side at this point and suddenly realized what was going on. So I go up and created a big scene.

"But these things happen to these kids all the time. And why is that? Prejudice and fear. Some people think it is pretty weird that I get involved with black and Hispanic kids. They ask me why I do it, and I tell them it's because these are the kids most in need of help."

Perhaps even more disturbing to Raffa is how little the schools seem to care for helping the underclass. Michael has turned into a fairly able student. During fourth period this year, he was hoping to take an extra math or English class and was pretty sure he could handle it. But the school has made him take a class on clothing because that was the only available course. "So they stuck Michael in a class on clothing," Raffa says, "and yesterday they taught him how to use bleach properly. It's crazy. You tell kids to stay in school, get a good education. But when they stick you in a class where they teach you how to bleach your clothes, you start to realize that the society doesn't really care much about helping you."

To Steve Raffa, however, the Urban Collaborative is the exception. "I just go to the Urban Collaborative once a week, so I don't know a whole lot about their teaching methods. But I do know they are doing a good job. They are catching kids at a tough time in their lives, a time when they could go one way or the other, and they are keeping them on track. I think there is no doubt that Michael would not have made it without the Urban Collaborative or without my help. I know that this school is helping nearly all the kids who go there, and many of them with more problems than Michael. The other schools, meanwhile, are just not cutting it."

Charles Walton is a state senator from Providence, one of only a handful of African-American politicians in the state, and an outspoken proponent of the Urban Collaborative. "I don't lend my name to everything," Walton says. "But I started early on with the Urban Collaborative, and I see no reason to end my support. I got involved with the school to help turn around this city's appalling dropout rate. I'm concerned that these youngsters do not have any alternative and will fall into a life of despair without help. And my basic feeling is that any youngster who is in the program and has not dropped out is a plus. Very few black politicians are committed to things like this mostly because the needs in the urban areas are so tremendous, one-half of which we can't do a damn thing about. I'm always having to react to things, which is not very satisfying. I give time to the Urban Collaborative on the belief that it is worthwhile to help stem the dropout rate, especially for blacks and Hispanics and other immigrants.

"I also have no faith that the educational institution can ever straighten out its problems," he continues. "There will always be a need for the Urban Collaborative given the systemic problems we have. It's discouraging to continue to see the plight of immigrants who are trying to acclimate themselves to a new culture only to be beaten down by racism. It's a hell of a situation." Walton said if he could offer advice to the U.S. President, he'd tell him this: "If you have to do one thing in the urban agenda, forget welfare. Put your money into education. Build a better system, starting with Head Start programs, and work your way up to high school. I am grateful for the Urban Collaborative. But it is only one school trying to shore up a very weak system of education. We need to make education more meaningful and valuable to *all* inner-city kids, and we need to do it now."

Rick Richards, as an evaluator for the Rhode Island Department of Elementary and Secondary Education, talks about the time he spent evaluating the state-funded dropout prevention programs, of which there are seven. The programs, he believes, are valuable, but of all of them, the Urban Collaborative stands out as the most ambitious and noteworthy. "I spent some time in the school and came away with a very strong impression of the Urban Collaborative," Richards says. "After you visit most programs, you don't really come away with a strong sense of them. Most of them are just add-on programs in traditional schools. But the Urban Collaborative, in the first place, is a self-contained school separate from any other program. And this makes one realize just how serious the school is about its mission. It takes kids out of the context in which they have failed in the past, and it is committed to creating a new context in which these kids can succeed. And I think that message comes through.

"I also spent a lot of time in the classrooms, trying to figure out how they teach, and I was very impressed. They have clear goals for the students. And they work individually, so that the commitment isn't to a particular curriculum, but to teaching individuals. It's not exactly a tutorial program, but it is much closer to a tutorial than what one finds in the normal public schools, or even in private schools. And this is what makes the school unique." Other programs, he points out, try to tailor schedules to individual students. But inside the classroom, the teacher primarily lectures to or teaches to a class, a practice that assumes that everybody is at the same skill level and has the same background. And this is just not true. The reason kids fail in the first place is that, for whatever reason, they are out of step with the rest of the class. "At the Urban Collaborative," he says, "the goal is not to put them back into the same curriculum that they came from but to actually teach them something, teach them skills and values. And from what I can tell, the school has a better curriculum than the normal public school. I think that what they teach is much more related to what students need to know, and they teach it in a way that is more interesting. Because of this, I think that the Urban Collaborative is revolutionary. It is much more a statement of what education should be than it is a dropout prevention program."

Earlier in the year, he openly questioned the value of a pull-out program like the Urban Collaborative for the problems its students face trying to fit back into mainstream schools. While he still sees problems, he is more inclined now to say the problem lies with the mainstream schools, not with the Urban Collaborative. And he also believes that there are solutions to this problem, solutions that can be worked out over time. In short, there is no reason to dismantle a good program because of the mediocrity of another program.

"Dropout prevention programs," Richards concludes, "will often be the place where people begin to think about what is wrong with education, in large, as opposed to how we fix up the problem of certain kids. And I think that in every dropout prevention program, you'll see that tension to a certain extent. You'll see people who are desperately trying to fit kids into the system. At the same time, the people in the programs understand how difficult it is for certain kids to operate within a system that isn't really built around their lives and interests and needs and abilities—their way of learning. Dropouts, then, are the ultimate challenge to the validity of the philosophy of how you operate a school. They are saying that what goes on in school is irrelevant to their lives. They are saying this approach to education doesn't work. If we accept the premise that as a society we have to do something for the disenfranchised students who drop out every year, then more Urban Collaboratives have to rise up. It is the only clue we have about how to conduct urban education successfully."

15

YOU WANT TO KNOW HOW HARD IT IS TO MAKE CHANGES IN public education? Ask H. Ross Perot. Of his efforts to reform Texas' public schools, the presidential candidate said, "It was the hardest, meanest, bloodiest thing I have ever been in." Coming from one who had smuggled employees out of Khomenei's Iran during the hostage crisis and who later learned just how vicious a presidential campaign can be, this is a telling statement. Unfortunately, it is also one many school reformers, including Rob DeBlois, understand all too well.

It truly is a complex business. Take a look at just one aspect—financing a new and different school—and you'll get a glimpse of the problem.

The cities of Pawtucket and East Providence graciously anted up for the Urban Collaborative in its first four years without much trouble. Pawtucket contributes the considerable annual sum of $115,000 to the program, but this money comes from state funds set aside for dropout prevention and literacy programs and not from local property taxes. The Urban Collaborative, therefore, doesn't have to compete with other Pawtucket school programs for funding, and, in these tough fiscal times, doesn't draw the ire of residents determined to keep property taxes as low as possible. East Providence contributes $57,000 to the program. Although this money does come from local property taxes, apparently the amount is reasonable enough not to raise many concerns. In addition, the Urban Collaborative is the only dropout prevention program currently serving East Providence. More to the point, East Providence School Superintendent John Degoes is one of the more progressive school leaders in Rhode Island; he has long recognized the need for better programs for poor urban students and has been a firm supporter of the Urban Collaborative from the start.

In Providence, where the majority of the Urban Collaborative's students and money comes from, the story has been markedly different. In the spring of 1992, the Providence School Committee voted to cut all funding for the Urban Collaborative, as it had done in previous years, because the school system was facing another major funding shortfall. The shortfall was essentially the result of tough times in both Providence and the state. This was exacerbated by the fact that the city refused to raise new taxes to compensate for the loss of state funds. To make matters worse, the school system had somehow forgotten to count its vocational students when figuring its 1992 budget. In all fairness to the Providence School Department, there was a great deal of confusion in the city at the time, with three superintendents serving in one year's span. Yet even if things were better organized in the city, the bottom line was still the same: like most school districts in the country, Providence relies too heavily on property taxes for school funding. In good times, funding alternative programs is easy enough. In bad times, they tend to get pitched overboard to lighten the load.

As he had done in other years, Rob DeBlois argued his case vigorously before the school committee, pointing out the school's success, its community support, and the obvious benefits to the students and the city. But at the start of the 1992–93 school year, it was clear that the Urban Collaborative would receive no funding from Providence. As the school committee saw it, something had to be cut, and lopping off the Urban Collaborative—a small, nonunionized program—was a relatively simple, clean way to save $430,000. Certainly it was easier than attacking larger programs that have union support and a broader constituency. The best Rob could do was to work out an absurdly complex plan in which the Urban Collaborative would survive the year on the funds from Pawtucket and East Providence, surplus funds from the previous year, a new dropout prevention grant it managed to secure from the state, and money supplied by private foundations and businesses. The gap left by Providence would be made up with a substantial, last-minute loan from Fleet Bank, with the loan's interest guaranteed by one of the supporting foundations. In turn, Providence had to agree to fund the school retroactively when, in the following fall, it received the $500,000 it should have received this year for vocational students. This is certainly not the best way to fund a school, but under the circumstances it was the best the Urban Collaborative could do.

In August of 1992, Rob was finally able to recall his teachers and inform parents and students that all was set for another year.

"I'm certainly happy we were able to survive," Rob says, "but it is extremely frustrating to operate this way. First of all, I'm just glad we didn't have to hire any new teachers this year. I don't think too many would have been interested in a school without funding. As it was, this fiasco will end up costing us an extra $15,000 in interest payments. With $15,000 I could run an afterschool tutoring program five days a week all year and buy 400 or so books for the library."

In truth, with all the hurdles and hoops the school has had to jump over and through to get financing and approval, it's a minor miracle that the Urban Collaborative exists at all. The problems began right at the start and have yet to let up. When Rob was first planning the school, Rhode Island's economy was healthy, riding the boom years of the mid-1980s. It seemed like an auspicious beginning. But during the spring and summer of 1987, all three superintendents in the participating cities happened to leave their jobs for varying reasons. Among other complications, this delayed the opening of the Urban Collaborative by one year. As a result, the school began in a very lean financial year. In those twelve months, the state went from boom to bust, along with much of the Northeast.

The flagging economy wasn't the only force trying to quash the school. Petty politics played along. Part of the process of getting the Urban Collaborative going as a public school included convincing the state legislature to pass a bill authorizing its creation. Most legislators were agreeable, but for circumstantial reasons, the Urban Collaborative was drawn into a battle involving another collaborative school proposed for a different region of the state. This other collaborative had run into serious problems because the state senator sponsoring its bill could not agree on some of the bill's language with the head of the National Education Association (NEA), one of the state's two teachers' unions. Since the two couldn't reach an agreement, the head of the NEA exercised his power to kill this bill. In these situations, a legislator can revive his or her bill by attaching it as an amendment to a similar piece of legislation. In this case the only similar piece of legislation was the bill to create the Urban Collaborative. As a result, Rob found himself having to mediate what amounted to a turf battle between the head of the NEA and a state senator over a few words and commas that had little significance—and that had absolutely no bearing on the Urban Collaborative. The whole episode was a pointed example of how the system can bring down a good program before it even gets off the ground.

By any measure, constantly fighting for funding and dealing with political battles is a difficult and awkward way to do business, and, for

Rob, is far more draining than dealing with the day-to-day trials of his students. And yet every year it has been like this, one problem after another after another—problems that have nothing to do with the merits of the school itself but with the vagaries of local and state politics. Between the first and second year, the Urban Collaborative was cut from the Providence budget completely. Intense lobbying of the governor, commissioner of education, mayor, city council members, school committee, and school department got the Urban Collaborative reinstated in the city's budget. Without Rob's relentless vigilance, there is no doubt the school would have died an early death.

Once, in a budget-cutting session between the school's first and second years, the head of the school board, soon-to-be-governor Bruce Sundlun, admitted not knowing anything about the Urban Collaborative. A school board member quickly informed him—or, rather, misinformed him—of the program, in effect telling him offhandedly, "I don't think it's particularly successful. I'm not impressed with it." Without further discussion, Sundlun decided to strike the school from the budget and move on. Afterward, an attentive reporter questioned the board member about her objections to the program. The board member had to admit that she had never formally visited the school. Her objections were based on a brief observation that led her to believe the students were not well supervised. One off-the-cuff comment and the school was on the ropes.

In order to get the funding reinstated, Rob DeBlois had to rally supporters—parents, students, teachers, and community leaders—to crowd into the next school board meeting to educate the board about the school's effectiveness and importance to the community. He also lobbied the school department and the mayor of Providence, Joseph R. Paolino, Jr. In the end, it was the mayor, under pressure, who saved the school the second year when he added five hundred thousand dollars to the school department's budget specifically to keep the program alive.

Since that time, the school committee has been well aware of the success of the Urban Collaborative. But even so, the members still have tended not to think of the Urban Collaborative as theirs, even though it is a publicly funded school and serves seventy-five or so Providence students each year. At the recent graduation ceremony, representatives from East Providence and Pawtucket school systems showed up to congratulate students from their respective cities. No one from Providence came.

The city's reluctance to support a successful program like the Urban Collaborative goes a long way in explaining why it is so difficult to offer alternatives in education and why, even when these alternatives prove successful, it is so difficult to keep them alive. The question arises: If a school has clearly demonstrated its value, if it employs many of the reform techniques urged by educators and researchers, if it has broad community support, if it is cost-effective, then why would it have to fight for funding? Why should it? One would think every school committee in the country would bend over backwards to keep programs like this going. One would think every urban school district would want to establish a similar program. As the Rhode Island Foundation noted in its 1990 Annual Report, "It is obvious the school's nurturing environment is the best thing in some of these kids' lives, and that it is transforming them into people with more confidence and self-esteem." In an editorial supporting the school and encouraging Providence to keep the school's funds intact, the *Providence Journal* called the Urban Collaborative "an imaginative alternative: A valuable experiment in reducing dropouts, and encouraging young people to develop their full potential. Providence needs to see this bright light stay lit."

Rob DeBlois and others have tried to point out the folly of cutting funding for the Urban Collaborative by reminding the board, and anyone else, that most of the Urban Collaborative students would likely drop out if not for this school, and in doing so they would cost the state far more money than it currently costs to educate them. The state pays $92,000 a year per student at its state training school—a youth correctional facility filled mostly with dropouts. Of course, we are not even considering the high cost of the unrealized potential in these children and the effect on those around them.

In May of 1992, the Rhode Island Skills Commission, under the direction of the indefatigable Ira Magaziner,[1] published a report full of recommendations for improving worker productivity, including suggestions for improving the educational system in the state. The report, "An Invitation to Act," is based on a national report titled "America's Choice: High Skills or Low Wages." The national report was the result of a commission of leaders from education, business, labor, and government challenging the nation to, among other things, create a revolution in the way our schools teach. "No nation can produce a highly qualified workforce without first providing its citizens with a strong general education," the report rightly insists. To do this, we need a "systematic commitment to educate all students and recover students who drop out of school."

Here are some of the commission's specific recommendations: that education should be student-centered; that schools, parents, businesses, and social services should work as partners to encourage educational achievement; that schools must be small and personal and community-based; that

---

[1] Ira Magaziner later went on to be the main architect in Hillary Rodham Clinton's national healthcare reform efforts.

schools should employ mastery learning as the criteria for promotion in grade; that schools should have as much autonomy as possible, with the freedom to manage themselves, including budget and personnel; and, finally, that teachers should have the power to tailor the program to their students' needs.

Does all this sound familiar? The Urban Collaborative has not had quite the success it wants with parental involvement—mostly because of the difficult lives most Urban Collaborative parents lead—but it scores high marks in all other categories. And it is light-years ahead of the mainstream school system.

Another report called PROBE (PROvidence Blueprint for Education), conducted under the auspices of the Public Education Fund, comes to similar conclusions as the Rhode Island Skills Commission. The report was prompted by the obvious problems in the Providence school system: low test scores, high dropout rate, low morale, and the inability of the system to deal with the influx of immigrants not yet comfortable with the English language. After an exhaustive study of the school system, "rife with factionalism and lax standards," the report concludes with a long list of criticisms of the current system, a list generated in part by the complaints and desires of teachers, administrators, students, and school board members. It also offers a thirty-nine-step plan for overhauling the schools. There were a few bright spots outlined in the report. These included three alternative learning programs. One program is a member of the Coalition of Essential Schools, a successful national network of schools established by Brown University's Ted Sizer, and another is the Urban Collaborative.

Edward Eddy, a former president of the University of Rhode Island and the PROBE leader, says that if the twenty-two-month study has proven anything, it is the need for change. "Everybody just wants change," he told the *Providence Journal*. "God, they want change." And, like the Rhode Island Skills Commission report, the PROBE report favors immediate change. Among other things, it recommends breaking up the large, monolithic schools into small learning communities, empowering teachers and administrators, and increasing parental involvement. Sound familiar?

The *Providence Journal* calls the PROBE report "a landmark study." Philomena Fayaujuoa, of the Rhode Island Urban League, says the study has uncovered glaring problems in the system and offers intelligent, workable solutions. The next step, she says, is for the city to find the moral courage to make the needed changes. Others, including State Senator Charles Walton, have publicly called on the mayor and school superintendent to begin implementing the recommended changes immediately.

On the national level, studies have resulted in similar findings. The Carnegie Council on Adolescent Development recently published an exhaustive report on middle schools, "Turning Points: Preparing America's Youth for the 21st Century." The list of recommendations included creating small learning environments, forming teams of teachers and students, encouraging healthy values and citizenship, giving teachers greater influence in the classroom and school, and involving parents and the community—all characteristics of the Urban Collaborative.

People have made the analogy between a good school and a successful business. It is wrong to think the policies of the business world can cure the ills of public education. But to the extent that business policies and methods can improve education, the comparison is valid. As in a good business, a good school needs the autonomy to deal directly with its customers (the students). It needs effective leadership and the accountability of everyone in the system. In their research for the book *Reinventing Government*, which highlights the value of entrepreneurialism in the public sector, authors David Osborne and Ted Gaebler discovered that the more successful school systems work because the educational bureaucracy has learned how to get out of the way and let individual schools and teachers do what they do best: teach. For a school system to be effective, they note, the school board should "steer the system but let others row."

In *In Search of Excellence*, a book-length study of successful businesses, authors Thomas J. Peters and Robert H. Waterman, Jr., point out that small companies breed commitment and efficiency. They tend to be more creative and responsive to the market. In short, the authors conclude, "Small is beautiful." A prime example of excessive bureaucratic waste—where size breeds inefficiency—comes from the Pentagon. According to the U.S. General Accounting Office, the Pentagon spent *$40 billion* on unnecessary items last year alone. One might call this waste shocking, but most of us have almost come to expect it from the Pentagon, where the lack of accountability, time and again, has led to absurdly excessive spending. The point here is that bureaucracies of any size often work against their own interests. What works for business can also work for schools, where flexibility and the human element in a small, autonomous school can lead to a better education. In education, as many reform specialists will tell you again and again, less is certainly more.

In the case of the Urban Collaborative, however, its greatest strength— its size and independence—is also its greatest weakness. It is a publicly funded school and, as such, the responsibility of the mayor, school department, and school board. But because it's small, and because it operates under a different principle than other city schools, it tends to be seen as an outsider, an interloper. A Providence school administrator actually said of another proposed new program that he feared it would become another successful program that the city would have to support. At a different point in time, he might have been talking about the Urban Collaborative. Such a statement belies a strange attitude toward new and different programs. More often than not, they are seen not as potential solutions to educational problems but as threats to the status quo—no matter that the status quo includes a dropout rate between 30 and 40 percent.

One could go on highlighting both the value of the Urban Collaborative program and the problems in Providence that have made the school's life miserable at times. But the point is not to bash this one city. Providence is not that much different from most other American cities when it comes to its approach to education—or anything else, for that matter. The point is that our layered system of government, regardless of its other successes and shortcomings, is simply not conducive to educational reform—even when it is clear to everyone that reform is necessary. So much conspires against new programs.

In most cases, the story of educational funding is a story of democracy in action, of people trying to make decisions in relationship to other people's decisions amid the various constraints and pressures to act one way or another. A school committee finds itself reacting to decisions made by the general assembly, the governor, and city hall. In addition, the committee must work within the confines of limited funding; already agreed upon contracts; federal, state, and local laws; various policies; and the often-competing political pressure from vocal constituencies. There is little room in all this to weigh the value of a new program against the merits of existing programs.

What follows is a simplified scenario of how things basically happened in Rhode Island around the time the Urban Collaborative was taxiing down the runway, waiting for takeoff. It's another way of clarifying the complexity of the situation. As you read it, put yourself in each person's shoes and ask yourself, "What would I do?"

The governor   You find yourself leading a state faced with a credit union crisis. A series of massively irresponsible loans has led to the collapse of the state's biggest credit unions. The unions require the infusion of tens of millions of dollars so that many residents of your state don't lose their life savings. This might be manageable in good times, but now the economy has gone sour and fewer tax dollars have been collected. To make matters worse, you've already raised taxes substantially in the previous year. You know the state needs money, but you don't dare raise taxes again, especially since this is an election year and you would like to keep your job for another term. The largest single line in the state budget goes to public education. So you take a closer look at it. You know it's not a good idea to cut funding for education, but you have to make hard choices. Cutting education funding, you realize, permits you to at least submit a balanced budget. And, thankfully, the question of who will make up the decrease in school funding will be transferred to others. To anyone who complains, you can simply say that these are tough times and that they are also going to have to make hard, but responsible, choices. You don't mention that those hurt most by your decision are members of a voiceless, powerless group—children.

The state legislator   You also must deal with the fiscal problems created by the current economic conditions and the credit union crisis. Because all politics are local, you know that you'll have to make up for lost revenue by raising local property taxes and cutting the largest line on your budget—educational funding. Local taxpayers will not be happy about either of these decisions, so you contemplate ways you can reduce this burden, lessen the cut. While you have to endure a reduction in education funding from the state, you fight to make sure your city's share of the smaller pie is as large as possible. In addition, you resort to a certain amount of budget gimmickry—early retirement incentives for state employees, for instance—and some accounting changes that make your budget look more in balance than it really is. Your fellow legislators generally collude with you on all these matters because they are in the same leaky boat. You readily take these steps because you know, in your heart, that you are not the cause of the problem. You are simply reacting to a bad situation.

The mayor   Like everyone else, you want to do what is best—but you also want to keep your job. Basically, you know that your goal is to avoid tax increases while still offering basic services to city residents. Your first step is to argue for as much money as possible from the state. You also scream about the rate of poverty in your city every chance you get, letting the state legislature and the governor know that your city has special needs, that the state's actions put you in an untenable position. What you don't say is that many of the city's basic services are provided by city workers who represent a substantial part of your support in a very close election victory during the last elections. You know, too, that these same workers are looking for a salary increase in the upcoming negotiations. You simply can't cut into these budgets or you'll end up appearing ungrateful (and unelectable). You try to do everything you can, but in the end you ultimately propose a property tax increase along with some reductions, including educational funding. It isn't the best of situations, you tell everyone, but you are just trying to be fair.

The city council member　　You have to vote on the tax increase proposed by the mayor, and the people in your district are just livid with anger. Most of the people in your district are not city workers, and only a small portion of them have children in the public schools. And even among these parents and guardians, a substantial number say they don't want more taxes. It's their number one concern. Given this situation, for you the decision is obvious: taxes should not be increased. In order to prevent a tax increase, you decide reluctantly that the education budget must be cut even further than the mayor proposed. Of course, you don't propose any specific cuts in the education department's budget. This is the responsibility of school boards, the mayor, and school department leaders.

The school board member　　You were appointed by the mayor and you are generally considered an able representative of the underclass, especially poor children. You already sent one budget to the city council and, after cutting it several times, said that it couldn't go lower. In fact, it is lower than you feel it should be. Nevertheless, you get a message back that you have to cut another $3 million (approximately 2.5 percent). Since this is a directive, you have to make hard choices. One possibility is to cut out school sports programs. Another is to cut the Urban Collaborative Accelerated Program. Sports, you know, are sacred in this society. You know, too, that some two thousand children participate in sports at some level in the city and that their parents are very active and vocal. You also vaguely believe that sports are important in school life. Then you look at the Urban Collaborative. You know the director and you know that he has been very good at finding money to keep the program alive, one way or another. You know, too, that the program serves only seventy-five students from Providence and that many of their parents are disconnected from the system. You believe that an alternative educational program like this is important, but you have to cut somewhere. You start by delaying the purchase of some textbooks, delaying maintenance of some schools. You cut your budget for school supplies. You increase the distance kids have to walk to school before qualifying for a free bus ride. You don't fill a couple of administrative positions. And you cut the Urban Collaborative completely, along with some other school programs, early childhood programs, and literacy programs. It's painful, but it seems the best solution given the alternatives.

The school superintendent   You understand all the events that have transpired in the state and city. Your job is to find a way to make the educational system work with the limited money you have been given. You have not been in the job a long time and don't feel you have quite the power or control that you hope to develop over time. Your wish is to prove that you are an able, responsible administrator. You would like to see the Urban Collaborative stay, so you start your search for cuts elsewhere. One good option, you think, would be to privatize the school lunch program. This would save the school district about $500,000, money that could be used to fund the Urban Collaborative. But this option is rejected by the school committee after a very vocal demonstration by the school lunch workers, who are unionized and who receive a nice salary and benefits package. In the meeting, no one disputed the fact that the school district could save $500,000 by switching to a private lunch service. However, all of the school board members know several women who are lunch workers. They know how much these women depend on their jobs, and they know that these women are generally hard workers. Pressure to keep these people also comes from outside the city. As it turns out, the entire statewide school lunch program hinges upon what happens in Providence. The city is the largest participant remaining in the publicly funded school lunch program (some other large school districts in the state have already gone private). If Providence goes to a private service, the state says it will get out of the business altogether and require all local school districts in the state to go private. It seemed like a good idea, but clearly the pressure on the school committee is too much. The lunch workers stay. Another solution would be to go with a private janitorial service and save even more money, but the current janitors' union is even stronger than the lunch workers'. You bravely decide to take a look at some of the union contracts; maybe you can find a way to save a few dollars there. But it turns out that negotiations are done by others, and deals are made that you simply have to live with. One of these deals gives lifetime Blue Cross, fully paid, to employees who retire from the school department. This one item alone, this year, will cost you more than the amount that could have funded the Urban Collaborative. In the end, having exhausted the possibilities, you decide you have to leave the Urban Collaborative out of your budget, but you tell the director that if he can get it back in through politics, you certainly won't object.

The school director   You understand the game. You've played it before (every year, in fact). However, you are getting tired of it. More important, all of the people you generally ask to attend meetings and rallies, write letters and make phone calls, are also getting tired. But you have no choice. You get on the phone during free moments in the day and every night after dinner to call business people and foundation heads who have influence in the city and state. You get press coverage any way you can. You even recruit students and parents for this purpose. You try to find out where you have connections to the mayor and school committee. As director, you do everything you can to get back in the budget. At the same time, you have to deal fairly with the teachers who have been laid off and who may want to look for jobs elsewhere. These are good teachers, many of whom could find other jobs fairly easily. You tell the teachers that you think things will be OK, but you can't be sure. They like the school and want to stay. But to protect themselves, they file for unemployment just in case. This filing is legal and appropriate, but you wince knowing it will also cost the school (and the city) more money in taxes in the event that the school does get its funding and the teachers are rehired. In the meantime, you also try to raise money for next year from businesses and foundations. You need to convince them to give some of their limited grant funds. You know this is asking a lot, since the number of grant requests have grown tremendously due to the poor economy, the credit union crisis, and the state budget cuts. The foundations and businesses would like to help, but they also wonder aloud whether your school will be around come September and whether or not they'd be wiser putting their grant money some safer place. You tell them that their money is needed now more than ever to demonstrate continued private sector confidence and support for the school. It's a tough sell, but most of them hang in there. Still, they wonder how long they should continue with a school that can't seem to draw steady government support. They also wonder what will happen to the school when you decide to leave. It's hard for them to imagine you'll stay much longer. This is tough, exhausting work. You thank them, hang up the phone, make your next call.

By all reports, the Urban Collaborative is worth keeping. You've gotten that point by now. It serves a real purpose, it is a great model for a school system in need of reform, and it fits the profile of the sort of school experts believe the system needs. Yet, instead of finding support, it has been constantly struggling for its own survival, constantly needing to announce itself and champion its own cause.

"Saying we will change our schools is one thing," says Rob, "doing it is another. The system is highly complex, overregulated and centralized, and notoriously unadaptive."

Is there any way to change all this? Is there any way to ensure the Urban Collaborative's survival without the school having to call out the troops every year, lobby until exhausted, and drum up the attention of the press?

It's hard to tell at this stage. It may just be a matter of the Urban Collaborative having to pay its political dues for a few more years before the city sees it as a vital part of its educational system. Perhaps the school's continued existence may even help generate systemwide reforms based on recommendations of the Rhode Island Skills Commission and the PROBE report. In the meantime, the battle continues.

It would be nice to think that the Urban Collaborative is going to make it. It would be nice to think that all the other successful experiments in education in places such as Chicago, Minneapolis, East Harlem, New Haven, and Dade County, Florida, will eventually lead to mainstream reforms. It would be nice to believe that all the reform ideas pouring out of universities—Yale, Stanford, Columbia, Vanderbilt, Brown, the University of New Hampshire, Johns Hopkins, and elsewhere—will shake our educational monolith to its roots. But this is not yet clear. What is clear is that, despite all the rhetoric about school reform, we still haven't found the collective will to make such reforms. Sadly, many school reformers are beginning to talk pessimistically about it all, wondering how often the message needs to be repeated before it sinks in. And that's too bad. Because until we do, a quarter or more of the youth in this country will continue to suffer, and the nation's future prosperity will remain at risk. We know what it takes. We know what students need. We know how schools should look and operate. Now we need to act as if our lives depended on it.

16

EARLY ON A TUESDAY MORNING IN LATE JUNE, A NUMBER OF
Urban Collaborative students show up at the Community College of Rhode
Island, a couple blocks from the Urban Collaborative. They're here to set
up the auditorium for the school's graduation ceremony. On the edge of
the stage is a boom-box blasting rap music by a band called Naughty by
Nature. Two students hang banners, including the red-and-black banner
that reads: "Too Legit to Quit," the school's motto. A girl carefully marks
off a series of rows as reserved seating for the students. The stage is sparsely
set with a podium and a few straight-backed chairs. Two other students,
Louis and Tory, arrive. Louis is wearing a double-breasted suit. Tory has
on a sheer blouse over a black tanktop, black spandex shorts, and bright
white sneakers. Her hair is fixed with great care and she is smiling, as is
Louis. They look around the nearly empty auditorium as if measuring how
it will appear in a half hour when the place will be filled with students,
parents, and guests.

"This is it," Louis says with unabashed pride. "This is really it."

In the atrium just outside the auditorium, a number of tables have
been set up for the lunch after the ceremony. A group of girls busily
decorate old jars with crepe paper to use as flower vases. Others cover
folding tables with sheets of white paper. The atrium is open, airy, and
flooded with a soft light from the opaque dome above. As the students
and teachers arrive, they gather here, at ease and clearly enjoying the
group's effort at dressing up for the occasion—though some, like Pablo in
his Nike high tops and an "X" T-shirt in honor of Malcolm X, refuse to
change their style for the ceremony. Peter Case arrives in a dark suit; John

171

Howard in a lighter blue suit. Maureen Farrell arrives in a flower-print sleeveless dress, though the formal effect is somewhat undercut by the thick set of keys hanging around her neck. She has an armload of flowers, which she deposits on the table for the girls to cut and arrange.

Jim Snead gathers a group of *a cappella* singers and leads them across the atrium to a quiet classroom for a last-minute rehearsal. A week ago, in frustration, he threatened to call off the performance when students didn't show up for practice, but the group has finally turned things around and are nearly ready. Jim rolls his eyes when another teacher asks about the group. Out loud he says, "We'll do fine," as if to boost the confidence of his singers.

Cati Martinez wheels Rob DeBlois in. Rob is wearing a tie and a light blue jacket. Of all the things Rob hates, putting on a tie and jacket rank near the top of the list. He flings his arms out wide and smiles. "Mela," he says to one girl, "you're looking great." Cati moves him into the atrium, where he offers comments to just about everyone along the way. Shortly, Cati leaves him with a group of teachers and walks off to talk with students, knowing that with many it will be the last time.

Cati admits that she is genuinely going to miss most of the kids. For her, the end of the year is the hardest time because it means she has to break the emotional bonds she has made with students during the year. Cati knows their suffering, and thus their triumph. "When I was growing up," she says, "the projects on Smith Hill in Providence were just a shambles. It was a crazy crazy place, and I lived just up the street. As a young girl, I used to hang out with all these tough monsters. Kids were always in trouble, always getting jumped by other kids, or getting in trouble with the law. I started wandering about at age ten or eleven. And I was probably a lot worse than most of these kids."

She says she hated school with a passion. "I had a horrible experience in school. The school didn't take any interest in me as a person, and that's probably what I needed the most. I was just another kid. I didn't have anyone I felt close to. So I ended up getting into a lot of trouble. I didn't care. I did a lot of drugs as a teenager. Then I got kicked out of my house and dropped out of school because I had to work. I was sixteen.

"Sometimes, these kids can be really obnoxious," she continues, "but I really like them and feel for them. I can look past what is coming out of their mouths at any particular moment, the cursing and the anger. I can look past the way they are acting because you've got to figure what they were going through that morning or what they are going to go through when they leave here. For those who stick it out, I can see a future, and

I can feel that there is hope for them." Cati bases part of this hope on the fact that she found her way back to school and earned an associate's degree from a technical college. "It's worth practically nothing," she says. "I'm paying through the nose for the two years of school. But it got me together. It got me this job. And it got me in the mode of furthering my education." She is looking to return to college and get a master's degree in education or social work. Her hope is to come back to help adolescents like those in the Urban Collaborative. "They are by and large good kids. They just need a chance and some adults who care about them. Just look at how well most of these kids have done here."

The mood—as at most graduation ceremonies—is generally cheery. It has been another long and difficult year for students and staff, and now it is time to celebrate their achievements. But two events cloud the day. The first is the possible closing of the school next year. All students are aware that the Urban Collaborative has lost its funding from the City of Providence and that there is a chance it may not get it back. Most of the concern focuses on where students will end up if they can't return in the fall. The prospect of going back to certain middle schools and high schools makes some shudder. "They've got to keep this place going," one girl says in near anguish. "It's just not fair if they close this school."

In support of the school during the funding crisis, a group of seven students had written a letter to the *Providence Journal,* saying "Before coming to this school many of us were thinking of dropping out, or already had dropped out. However, now we're looking ahead to the future with open minds."

As serious as the school's possible closing is, the other event attracts more attention. The previous afternoon, following the school trip to Rocky Point Amusement Park, two students got into a fight in a parking lot a short distance from school. Both boys, Ray and Arthur, have been on bad terms since early in the school year. Both have also been in their share of trouble in and out of school. Ray has worked steadily in his classes most of the year, and he genuinely wants to do well. But he couldn't seem to keep himself out of trouble. Earlier in the year he was suspended for throwing a rock at Jim Snead. Since then it has been one little thing after another. But basically the staff feels hopeful for Ray. He had done well in some of his courses and showed signs of wanting to turn his life around.

Arthur, on the other hand, has a basic contempt for all forms of authority, including the staff at the Urban Collaborative. He didn't do well in school, didn't even complete a year of work in his one year at school. At seventeen, he cannot come back next year, and halfway through the year, realizing he wasn't going to make it, he more or less, as Peter Case says, "let us know that next year he'd be dealing drugs on the street." Arthur is a smart boy and very strong. But it is often too painful for such kids to be presented with another chance when they feel the odds of failing are high. Arthur couldn't open up, Peter speculates, couldn't take another chance. He'd shuffle into class late, moving slowly, and glare defiantly at no one in particular. The message: Don't ask anything of me; I cannot and will not perform anymore. I'm just biding my time until summer.

As best as anyone knows, Arthur punched Ray, knocked him to the ground, then, literally, stomped on his head until Ray lost consciousness. When Ray came to, he was incoherent. Some friends helped him to the hospital, where it was determined he had suffered a severe concussion. Peter Case speculates that Arthur had been waiting patiently for this moment so he could leave his mark, let everyone know that "I am not one of you. I will not conform."

The students stand around in small groups whispering about the fight, retelling the story, trying to fix blame. Eric and Mark sit at a table with Tran, who has done very well at school this year. After they talk about Ray and Arthur, they talk about the future. Tran, who completed ninth and tenth grade in one year, says he would like to go to college. Eric, who has another year to go at the Urban Collaborative, says he would love to go to college, also, but feels less confident that he can make it.

"You can do it, man," Tran says.

Mark, more hardheaded than the others, says he might go off to community college someday, but that he does not enjoy school all that much. He's a smart kid, reads the paper every day and talks intelligently about the upcoming presidential election. And he has done very well at the Urban Collaborative. Next year, he is off to Hope Essential School, a new alternative high school program not unlike the Urban Collaborative.

Steven West comes over and joins the three boys.

"Cops," Mark says, shaking his head at Steve.

"What about cops?" Steve wants to know.

"All cops do all day is hang out at Dunkin Donuts," Mark says.

Steve smiles. "You just don't like authority figures."

"You've got that right," Mark says.

Carlos, a fourteen-year-old first-year student at the Urban Collaborative, stops by to say good-bye to his friends and reminisce awhile. He started the year in seventh grade and says he has almost finished eighth this year. Next year, he decides, he would like to do all of ninth and tenth, if possible. "It's going to be hard, but I know I can do it." Carlos looks around the room as if to make sure no one else is listening, then he says he really wants to catch up with his peers because he doesn't like being in class with such young kids. He's a big boy, closing in on six feet and two hundred pounds, and feels it's embarrassing being this big and still in middle school. He stayed back one year, he says, because of teachers who hated him. "Teachers at the Urban Collaborative really care about you. You can raise your hand and they'll come help you," he says, as if that is an amazing thing. "In other schools teachers only annoy you. Here they care. They give you more freedom. You learn to do the work yourself. But they are always encouraging you." He admits he got off to a slow start, but he has big plans for next year. And someday, he says, he wants to be a lawyer, or a policeman. "I want to do something to help out people."

A former student named Pablo stops by to offer his congratulations. Pablo was a student at the Urban Collaborative during its first year. Like so many of the students at the Urban Collaborative, he is a bright boy who had skid to the edge of the academic precipice, failing every subject in the seventh grade and missing 75 percent of the school year. He had come to the Urban Collaborative in part, he admits now, because the school started an hour later than other schools, and in part because he wasn't happy with failing. It took him a while to get back on track, but slowly he found learning engaging. He says he also liked the one-on-one attention he got at the Urban Collaborative. After two years, Pablo completed the seventh and eighth grade and half of ninth grade. He started working hard, became "focused" on school. He was sixteen, and two of his good friends dropped out of school. Pablo knew he didn't want this.

At the beginning of this year, Pablo entered the tenth grade in Central High School, a school with two thousand or so students, a school known among students for its problems with drugs and fighting. But he has done well, made the honor roll each quarter and held a B+ average through three quarters. Now he's not only talking about college, he's talking about law school. "The future's not bright if you don't have an education," he says, "if you don't have a goal."

Eventually, everyone filters into the auditorium. The lights go down. A student named Craig walks up to the podium set to the right side of the stage. He stands poised, addresses the crowd in a steady, strong voice, welcoming everyone to the closing ceremony. He and a girl named Keri are running the show. No adults are present on stage. A group of seven students walks reverently on stage and one at a time welcome everyone in a different language: English, Portuguese, Spanish, Cambodian, French, Italian, Russian, and sign language. This is followed by opening remarks by Dr. Richard Charlton, president of the Urban Collaborative's board of superintendents. Charlton offers up a number of superlatives about the school and its staff and students. In particular, he praises Rob DeBlois as an "outstanding man with outstanding traits." To the students, he says, "You've enjoyed success because of him." Everyone applauds vigorously.

Next, a group from the sign-language elective signs along with a recorded song, "Love in Any Language." Their movements are graceful and sure. Three students, one of whom is pregnant, step forward for short solos. Afterward, a girl named True walks on stage alone. She is dressed in a long, flowing African robe and wears a ring through her nose. Last year, True had agreed to sing a solo at the closing ceremony but got so frightened she ran off stage in tears. This time, she stands in center stage and fixes her stare above the audience. The music to the song, "The Greatest Love of All," comes on, a song True has chosen, and she joins in softly with the vocals, swaying slightly, her hands held behind her. Slowly, her voice rises to a rich crescendo. "I decided long ago never to walk in anyone's shadow," she sings. A woman in the back of the auditorium smiles and says, "she's got that right." By the end, True is belting out the song with a strong and melodious voice.

Afterward, the crowd gives her a standing ovation.

The guest speaker for the ceremony had to cancel at the last minute, so Rob asked Valerie Tutson, the drama teacher, if she could tell a story, do something to entertain and enlighten the group. Valerie, never one to shy away from performing, happily agreed—despite little time for preparation. Now she hops on stage and begins telling a story about two boys who have graduated from school and are off on a journey to find a wise old woman whom they plan to trick. They've heard that she can answer any question. So they decide to bring along a bird and, holding it behind their backs, ask her what they have in their hands. Surely she won't know the answer, and they'll have a good laugh at her expense. But things become more complicated than they boys expected. For one, the journey to the old woman turns out more difficult than the boys imagine. At one point, they have to hack their way through dense thornbushes using only their hands. All the while, strangely enough, an old man sits and watches them, calmly paring food with a knife. When the boys finally break through, they turn to the man and ask why he didn't help them. "Because you didn't ask," the man replies. He stands up then and breezes through the opening the boys had made.

It turns out, as well, that the woman they plan to trick is wiser than they think. When they arrive at her home, they ask the prepared question.

"What have we got in our hands?" they ask.

"A bird," the woman says.

Nonplussed, the boys huddle, then ask, "Well, is it alive or is it dead?" They figure they've definitely got her now. If she says it's alive, they'll simply strangle it. But the woman knows how to respond.

"The answer," the wise woman says sagely, "is in your hands."

The story has no clear moral, but Valerie knows where she is going with this one. She lets the words hang in the air. "The answer is in your hands." What is the moral? First, that there are knowledgeable adults in this world who can help you and offer valuable advice and assistance—and that you shouldn't be afraid to ask. And, second, what one makes of one's life, ultimately, rests in one's hands. Take control.

This has been the message of the Urban Collaborative all year. The combination, the staff will tell you, is extremely important. To love oneself, as True has sung, is good. But it is not everything. These kids need guidance and mentors.

Next, Jim Snead announces all the accelerations for the year, and the staff hands out roses to each student who is leaving. At the top of the list is Louis, who has completed two years' work in one. Afterward, Louis gets up on stage in his double-breasted suit and talks briefly about the Urban Collaborative and what it has done for him. "This school has helped me know what I want to do in the future, which is to be an engineer," he tells the crowd. "The school has helped make my future look brighter, and I thank everyone on the staff for their help."

Afterward, Tran reads a statement written by Maria, a student too shy to address the group. "Because the staff has been hard on me, because the teachers have pushed me, they make me feel like I can do the work," Tran reads. "I didn't want to go to the Urban Collaborative at first. Then I learned I could catch up. So I decided to take a chance, and I'm happy I did. I learned that if I did a lot of work and didn't get into trouble, I could make it. Next year will be my most important year ever. But I know now I'm going to graduate from high school if I work as hard as I have here. At one time I really didn't think I was ever going to get through high school. But now I know I will. The Urban Collaborative has helped me realize I will be fine in life."

Jim Snead's *a cappella* group takes the stage and pulls off a more than passable rendition of "Hard to Say Good-bye," by the group Boyz II Men. This is followed by True's final solo, "One Moment in Time," which she performs with even more poise than before.

Rob is wheeled to the front of the auditorium below the stage. The audience gives him a standing ovation, and when they quiet down, Rob simply tells the graduates it is time for them to move on, that he is proud of the work they've done, that he is proud they have stuck it out. Now, he says, they need to take charge of their lives and remember what they have learned. "Take care," he says, concluding his short address. "We love you."

Afterword

A GREAT DEAL HAS OCCURRED AT THE SCHOOL SINCE THIS snapshot was taken—and, I am happy to report, much for the better. In essence, the fruits of all the early struggles have finally come to bear.

The school survived those early, white-knuckle years of repeated funding cuts. Now it finds itself on firm financial ground, largely due to the support of Providence's superintendent. The school is in the enviable position of being a primary innovator in Rhode Island public education. Perhaps the highest honor came from the Carnegie Foundation, which named the Urban Collaborative a "Lead School" in Rhode Island—that is, a school considered to exemplify the best of middle school philosophies.

In the fall of 1996, the school moved into its own building for the first time. The purchase of the building, like every other event in the school's life, was a complex process that required, among other things, the readoption of the Urban Collaborative by the three participating school committees. In signing the agreement, the cities of Providence, East Providence, and Pawtucket, in effect, expressed their confidence in the school and a willingness to commit for the long haul. In an interesting twist, the City of Providence backed a $1.5 million loan for the school building. As long as the Urban Collaborative stays in business (which Providence can ensure by sending students), the city doesn't have to worry about assuming the loan. Ironically, Providence now has a financial incentive to keep the school alive.

In addition to receiving this outward recognition, the Urban Collaborative has continued to improve upon its internal mission to branch out in new directions. Key among them is an extensive community service program and a career mentorship program. The latter is supported by a private foundation grant and involves placing some fifteen to twenty students at part-time job sites around the state where students work closely with mentors in various professions. To help other students through the summer, the school has arranged for them to participate in a highly successful summer program that combines recreation and interdisciplinary studies. With the assistance of another grant, the Urban Collaborative has begun a desperately needed network of urban teachers in Rhode Island who want to improve their difficult craft. Finally, the school has begun a pilot program in Providence to help special education students participate in the Special Olympics—this with a grant from Special Olympics International.

All of the improvements stem from the school's internal expectations that it will continue to evolve and improve—a philosophy that one can trace to the school's site-based management system. Recently, Rob DeBlois visited several schools to observe special education classes. These were public schools with good reputations, but Rob came away distinctly unimpressed. "Afterward, I spoke with the teachers and they talked about what they had done and why," he recalled. "But it surprised me that none of them spoke about what they would like to do to improve the classes. They didn't seem to have any clear goals. At the Urban Collaborative, by contrast, you could not have a similar conversation with a teacher without that teacher putting the class in perspective of some larger goal, in context of where they would like to be, how they hope to improve. You could not help but get from them what I describe as 'a sense of excited discontent.' "

This excited discontent relates to improvements in curriculum and instruction, school culture, and discipline—very basic, yet essential, things that have to do with what kids learn, how they learn, and the role teachers play in the process. In a sense, this is what makes the Urban Collaborative tick. It's what makes it better this year than last, and what will make it better in the years to come.

Many of the teachers described in the book have since gone on to other challenges. Pauline Hilgers moved back to her home state of Missouri, where she still teaches math (and raises a son of her own). Peter Case got married in 1995 and is enrolled in an architecture program at Rhode Island School of Design. Jim Snead took a job in the Providence schools teaching science and coaching wrestling (and remains in close contact with the Urban Collaborative). Cati Martinez gave up her job as Rob's assistant to complete her own education. She is now in her senior year in the Marine Studies program at the University of Rhode Island. This past summer she won a fellowship to study migratory patterns of certain fish in Puerto Rico for the creation of a marine sanctuary. John Howard left to create his own nonprofit organization that connects businesses with inner-city schools. He continues to run the Urban Collaborative's career mentorship program, a program he started while teaching at the school.

Of course, others have remained, including Chris Cuthburtson, who now has a son, Lynne Abbott, Al Lemos, Valerie Tutson, Connie Zeeland, and Aisha Abdullah Odiase. Interestingly enough, through her work as office secretary (read: mother, counselor, teacher, disciplinarian, problem-solver, friend), Aisha has become so involved with the education of Urban Collaborative student that she ran for and won a seat on the Providence School Board.

And then there is Rob DeBlois. He's still in charge, still fighting for the school and for better urban education in America. For his work, he has received an honorary doctorate degree from Rhode Island College and a community service award from the Providence Community Center. Through the Carnegie Foundation, he is taking part in the national dialogue on school reform. In a way, he has proven to be the ideal leader of a school for children at risk of dropping out. Certainly he has the tenacity, the persistence, the fearlessness to push for the necessary change. But his handicap has also proven to be a valuable asset. Early on, Rob's injury taught him that, if he were to live a full and productive life, he would have to rely heavily on the help of others. People help him up in the morning, help him shower and dress, help him eat, help him to school, help him from van to office to classroom, help him write down his thoughts, help him home and into bed at night. In short, it forces him to be pragmatic, to ask for help from anyone who is able, and this is exactly his approach to helping the disenfranchised children of Providence. He has drawn support from every direction he can think of—from the cities and state, from the public school system, from private foundations and industry, from friends and family, from educators and educational organizations, from the Providence community. He has learned how to draw people together for a common cause. Of course, he admits that his wheelchair has been a valuable prop in all this; people find it hard to say no to a man in a wheelchair asking for financial assistance for his school.

It is also interesting to consider the lives of the Urban Collaborative students following their commencement. It's not all great news—but then the school never expected it would be. The goal has always been to help as many as possible and to find a method of education that works best for the majority.

Since the school's founding, approximately four hundred and fifty students have passed through its doors. Of that number, two have died of gunshot wounds and one of disease. One has been charged with murder. A handful have spent time in the state training school for one crime or another. An estimated seventy-five students have become parents, some with more than one child. About ninety dropped out of high school, though half of these eventually returned or enrolled in GED programs.

But the majority has hung in there. Some three hundred and sixty students have made it through high school. Following high school graduation, they have entered the job market, military service, programs like Americorps, junior college, and college—some with plans to be teachers.

The good news is that the Urban Collaborative Accelerated Program will continue to do its best with the small group of students that comes its way each fall. And one hopes that the lessons learned here will help others improve the quality of education we provide for all children at all levels. Indeed, one hopes that readers of this book will begin thinking optimistically about America's ability to offer poor children a brighter future through thoughtful, flexible education programs. But the dike is huge and the many leaking holes are more than one small school—or even a hundred small schools—can easily plug. Since the Urban Collaborative first began, the number of poor American children under the age of six reportedly increased by one million. Do the math; you'll understand.

So the story continues. Rob DeBlois and the Urban Collaborative continue their work, as the rest of us search our souls. My hope is that after you close this book, you'll think about a man being turned over in his bed late at night by his dedicated wife. He can't move his limbs. And this night, he can't sleep. His mind is racing. He's thinking about the parents he needs to call in the morning to encourage them to get their children to school on time, to encourage them to turn off the TV at night and sit with their children as they learn math and history. He's thinking about the pregnant girl who has been kicked out of her home—how he can encourage her to stay in school and help her find shelter and proper prenatal care. He's thinking about what he'll say to a young boy whose father has just been arrested for selling drugs. He's thinking about the CEO of a local company who might be able to provide financial support or perhaps take on a student apprentice for the coming summer. He's thinking about his meeting with a bank officer and how they can find a new way to finance needed improvements to the school. He is facing a darkened ceiling. He is thirsty but cannot get up to get a drink. He tells himself to be patient. Beside him his wife is already asleep again. His children are asleep in the next room. Out the window there is a hint of daylight. It comes so slowly when you're awake to watch. But it comes. And that's all he needs to know.